The
American Girl

Center Point
Large Print

**This Large Print Book carries the
Seal of Approval of N.A.V.H.**

The
American Girl

KATE HORSLEY

CENTER POINT LARGE PRINT
THORNDIKE, MAINE

This Center Point Large Print edition
is published in the year 2016 by arrangement with
William Morrow, an imprint of HarperCollins Publishers.

Copyright © 2016 by Kate Horsley.

All rights reserved.

The text of this Large Print edition is unabridged.
In other aspects, this book may vary
from the original edition.
Printed in the United States of America
on permanent paper.
Set in 16-point Times New Roman type.

ISBN: 978-1-68324-200-0

Library of Congress Cataloging-in-Publication Data

Names: Horsley, Kate, 1952– author.
Title: The American girl / Kate Horsley.
Description: Center Point Large Print edition. | Thorndike, Maine :
Center Point Large Print, 2016.
Identifiers: LCCN 2016040394 | ISBN 9781683242000
 (hardcover : alk. paper)
Subjects: LCSH: Large type books. | Psychological fiction. | GSAFD:
Suspense fiction.
Classification: LCC PS3558.O6976 A84 2016 | DDC 813/.54—dc23
LC record available at https://lccn.loc.gov/2016040394

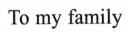
To my family

The
American Girl

Quinn Perkins

AUGUST 5, 2015

Video Diary: Session 6

[Quinn, a girl of seventeen, sits on the edge of a hospital bed wearing a white gown. As she talks, her bare legs kick the frame of the bed and monitors beep softly in the background]

You ever have one of those Magic 8 Balls as a kid? Yeah, pretty retro, I know. I remember asking mine if Adam Epstein was planning on taking me to senior prom. It said, *Don't count on it,* so I sat on my little pink bed with the daisy-pattern comforter and shook it again and again until I got the answer I wanted.

Um, my mind keeps circling. Back to that Magic 8 Ball. See, if I can remember those details—my room, the pattern on my comforter—then why can't I remember all the other things that are so much more important? The therapist who gave me this camera told me to keep a diary. He gave me some exercises and helpful advice, too: "the mind is a mysterious place" kind of thing. But in the end, I guess, he found it just as frustrating trying to get inside my head as I do. Everyone seems to.

[Quinn moves closer to the camera and stares into it]

I'm that 8 Ball, y'know. Shake me once—one answer bubbles to the surface. Shake me twice—I say something different. Might not be the thing you want to hear, though. I can't help it. All those sharp little shards inside me could be answers, but they've come loose. Now I see them in fragments that don't make any more sense than my nightmares do.

Those puzzle pieces are all in there somewhere. I know it. They're waiting for the right person to fit them together. That must be why they keep shaking me over and over and over, asking the same question:

"Where is the family?"

[A nurse walks into the frame and adjusts the sheets on the bed. She glances at the monitors, notes something on a chart hanging from the bed and leaves without speaking]

I'm back. Anyhow, sorry. Didn't mean to sound crazy there. Dunno what's come over me since . . . well, since whatever happened. But I want to help find them. So here goes. I'm telling all of you—the therapist and the police and everyone— what I remember about that night.

I woke in the woods. I don't know how I got there. I could see my hands in front of me in the dark and that was all. I was only sure of one thing—I had to get away from that place.

I got up and I didn't know which way to go. I kept spinning around in circles, but the trees looked the same every way I turned. There was a full moon, I think, and I had the idea that if I kept it on my right, I'd get to where I needed to be, so . . . I started to walk. Then I realized I was barefoot. These sharp little bits of stuff dug into my feet and I had to pick my way along on tiptoes. I walked a few steps. Then I heard the sound of twigs cracking. Yeah, uh . . .

[Pause]

It sounded like someone was behind me. God. This horrible thought came into my head like there'd been something back there in the dark I was scared of—really scared of. That something terrible had happened to me. I had this thought, *They'll start hunting for me soon.* That thought was like . . . well, it was like wooden letters spelled out in my head. Yeah—just a sentence with no explanation.

The footsteps came closer. I hid behind a tree. I tried to think what to do. Then I just started to run. It felt as if I was moving in slow motion, like my mind wasn't really moving my legs. I fell, hard. I can still . . . well, it throbs . . . The ground punched me in the face, I think.

[Laughs]

Which is how I got these cuts around my lips, I guess. I remember blood in my mouth, getting up, winded. My knees and my tongue stung 'cause I bit them. I was getting more and more stressed. I wanted to stop somewhere. Prayed someone would come and help me. All I could do was keep going and not look at anything like the dark or the trees. They were pretty scary.

I just knew I *had* to keep running. I ran and ran. I didn't know if anyone was behind me or not. Maybe I should have looked around or something, but I couldn't stop long enough to listen. Then the sun started to rise. I remember thinking it looked like melted metal running down between the trees. Would've been pretty if I hadn't been so terrified. By that time, I couldn't feel my feet anymore. All of a sudden, I heard, um, a river rushing by, I thought.

So I ran towards the sound, but there was a slope I didn't see and I stumbled down it. Then I saw where the noise was from—not a river, but the road. Well, more of a track. I followed it for a while. I don't know how long. My feet really hurt. I was cold, shivering. I kept looking over my shoulder all the time, hoping someone would come.

Then I heard this sound . . . tires on the road and I saw a red car coming, so I ran to it, waving my arms and shouting and stuff, but the driver just kept on going and the headlights blinded me. I kind of knew it would hit, but I couldn't move. I just . . . froze.

[Quinn laughs softly]

Do you find all of that as hard to make sense of as I do?

Well, you can "ask again later" if you want to.

Molly Swift

JULY 30, 2015

It's two days since they found her. The papers say she was wandering on the road, barefoot and bloodied, her mouth open in a scream the driver couldn't hear. He slammed the brakes but didn't stop in time; he hit her and took off.

As fate would have it, a German tourist couple was parked on the top of a hill along the road, filming a panorama of the sunrise over the lavender fields. In the midst of their early-morning filmmaking, the camera panned towards the road—and caught the whole accident, from the moment she walked out of the woods. She was lucky, I guess. If they hadn't spotted her, who knows how long she would have lain there bleeding.

According to *Le Monde*, the tourists ran to help and rushed the unconscious girl to the hospital here in St. Roch; but by the time the doctors wheeled her into intensive care, she was in a coma. Shaken, the pair returned to their holiday flat and watched their French sunrise video. They were shocked afresh by the sight of the girl lying crumpled in the road, the way the red car sped away, the scene captured as they ran downhill to help her—filming as they went.

That's how the video went viral. The Good Samaritans saw that glimpse of red car, the hint of a plate (a nine? an *E?*), the merest blur of a man's face, hair dark, sunglasses on. They decided the best thing to do was upload the clip to YouTube. It spread to Facebook as one of those long status updates calling on the public: "find this monster," "help the #AmericanGirl."

She wouldn't have made the headlines except it was a slow news week and the story of an American girl abroad for the first time, alone—a mystery girl who walked out of the woods— spread in the way stories do nowadays. In the video, there was that hint of foul play: not just a hit-and-run, after all, but something darker. Otherwise, why would the girl be half naked and screaming before the car ran her down? Soon the clip was trending on Twitter and dominating the insistent worm of text that slithers across the bottom of your TV during the news. It became one of those stories everyone's curious about, one of those mysteries everyone wants to solve.

That's why I'm here, me and the handful of other hacks camped outside the Hôpital Sainte-Thérèse in St. Roch, where the nuns come and go at inhospitable hours, murmuring prayer and giving no sound bites. I'm the most recent arrival, late to the party, crashing in uninvited as usual. Well, not quite uninvited. I was in Paris when I heard the news. First holiday in years, and then this story broke.

I was intrigued. I called Bill to tell him about it and he said, "Why don't you go? Cover it for the program. We'll do an episode on it." Dangling the thought, a whole episode with me at the wheel.

I said, "Go away, Bill, I'm on holiday," but I found myself thinking about that American girl, all the more so because the video was impossible to get away from.

Of course, the other journalists will state the obvious: the facts, the theories, the local gossip. But this is *American Confessional*—"the truths no one wants you to hear"—podcast once a week on iTunes in a series of audio episodes topped and tailed with our melancholy signature music. We're interested in the big themes: police brutality, political corruption, contemporary loneliness in the toxic age of the internet. We've gathered quite a following for unpicking the kind of unsolved mysteries that fascinate the American listener (well, the HBO-loving, *New Yorker*–reading kind). I like to think the show's motif of moral inquiry emerges through the interviews I do. I don't judge or comment. Bill and I let our audience decide the guilt of those involved as if they were investigating each case from the comfort of their armchairs.

So we're going for more of a think piece on this one: a young American girl coming of age, going into the world on her own only to encounter the unkindness of a stranger. Then cue the ominous music, delving into her life via her social media profile and those that encountered her here. I could see how it would work with our show, too: ragging on law enforcement always draws listeners, so we could condemn the local police, too corrupt or incompetent to find the guy in the car or examine the video before it spawned a legion of online vigilantes.

I was also the only journalist with enough guts to sneak into that hospital and make my way past the nuns. As a former Catholic-school girl, I'm not scared of nuns, which served me well when I encountered the severe-looking nun manning the hospital's reception desk. When I asked what room Quinn Perkins was in, she muttered something dismissive in French. I could see she was tough, probably prides herself on getting rid of people; but then, I pride myself on being a professional liar.

"Could you please repeat that in English?" I said with a smile, holding my ground.

"Family only allowed here," she barked, "no person else." Then she paused, glaring at me over her half-moon specs. "You are a family member of Quinn Perkins?"

What, because we're both blond and American?
I thought. It was lucky for me that she made
that assumption. A little too lucky perhaps. I
fought off the impulse to look over my shoulder
when I smiled back at her and answered,
"Yes."

Molly Swift

JULY 30, 2015

I felt bold in my lie, but I expected to be found out any moment. I followed the receptionist's directions to the girl's room as quickly as I could without looking as if I was hurrying. I came to the room, and stopped at the threshold.

From the newspaper stories, I'd imagined she would be in a tent of plastic, tangled in tubes and wires, barely visible; but she lay unfettered by machinery, neatly tucked under starched white sheets. Her face was bruised from the accident, her head shaved on one side. A run of stitches tattooed her scalp like railroad tracks: the place the car hit, the blow that knocked her clean from this world into dreamland, some gray space where she couldn't be reached.

It always happens when I'm working on a new story: that moment when the person I've been researching transforms from a news item into a human being. I'm used to it, so I'm not sure why it hit me harder this time. Maybe because I was far from home and she was, too: the girl in the bed, the girl called Quinn Perkins, was all too real to me now. Bill had told me to take some footage with the little hidden camera he bought me years ago for my undercover work. It was pinned to my lapel, switched on and filming. He'd asked me to find a chart if I could and photograph that—to document the room, the nuns, the state the girl was in.

Instead, I found myself turning off the camera and, almost as if in a dream myself, falling into the plastic bucket seat next to her bed. I sat watching the rise and fall of her chest, even and slow, and felt a strange peace descend, like watching a child sleep. With her bruised face, her half-shaven head, and black scabs crusting the stitches, she looked worlds away from the fresh-faced teen in the photographs.

I found myself pondering all over again how she came to be walking out of the woods that gray July morning. I imagined how her legs would have been bare and dirty, her feet cut to shreds when she wandered down the middle of the dirt road, her blond hair stringy with blood. Why? This question intrigued me far more than the driver of the car.

The video footage the German tourists took of her was so shocking it looked like something from a handheld horror movie. That, and the mystery of her identity, seemed to be why the video spread so far so fast. Stills taken from clips ended up on the front pages of French papers. Soon *"La fille Américaine inconnue"* bled through Reuters and Google Translate, becoming "Mysterious American Girl Found."

Eventually her father, on holiday in Tahiti with his very pregnant fiancée, recognized the face of his daughter and called up to claim her. She was given a name: Quinn Perkins of Boston. She had come to St. Roch as part of a study abroad program that placed her with a local family called the Blavettes—a schoolteacher mom, her son and daughter—presumed to be away visiting an ailing relative in some mountain area with no phone reception. Their name came out when the police released details of the case.

The news feed on my phone said Quinn was running out of time, that after the first twenty-four hours of a coma the chances of waking plummet. From the chart at the end of her bed, I could see that this particular coma had been rated a "7." Google told me that made her chances of recovery about fifty-fifty. She should have had relatives there, talking to her, playing her music, stroking her hand. But the visitor list near the door told me she had no one—Professor Perkins hadn't yet rushed to her side, which was odd. Not just odd, heartbreaking. A plane would get him here quickly from anywhere in the world.

They say that sometimes the feeling of touch, the sound of speech, can jolt a person from this dream state, wake them like a kiss in a fairy tale. And so I found myself reaching for her hand, taking it in mine. I touched her hand almost reverently. Time unspooled until I didn't know how long I'd been in that room with the softly bleeping machines, the sleeping girl, her mystery sealed inside, pristine. All of a sudden, her hand twitched, the fingers wriggling inside mine. I squeezed it again, but this time nothing happened. Still, I couldn't help thinking, *She moved.*

"Only you know how you got here," I said softly.

A hand touched my shoulder. As startled as if I'd been sleeping myself, I looked up to see the habit of a nun, crisp white folds around a surprisingly young face.

The nun's brow was creased. Her pale eyes looked nervously down at me through frameless specs. "Poor thing, she has been alone. We are so glad her family is here finally."

"Yeah." I smiled, hoping she didn't want to know exactly what family I was.

She checked the charts, the machines, making little ticks on a chart as she did. Faintly, I heard her singing a French song under her breath. I sat tensed, wondering if I should make my excuses now and leave before she started asking me questions I couldn't answer.

She was in the middle of adjusting Quinn's sheets when she turned to me and said in very precise English, "Have you heard? It is so terrible. Now they think the family of Blavette is missing."

"The family she was staying with?" I asked, managing to sound genuinely shocked because I was. "I thought they were visiting some relative."

"No indeed. The grandmother has been in touch and has not seen any of them since Christmastime. The police have just searched their house again and found something perhaps, because they are putting out a news bulletin to say this family is missing. It is on the television now."

In the reception area, a crowd had formed around the television. I couldn't see the images except for a flicker of color between their heads, but I understood enough of the rapid French reportage to confirm the nun's story: the Blavettes had been declared missing. The search was on for them as well as the hit-and-run driver. Two mysteries to solve for the price of one. When I walked into the hospital parking lot, I noticed that most of the other hacks had gone, perhaps to the gendarmerie to hear the press release. I had other plans.

Quinn Perkins

JULY 12, 2015

Blog Entry

It's midnight. The family is out. Noémie's at a party in the woods. Madame Blavette is on her date with Monsieur Right. I'm alone in the house in the middle of the French countryside, tucked into my lumpy bed that smells of bleach and jam and sterilized milk. A latchkey kid still, just in a different country. Through the slats of the wooden shutters, I can hear cicadas thrum, a thick carpet of sound, unbroken. It's comforting somehow, though I'm almost too sleepy to work on the blog, sleepy and a bit drunk still, from cider and beer and cheap rosé all swilling together.

My phone beeps: one new message. I see the number and the knots of my spine draw closer together. The sweat on my face and chest grows cold. That number. It's the one I mentioned a couple of posts ago, the one you guys all said you were worried about (I remember*loserboy38* suggested adding it to *Contacts* under "Stalker," but that was too creepy, even for me). So anyway, consequently it just comes up as just a series of ones and nines and fours and sevens. Sometimes the number series sends texts, photos like that one I posted up Thursday—the blurry photo of me sunbathing. There was another: my hoodie up, my school bag on my shoulder, and my sneakers kicking up dust on the road back to the schoolhouse. It creeped me out too much to post.

This time, it's just a single emoji, a winking face. I delete the whole message thread, like always, and at that moment, a notification pops up, a Snapchat from *lalicorne,* some random person I only half remember adding a week or so ago because I thought it was a friend of Noémie's. But they haven't chatted me yet and the profile image is one of those gray mystery man icons so you can't even tell if it's a boy or a girl. I open the app and swipe onto the chat thread to see what they've sent.

I tap on the pink square and a video loads. The film is dark, hard to see, but I hear a noise like heavy breathing. A muffled scream startles me. I grip the phone harder. A girl's face appears, too close up to see in detail. The film is choppy and moves so fast it's hard to take in before the timer in the top right corner counts down. The girl's breathing hard and there's something—a plastic bag, maybe—stretched over her face. Three . . . two . . . one, and the screen goes black, the video vanishing forever as Snapchat deletes it and, with it, the girl.

For a long time after that I sat on the floor. The curtains were open and outside I could hear the constant cricket machine, see star-shine countryside black with no light pollution to reassure me that I was anything other than alone. Mme B says this place is haunted. I don't think I believe in that stuff, but sitting there alone in the middle of the night, I knew what she meant, like I could almost hear the laughter of the people who lived here before trapped in the walls, behind the brick, the ghost of a good time.

I started to make up explanations to comfort myself—that it's Noémie's doing, a practical joke or some really weird junk mail. After a long while, I reached for the phone, half hoping it was all some weird dream, half wanting to see it again and find out that it's really just a clever advertising campaign for a new handheld horror movie. But somehow I know it wasn't a horror flick clip. It was too real for that. When I do pick up the phone, the video's gone. Snapped into an untimely death in the virtual void, because it's Snapchat, of course. All messages are instantaneous, ticking down the moments it takes you to read or watch them like a fuse on a bomb and then they're gone.

She's gone, as if she was never there, and I'm sitting with my back against the door, typing this on my blogging app. And here's a straw poll: What do I do, guys? Who do I tell? Anyhow, I need to go now, to check the house, to lock the door. Something instead of sitting on the floor, feeling scared and alone in the middle of nowhere, waiting for them to come home.

Molly Swift

JULY 30, 2015

As I drove along the dusty main road of St. Roch, my skin still hummed from the excitement at the hospital: being mistaken for a relative, the plot twist with the Blavettes, seeing Quinn. I came to the part of the road she must have walked along, the jagged points of trees looming like arrowheads dug from a riverbed.

In the YouTube clip, right before the accident, Quinn makes no effort to dodge the car hurtling her way. Afterwards, she lies in the road, mumbling words you can't quite catch from the choppy audio as the tourists got close to her, filming all the time, though a number of comment threads have speculated on what she was saying. Heading towards the line of trees, I couldn't visualize the pixelated image of her prone body that was reprinted in all the papers. In my mind's eye, she shimmered as she walked out of the forest, her pale fingers beckoning me on to the dark trees.

My rental car squealed around a turn in the road and towards the house. I wasn't yet used to driving on these kinds of roads; it amazed me that I could be in town one moment and the next in the heart of farmland, driving down little sewage runnels between rows of squat olive trees or lavender or yellow rapeseed flowers. The Blavette house came after a turnoff for just such a nothing little lane. Opposite it was an orchard, where the apples were growing red and dark and glossy as poison fruit. A sprayer moved between trees, dispensing real poison that ran into drainage ditches and misted the air. This was the place where the American girl had been staying, where her vanished host family had lived for generations—it wasn't hard to find. Google, the great democratizer of freelance detective work, told me where to go for a bit of trespassing.

I stopped the car and lit a cigarette, hoping the air around me wouldn't catch fire in the fug of pesticide. I smoked hard, letting the engine idle while I sized up the house. Like Quinn, it was different from the pictures I'd seen, idyllic shots that must have been stolen from some holiday rental catalog. Paler, sadder, more elegant, and more ruined, it peered from between the trees, a witness to who knows what.

From my left came a rhythmic clipping noise. I climbed out of the car, keys clenched between my fingers Boston walk-to-your-door-from-the-bar style, cigarette hanging from my mouth.

An old man ambled from the side of the house carrying a pair of garden shears. He was ancient and white-bearded, clipping away at the leaves of a vine climbing the side of the house, and at first he didn't see me. Like some scene from a French Pathé reel, he was timeless, whistling to himself as if nothing untoward had happened in the village of St. Roch. I got back in my car and crawled over the pebbles of the drive, slowly so I wouldn't give him too much of a fright.

He must have been pretty deaf, because it took him a long time to turn around. But when he did, he looked more scared than I was when I spotted him. I let out a sigh, laughing at myself for succumbing to the gothic fantasy the place suggested. He nodded to me. I got out of the car and walked over and for a moment we stood and looked at each other, caught in the embarrassing free-fall between people who never listened in language class.

Eventually I broke the silence, introducing myself in shaky high-school French. *"Bonjour. Je m'appelle Molly."*

"Ah, bonjour." The man took off his floppy cloth hat and held out his hand, gnarled and thorn-tracked as my grandpa's were. *"Monsieur Raymond. Enchanté."* He murmured more words to me in a sweet old man crackle. Their meaning was lost on me, but I gathered from his accompanying gestures that he hammered things here and may have recently cut something with a pair of giant scissors.

"A gardener?" I asked, smiling, "For the family?"

He looked at me blankly with milky blue eyes like sucked sweets. I wondered if maybe he didn't speak English.

And then he intoned in a gentlemanly crackle (twice as charming for being in Franglais), "I take care of school and, as well, this house while the family . . ." He thought for a moment, then flapped his hands like birds flying.

"Are away." I nodded. *Take care of school.* I remembered reading something about a school in the reports on Quinn. "You the caretaker?"

I fished for a cigarette so that he saw no trace of surprise or anything else on my face. "When do you think they're coming back?" I flicked my lighter wheel, eyeing him through the smoke. From my years of interviewing people, looking for the real stories under their words, I know everyone has little tics, little tells. For most, it's easier to tell if folks are lying when you know them. But actually, when you've been at it a while, you find yourself cold-reading people all the time without meaning to. You had the money for a ticket all along, old lady at the *métro* stop—yeah, you. And, taxi driver, I see you in your rearview, and no, you *don't* know the way.

But as far as I could make out, Monsieur Raymond was not lying. He shrugged. "They go away often. Are you a friend of theirs? I only live over there, yet I have never seen you." He pointed to the primeval forest, its dark shapes gathering form and substance as the dusk crept in.

"You live in the woods?" I asked in the hope of distracting him.

He smiled. He liked that question. In my experience, professional weirdos work hard to generate notoriety—locally he is *Raymond, that crazy man living in the woods.* I bet he's the one who originally spread the rumors about what he gets up to out there all alone.

"On the edge of those," he said, pointing vaguely, "that very far edge of school field. You look hard you just see my chimney—she's smoking."

Straining my eyes, I did see it, though before it seemed like just another dark point in the tree line. I felt an involuntary little shiver of glee rattle up my neck at the idea of a childhood myth made flesh—the creepy old guy in the shack in the woods. I'd finally met him.

As if he could read my mind, he said, "Yes, I am there always. Keeping my eyes in things. I see a lot of things here."

"Like what?"

Tapping his nose. "Everything."

I dragged on my cigarette, letting the smoke burn and twirl in my lungs, exhaling. "Did you see her—the American girl—when she came out of the forest?"

He looked at me strangely, cutting his eyes at me under snowy lashes. Very blue eyes, betraying a much sharper mind than he let on.

"*L'Américaine?*" He patted his pockets, pulled out a packet of Drum Gold, took a pinch, and flicked it into a paper, rolling and licking in one seamless gesture so that the cigarette seemed to grow out of his thorn-pricked, nicotine-stained hands like pale elongated fruit. "Sometime I feel sorry for that girl."

I flicked my lighter and he dragged hard, cheeks puffing out to show the impressive spider veins of a lifelong drinker. "Why's that?"

He shrugged. "*Sais pas.* Just . . . well, there was something about her. How you say? Soft? Like a fruit, that you know." He gouged his fingers as if he were squeezing a peach. "But then I only met her possibly twice."

"Sweet girl," I said, smiling.

"*Ouais.* But then so are all the girls they keep here, aren't they?"

Molly Swift

JULY 30, 2015

For the first part of my life, I grew up in a family that, to the casual onlooker, resembled a Norman Rockwell painting. Dad was a senior partner in a Boston practice who could afford not only an apartment on Beacon Hill, but the beachfront house in Maine where my sister and I spent the best summers of our childhood. Mom was a part-time paralegal secretary and domestic goddess of Martha Stewart proportions. My sister, Claire, and I were brats: she the mean teen homecoming queen; me the band-camp-loving nerd.

The summer I turned thirteen, a letter arrived. I never knew exactly what it said, but I remember Dad's hands shaking as he read it, Mom's angry nagging curdling the hot August air. I was used to their ups and downs. I think I took my bike out for a ride around the coast instead of worrying. In any case, the malpractice suit that ate up everything we owned took its sweet time. It was another year before we'd gone from living like princes to crowding into my Jewish grandmother's stuffy brownstone, torturing her cats. When she threw us out and we began a stint with my Catholic paternal grandparents in Boston's South End, I began to notice the comments friends and relatives whispered as they sat around the big kitchen table: "Col's losing his way and he needs our prayers"—a Catholic way of saying that my father had gone nuts.

We moved back to Maine, to the northern woods that smell of hemlock and balsam, the setting for Dad's new purpose of refashioning his bankrupt life in the image of Thoreau's. By which I mean that he tumbled, babbling, into Grandpa Swift's old timber cabin on Chesuncook Lake and used what money remained to stock-pile AK-47s and all the canned creamed corn you could stand. Out in those woods, while Dad snared rabbits and speared trout, Mom discovered a taste for home-brewed beer and I became a delinquent. It was easy to do since my dad's transformation into a wild-eyed survivalist meant that the materials for mischief—knives, rope, power tools—were all around me. By the time I was Quinn's age, my favorite hobby was stealing weed killer and a bag of sugar and rolling my own fuses from cigarette papers so I could blow the fuck out of the earth that trapped us in that madhouse. My sister—through a rock solid combination of grit and conformity—came out of that life pretty normal. She learned to blend in, to agree, to hide the crazy. I didn't, or couldn't. I've always been the black sheep, though over time, life has sanded the rough edges off me.

On the positive side, Dad's questionable parental supervision taught me three crucial things: how to blaze a trail, how to hot-wire a car, and how to pick the toughest locks. Joyriding in cars, carving arrows in trees, and breaking into barns to scare sheep haven't been all that useful in furthering my journalistic career, but the ability to pick locks? Handier than you might think. Filing cabinets, abandoned warehouses, creepy *Silence of the Lambs* lockups are not a problem as long as you've got a bobby pin, or in my case a little black bag of hook picks, pins, and paper clips. I pulled it out, ready to take a look in the Blavette house.

I needn't have bothered. My evening's trespassing was made a whole lot easier by the fact that either the police or the caretaker had left the back door open. It was pitch outside now, the stars sharp and bright as police spotlights. It didn't quite look like a crime scene yet, but you could tell the police had been poking around from the big-booted footprints scattered around the floors, the occasional coffee cup left to stain surfaces. Once I was sure Monsieur Raymond wasn't still lurking around, I took a deep breath, peeled away from the doorway, and crossed the hallway to the stairs.

36

At the top of the stairs was a bedroom. The large bed told me it was probably the master, and the matching rose-pattern wallpaper and curtains suggested a woman had decorated it. I tiptoed over the pastel rug towards the bed, as cautious as if I might find someone sleeping there. On the nightstand sat a framed picture of the Blavette family, when the husband was still on the scene. I snapped an iPhone photo and moved on, flicking my torch over the ointments and powders on the antique dresser, illuminating the dark spots freckling the mirror. Without its people, the house felt frozen in time, like the ballroom of some lost ocean liner.

I crept out into the dark well of the hallway and walked on, identifying the various bedrooms, all with objects and clothes left strewn across beds and floors. First was what I decided was the son's room, the door decorated with a photo of twenties Paris and a map of the stars; inside, a guitar, a basketball hoop, and thick textbooks. Save the French titles of the books, it could have been the room of any American college-age boy. Next was a young girl's innocent bedroom: a world map dotted with photos of pen pals decorated one baby-pink wall and the shelves were crowded with pony figurines and books about ballerinas.

The guest room was bigger but had less character, its floral walls and drapes echoing the master. It smelled of lavender and cigarettes. Weirdly, the wardrobe and desk were clean; where had Quinn's clothes and things gone? I snapped a few pictures but found nothing more useful than some old book about the history of the local caves and a half-written postcard addressed to someone called Kennedy. "Hey, dude!" it began. "Missing your face. So awesome . . ." My heart sank a little at the way it tailed off mid-awesome, as if something had interrupted the writer. On impulse, I stuffed both the book and the card in my bag.

At the end of the hallway was another door I hadn't tried yet. I twisted the handle. It moved, but the door didn't open. I had just knelt down to look through the lock when there was a noise downstairs, like the scrape of a chair. My hand fumbled my keys from my pocket. I pushed my sharp little front door key between my forefinger and middle finger, straining my ears towards the stairs. As I tiptoed down them, I heard a noise from outside, a sharp bark, like a fox. Maybe it was that I'd heard. In a place like this, it wasn't surprising my mind was playing tricks on me.

I was just creeping back into the front room when I heard tires gobbling up gravel and saw the lights of a car. It pulled to a halt. The thrum of an engine stopped and the headlights went out. A door slammed. I stopped in the hallway, just listening. A ring tone sounded outside, then stopped and a man's voice began speaking rapid and low in French.

I turned around in a slow circle, thinking about the house, the windows, the doors, the ways out. The only option was that back door. I tiptoed to it, trying to keep my steps light, my breathing calm. Outside, the voice stopped talking and the man cleared his throat. I glanced behind me to see the front door handle beginning to turn.

Quinn Perkins

JULY 13, 2015

Blog Entry

Back home in Boston, this blog is all about coming up with creative ways to make my boring life seem interesting. I:

- tell weird stories that are semibased on my antics
- post bloodthirsty stories about zombies and hell beasts
- quote lines from classic horror movies of the '80s
- write trashy tabloid headlines to caption my most awkward moments

I guess it's how I met you all, horror fan friends, who always write bloodthirsty comments on my Monsters of New England posts: *My Rockport Devil Sighting*, *What Mothman?* and my most popular post ever, *Lizzie Borden and the Fall River Witches!* Earlier in the year, I had so many great chats with talented writer friends like *PoeBoy13* and *dreamswithghosts* that I got up the nerve to send some of my horror stories out to zines and even got "Lila on the Ceiling" published in *Splatterpunk*! (It's that one you all said reminded you of early Stephen King—oh, how I would *love* to be Stephen King one day!) I thought my travels in France would give me the perfect chance to develop my skills with some travel writing, and find some new spooky places to do a little urban exploring, dig into the local legends.

Turns out I didn't need to leave this house to find the darkness. It found me. It's weird to think that this blog used to be all about a wannabe writer with no life experience to write about. Now that life in France has taken a dark turn and real stuff has happened, I should be unblocked, but I'm not. Now for once I find myself wishing my life was more ordinary.

It's almost dawn and I've given up on trying to sleep. I've taken my meds early—clonazepam, Wellbutrin, Depakote, lorazepam—hoping to calm down, but they didn't make me any less anxious or depressed, so now I feel drowsy *and* stressed.

In the cold light of day, it will seem less scary, I guess, but I still have that papery feeling. Like something's about to go wrong. I've turned around and around and around in the starched sheets all night and haven't actually slept. That video thing freaked me out way too much.

Any suggestions, people? Maybe y'all are asleep.

At least Noémie's home now. I heard the noises of her door creaking open, the whisper of her clothes falling to the floor, the rusty metal groan of her climbing into bed. I felt such relief to hear those familiar sounds, so much that I almost went in to tell her about what happened . . . but I didn't know what to say. The video is gone. I put the text message into Google Translate. It said, *This is real.* That's all. Pretty weird, huh? And I don't know her well enough to guess how she would react.

Though after three months here, I should, right? I came here just after Easter, hoping to complete my very last quarter of high school speaking fluent French. Since then, I've walked with Noémie each day to the shiny new lycée for fast-talking French lessons and head-spinning economics lessons (not sure if the latter is useful preparation for being an English major at Bryn Mawr in a couple of months, but Noé's studying it for her baccalaureate so I'm tagging along). Each weekend—as stipulated by my study abroad program—we've gone on an odyssey of cultural discovery in Charente-Maritime: exploring the Vieux Port, the amphi-theater and the big old church in La Rochelle, the museums of commerce and automata and the *son et lumière* at the castle (that place about a hundred times!). The Sacred Heart Travel Scholarship promised a chance to "soak in the French way of life through full cultural immersion, expanding academic horizons as much as comprehension."

If anything, I have less comprehension. Noé is more of a mystery to me than when I arrived. Back in April she seemed excited to have an American friend, giving me friendship bracelets and mixtapes, throwing me parties. Since the holiday started, she's been quieter, staying in her bedroom a lot . . . *sang-froid*, maybe, or plain old-fashioned dislike. We were hurled together by the freak weather conditions of cultural exchange, matched by an educational eHarmony through a database of hobbies that couldn't possibly tell if we had much in common. Secretly, though, I think we have too much in common—living in our heads, not being, as the French say, *bien dans sa peau*. It makes for a lot of awkward silences at dinner, that's for sure.

It makes for being lonely. I even tried to phone my dad, but I think he's too busy getting ready for the trip to Tahiti with Meghan. They're superbusy, anyway, preparing for the new baby, the tiny half sister or brother who's arriving just in time to fill in for me when I go off to college. Pity that kid! I mean, Meghan's nice enough. I'm sure she'll make a good mom. She turns twenty-five in a few weeks, so she'll be exactly half Dad's age by the time she goes into labor. He was supervising her PhD when they started sneaking around, and I think she thought he was a catch.

She came to dinner once before they knew I knew and after a bottle of wine she told me "your dad is such a good listener, even when I talk about my feelings." Then I *really* knew. Though I still didn't know whether to hug her or warn her to get out while she could. So I just topped up her glass and later, in my room, I looked at some old photos Mom took of me and Dad for some photography project or other and tried to see if he listened to me back then, if we were close. But how can you tell? Just because people smile for photos doesn't mean they're happy.

Poor Meghan's learning the hard way now. Postmarriage, prebaby Dad is an absent presence, working late, drinking hard, teaching summer school so he doesn't have to spend time with anyone who's not an adoring student. I remember feeling bitter when they got engaged and thinking, *One day he'll blame you for everything like he blames me.* Like he blames me for Mom dying and for losing it after she did. Now that it's come true, though, I just feel sad for her.

Anyhow . . . to make a long story short, I didn't talk about the stalker/message situation with

Dad or Meghan or Noé or anybody. In the end, I just spent the whole night feeling totally paranoid, making a bullet-point list of suspects (in other words, a list of all the people I've met here so far):

- Noémie Blavette
- her mom, Émilie
- Marlene who works at the café
- Émilie's British friend Stella
- the school caretaker, Monsieur Raymond
- the local kids who hang around the pool

Seriously, though, I can't think of any reason any of them would send me snuff movie texts. After all, I'm just an ordinary girl who happens to be a long, long way from home.

Molly Swift

JULY 30, 2015

Halfway back to the hotel, a pair of headlights glared in my rearview mirror, burning full blaze. I shielded my eyes. The car came closer, going faster. I craned around, blinded by the lights. Behind me, the car was almost touching. I braced for impact, squeezed my eyes half shut. I heard the engine rev, the rubber squeal of the tires swerving around me. As it flew past, it swiped the side of my rental, jolting the car.

I almost steered into a ditch but I didn't stop. I kept on driving, forcing the little car back on course. I could feel the sweat streaming down my collar. By the time I was straight and steady again, the red taillights of the other car were just visible in the distance like the eyes of a demon dog. Then they left me in darkness.

Everything around—the white moths shivering in the headlights, the treetops soughing in the wind, the bats, the night noises—fucking everything gave me the creeps. I drove on instinct alone. No higher brain function available. Just getting towards people, lights, civilization as fast as I could, away from the silent house and whoever was in there with me. Twice I drove into one of the loose-dirt ditches that run the length of the narrow roads, once out of sheer nerves, once because a car came straight at me around a bend, headlights blazing, radio blaring. We almost crashed. I swerved. It was only sitting in the ditch, the other car's horn blaring angrily into the distance, that I realized I was on the wrong side of the road. I sat, took a deep breath, took out a cigarette.

I pride myself on my stoic nature. I always have, from my tree-climbing, bottle-rocket-building childhood onward. I talk straight. I swear loud. I honor promises. Like John Wayne, but female and much less right wing. If you asked me to describe myself in a word it would be *tough*. Or *bitch*. Or maybe *tough bitch,* but after the scrabble out of the Blavette house, the headlights on the way home, it took a full ten minutes until my hands stopped shaking enough that I could light that cigarette.

I couldn't help wondering if it was Monsieur Raymond who had opened the door at the house, followed me along the dark road. Take it from your unreliable narrator: there was something creepy about that creepy caretaker. No way of knowing for sure, though.

My phone binged at me from its plastic rest on the dash. A message popped up—Bill asking if I was still alive.

I tapped to call him. He picked up after two

rings but didn't say anything. "Hey, Bill. You good?"

"Who wants to know?" He sounded cranky. A couple of days without checking in, and already the sarcasm had begun.

"Me, Molly," I said with a laugh, taking a drag of my cigarette, my eyes flicking nervously to the rearview to see if anyone was there. "You losing the plot without me there?"

"Flattery will get you everywhere, you know," he said in the deadpan tone I knew and loved.

"That how I ended up working for you for peanuts?"

"Ha. You got anything on this girl yet?"

"Yeah. But listen, I gotta go," I said, turning the ignition.

"You okay? You sound . . ."

"Call you later." I hung up and turned out into the road.

I knew St. Roch was a short drive from the Blavette house, but nonetheless it seemed like a very long while before my poor car juddered to a halt outside the Overlook—the seen-better-days hotel Bill had booked me a room in. Actually, the only hotel in town, a grand old turn-of-the-century building with a comfy three-star hotel inside. Its original name, Le Napoléon, better befit its air of seedy hubris.

But I love a fleapit, and the Orwellian level

of journalistic commitment it implies. I love that you meet people from all walks of life, that you can drink out of a paper bag or eat pizza or smoke cigarettes (hell, probably even crack) in your room. Most of all, I love that there are people inside and the lights are always on.

After the trauma at the Blavette house, I felt that life owed me a pack of Gauloises and a whiskey. My room in the Napoléon can just about sustain a guest edging around the single bed to turn on the TV or open the door, and the pissoir is so closely situated that you can practically use it from the bed if you've got good aim. You can also turn the TV on with one toe as you smoke out the window. So instead of going straight to my room, I walked past the bored desk clerk playing Angry Birds, past the wolf pack of journalists decamped from the hospital to the hotel bar. As soon as I reached that comforting oasis of wood and free peanuts, I ordered a double JD.

I stared into the drink, my pale, freckly face suspended in the dark liquid like a bad moon rising, my hair wild. Not a good look. Turning to my phone, I checked for messages, pretending to myself that I wasn't still shaking. There were two: one from my mom and another from Bill. I texted Mom that I was really fine, and left Bill for later.

Playing silently on the TV over the bar was a

news bulletin about the missing Blavettes, showing the faces of the mother, the son, the daughter. Pictures harvested from their Facebook accounts just as Quinn's have been. Photos showing smiling faces, glowing tans, people with places to go and everything to live for.

Back in Paris, when the #AmericanGirl story broke, I did as much Googling around as I could on my phone. News about Quinn was easy to find. Deeper searches led me to a dedicated subreddit as well as a concerned group of Facebook well-wishers, online supporters for this viral heroine having sprung up overnight like chanterelles. The main theory of the subreddit armchair detectives (the very same sweetly fanatical cellar-dwellers who tune in to my show each week) is that the family went to visit a relative, to get away for a weekend. They've been roundly criticized as irresponsible for leaving a foreign exchange student in their care to wander and wash up broken. Now the police have declared them officially missing, the clock will begin ticking, as it is already ticking for the girl.

After messages, I flipped through the photographs I'd taken with my iPhone, glancing at dark and poorly composed images of the woods, the house, the bedrooms in darkness. The one that made me pause longest was the photo of the photo on Émilie Blavette's nightstand, so different from the fake-smiley Facebook ones issued by the police. In the picture from the nightstand, Émilie looks happy. She hugs her husband close, though he stands more aloof, all French and cool in his sunglasses and crisp shirt. Young Raphael leans his head on her shoulder, a gangly fourteen-year-old momma's boy. Noémie at twelve is a chubby little thing, cute in her pigtails and halter top, hugging Daddy tight.

How does a whole family disappear? Leave the face of the earth without a trace? From reading the news and snooping at the house, I know this: one minute the Blavettes were a normal(ish) happy(ish) family—the son a star athlete, just beginning his university career in film-making, the daughter a shy girl who loved ballet and ponies and boy bands, the mom a former head teacher. One minute they were going to the beach, posing for smiling photos, the next, gone. And what of the American girl, who they'd invited to be part of their family for a summer? How did she fit into this picture?

I took advantage of the better standard of Wi-Fi in the bar to check out Twitter (#AmericanGirl still trending, video still viral) and Facebook. I'd already had a brief look at Quinn's page, but now I looked again, noting her relationship status: "it's complicated." Her privacy settings meant you couldn't see much: a profile picture of her with the Blavette boy and girl arm in arm on the beach with the sea behind them, tanned, grinning happily, Quinn in the middle, squeezed between the siblings. They must have been pretty buddy-buddy to get to the profile pic stage. Behind them lies Quinn's cover image of herself standing in the middle distance on a Boston lake in winter, black-clad against the snow and ice, serious-faced, a forlorn contrast to her seeming happiness in France. The only other thing I could find is a little clip| of her waving pom-poms at some high-school football game, blond hair bouncing. A different Quinn again. This version seems like the sort of popular airhead whose high-school yearbook reads like the story of her, whose bed would be surrounded by get-well cards. The "Mean Girl" type. I found myself wondering which image is the real her, or if any of them were.

Thinking back, I didn't see one get-well card; and that fact only deepened the mystery surrounding her. The American news had said a lot about her father, Professor Leo Perkins, head of classics at Harvard. It also mentioned that she was an only child whose mother had died years before. A fresh Google search revealed a Spotify with a bunch of playlists and an Instagram with more pictures. I looked at her snaps of a pool, a beach, the woods, a club full of young people partying, trying to make sense of the captions—*Picnic at the beach, Noé, Raffi and Freddie, Adventure at Les Yeux* and the hashtags #funtimes, #selfie, #thuglife.

By two in the morning, the barman was yawning and giving me a weary look as he polished beer glasses and swept peanut shells off the bar and into my lap. Finally, even this exquisitely polite individual lost patience and asked me to go. I was about to head upstairs when I remembered that in my fearful rush, I'd forgotten my notes in the car. Good time to nip out for a smoke, anyway.

In the parking lot, I teetered along, suddenly realizing how drunk I was. It had been raining and the streets were gleaming. As I came closer to my car, I saw that the passenger door was ajar. Had I forgotten to close it? Kicking myself, I tottered closer, hoping that wasn't where I'd left my file of clippings on the case.

It was only when I reached the car that my eyes adjusted to the dark and I saw that I hadn't forgotten to close the door at all. Someone had jimmied it open with a piece of metal, or something—you could see it from the tiny scratches in the paint job around the handle. Pulling it open, I saw my file was gone.

Quinn Perkins

JULY 13, 2015

Blog Entry

Today we went to the pool. Again. Noémie took her bike and I borrowed her brother Raphael's. He's been studying film in Paris at the Sorbonne, so doesn't really live in the house anymore, but is coming home for the summer. He's kind of the local hero in St. Roch, the all-star football player, the guy that got the scholarship. Some days he's all you hear about, especially from Noémie's mom, who's fond of getting the family albums out. Noémie must get sick of it—I mean, I've only been here a few months and I'm already a bit sick of hearing how amazing and handsome and smart and athletic he is. At the same time, after looking at about a million photos of him over the last few months, I'm not sure I don't have a bit of a crush on him. After all, I practically know him already.

So I borrowed the all-star's bike and we cycled along the dusty country road dodging Vespas and farm trucks, the boy saddle punching my girl butt with each pedal stroke. And then we were there: the pool, with its rusted green fence, its siren song of blue, its golden boy flesh pulling us through the rose-tangled gates.

In St. Roch, the pool is the place to be. There aren't many teens in this town, maybe twenty or so around my age and a little bit older. There aren't any jobs either: some really big scandal happened years ago from what I've heard, and it almost shut the place down. Now it's the southern French equivalent of one of those American ghost towns that used to rely on coal mining and then the mine shut and the people left. You might think that in a rural town surrounded by idyllic beaches, teens would tan there every day, but no jobs means no transport. You need a car to get to the beach and almost no one has one.

Plus, no adults go to the pool, so it's like this secret clubhouse where kids can smoke and get up to mischief. When I saw the photos on the study abroad site, the town seemed so picturesque and "so French." Over the past few months, I've come to find those advertising-perfect images funny in a sad way: they're such blatant lies. In reality, this place is dying, everything around fading and breaking as residents abandon it and tourists find better places to go.

The kids I've met here feel trapped, as if they'll never go anywhere else or find anything better to do, so they make things worse by vandalizing everything, even the pool, where, unless it's raining, they all come after lunch and lounge on the burned grass around that little rectangle of blue. Surrounded by the looping hate speech of their graffiti, they smoke and gossip and flirt and play guitar, and they swim, dive, dunk, splash, all day every day, all summer long. I guess it's okay, if you're good at flirting and swimming and tanning, if you're not feeling totally paranoid about who's stalking you.

(I know, I know. You all said to chill out and relax, and if it happens again to tell an adult. But wouldn't you be just a *tiny* bit freaked?)

We strolled in, not greeting anyone too enthusiastically, not letting our eyes fix on anyone beautiful, boy or girl. To me, the one outsider, they all look so at home there—as if they sprang up in the night, flesh fresh from the wrapper. Twenty pairs of fake Ray-Bans turning to watch us walk in before losing interest.

This early, the pool is empty except for two acid green noodles and a busted pink inflatable raft. We reach our usual spot under the olive tree and kick off our flip-flops, shake out our towels, ditch the baguettes Émilie made us take in the nearest bin. "Get Lucky" is playing on somebody's mini-speakers as we strip off, stretch out, already breaking out the tanning oil. As usual, a knot of sinewy guys is looking our way, their eyes popping like the Photoshopped colors of a soda ad because their skin is so brown. They're hot, but all I can think is: *Is it one of them?*

One is offering his hands up to the service of our un-sun-creamed backs, grinning straight-white-toothed, eager and horny. This is Noémie's doing, not mine. Berated at home and by her own account hated at school, she is Queen Bee at the pool. And it's not hard to see why: she totally has that French chick thing going on: the smooth tanned skin, cool, short-cropped hair, beestings of tits (French titties, I call them). Lounging by the pool in her bikini, smoking American Spirit and shooting the shit, she's all *sang-froid.*

The guy with the hands—Freddie is his name—takes pride in his work. It's a weird feeling, but not a bad one. When he undoes my bikini top, though, and gestures that I should turn over so he can do my front, I shake my head, feel my face flush. Noémie rolls her eyes at me as if to say, *Prude,* or whatever the French is for that, and beckons him over. I want to tell him to tuck his tongue back in. He's her flunky. Neither of us would ever date him.

After an hour of sunbathing—and you could set your watch by this—Noémie says, "Let's play the game."

So we obey her, playing the daily game of dunking each other in the pool, seeing who can hold their breath the longest. The St. Roch boys *love* these games of dunking. Me, not so much. But Noémie eggs me on, shooting me a disappointed look every time I try to drift towards the sidelines. She's a pro at the old peer pressure.

I'm holding my own until Freddie comes up behind me and dunks me hard and for a long, long time. I start panicking. Chlorine burns my throat and eyes. Starts stripping out my sinuses.

Alone down there where no one can hear me scream, I flail, kicking his leg, clawing his arms. I start to think—no, I start to *know* I am drowning.

Molly Swift

JULY 31, 2015

The only things taken were my notes on the case, though actually, it was that choice that worried me. Why would anyone break into a car, not to steal it, not even to take the GPS—still sitting brazenly on the dash—but to take my lousy papers? I thought about the noise in the house, the headlights following me home. Maybe whoever was behind me on the road had followed me here.

"It looks to me that someone has cracked up your car," said a French-accented voice at my elbow. "Have they also taken your things?"

I turned around, poised to take a swing, and saw a man in a panama hat and a crisp white suit, smoking a purple Sobranie and looking pretty pleased with himself for his observation.

"Computer printouts," I said, "which were worth nothing. It's more just . . ."

". . . stressing, I know," he said, his eyes twinkling sympathetically. "There have been a few break-ins around here. The hotel should have warned you."

"That would've been good," I said, slamming the door. It bounced open again.

"It would seem the locking parts are broken," said the man. "I may have something that will be of use in this."

"I'm fine, really," I said.

"It's not a problem," he said, lifting his hat briefly to reveal thinning blond curls.

It seemed rude to say no twice. He walked a few feet, opened the trunk of a green Figaro, and pulled out some cardboard and gaffer tape. *How convenient,* I thought. It just so happened that he was out here when I found my car and that he had the very things I need to fix it. I squinted at the Figaro, trying to see if the headlights looked familiar from the road to St. Roch. I was still a bit bleary from the Jack Daniel's and it was hard to tell. I got my keys ready between my fingers to be on the safe side.

When he came back, grinning with DIY man-pride, I said, "So how come you were here in the parking lot? It's nearly three A.M."

By way of answer, he took a drag of his cigarette. "We are both working on catching the lung cancer, I think. Here . . ." He handed me the tape.

I accepted it, not completely convinced, and bit off a length of silver tape. Together, we forced the door to stay closed with one of the most haphazard repair jobs of all time.

"Looks like a pirate with a shitty eye patch," I said.

"Of course it is." He smiled glassily, looking like he hadn't a clue what I was saying. "Are you staying at the Napoléon?"

I nodded. "You, too?"

Mr. Panama Hat smiled charmingly with one side of his mouth, and I felt surer than ever that he was either my stalker or a journalistic rival. Still, he seemed harmless enough for the moment, so I waited while he put his tape back, and walked back to the Napoléon with him. A few steps from the door, the rain started coming down hard. Before I knew it, my knight in shining armor was sweeping his coat off, holding it out to protect me like something out of a Robert Doisneau photograph.

When we were safely inside the doorway, he laid his hand on my arm. "I can see you are shaking." With a little bow he pulled the door open for me.

"I'm fine," I snapped. Chivalry frightens me.

"Really? It might do you good to drink one more Jack Daniel's for the road, to steady your nerves?" He smiled his charming smile, his face moving too close to mine.

"What do you mean 'one more'? How do you know what I've been drinking?"

"You've been in the bar for a while," he said with a laugh. "I did see you before, and now you are weaving a little. It is part of the reason I helped you."

"Well, don't," I said. "I can hold my drink and I don't need some two-bit Jean-Paul Belmondo impersonator holding doors open for me."

I strode through the door to the old-fashioned brass elevator and jackhammered the button. It was stuck.

Monsieur Tremblé, the concierge, walked up. "All is well, mademoiselle?"

"No," I said. "That gentleman over there has been bothering me. He—"

"That gentleman—" Tremblé gently released the button "—is Monsieur Valentin. I'm sure he would only be meaning to help."

The elevator arrived and he pulled open the delicate birdcage.

"Thank you, Tremblé." I smiled weakly and stepped inside, thinking that I knew that name from somewhere.

Monsieur Valentin. Inspector Valentin. I'd just missed a golden opportunity to have a drink with the detective in charge of the case. I could have drunk him under the table, charmed him, pumped him for information, and captured it all on video. Instead, I verbally kneed him in the balls. Typical.

Quinn Perkins

JULY 13, 2015

Blog Entry

Hands burrow into my armpits, close on my upper arms, strong as a vise, pressing into me. Hurting me so I want to yell. But I can't because my mouth is full of water, my lungs burning, chest, flesh heavy as lead. The hands squeeze me, wrench my flesh, and I am fighting tooth and nail, fighting for all I am worth, sucking the water deeper and deeper, my nose, my throat on fire.

And then the hands haul me to land and I flop on the concrete oven shelf at the side of the pool, its grit raking my flesh, then I lie still, weirdly still, no longer fighting at all.

The field of my bright-light-spotted burning blur vision darkens. Something is over me, on me, blocking out the sun. Someone. Vaguely, I see a tanned face, dark eyes, lips. Then the lips are on mine, blowing, and strong hands pump my ribs. I cough, splutter up water, choking, wheezing for air. Lips press mine again, soft and hot against my freezing lips, breathing harsh life into me. I cough harder. More water comes out. The man moves, turns me on my side. It strikes me that he is fully clothed in black and I have the surreal thought that the ghost of Johnny Cash just saved me from drowning.

My ears pop and the world shrieks again. Voices crash against my eardrums, angry, cacophonous. Waves of sound, argument, some angry exchange in French happening over my head that I am way too out of it to translate. The squall of words ends as suddenly as it started. The hands are on me again, under me, lifting my waterlogged floppy fish body. Johnny Cash cradles me against his black-clad chest. I blink and stare up like a baby. His face is all I can see and he is beautiful . . . and familiar somehow.

He frowns down at me and I hear my voice all high and dreamy. "Am I dead?" My own voice betraying me.

He grins and says, "That's terrible."

"What?"

He's laying me down on a towel at this point, my own towel under the olive tree. Other faces jostle behind him to look at me. Noémie, Freddie, Sophie, Romuald. They are blurry, out of focus. Then I see Freddie, who nearly drowned me, and I look away, look back at Johnny Cash. Less Johnny Cash now that I'm gazing up into his dreamy brown eyes, more James Franco. He has the tousled dark hair, a stubbly beard, and cute crinkles in the corners of his eyes.

"Terrible," he murmurs, leaning close to my face so only I can hear, "to almost drown and then the first words you come out with are cliché."

I smile up at him, even though my ribs ache and my eyes sting and my throat burns. "So the next time I have a near-death experience I should—" cough "—stop watching my life flash in front of my eyes and take a minute to come up with a better line?"

"Ah, irony. You must be feeling better. I am officially no longer needed here." He pretends to get up and then kneels down closer, grinning again. He smooths strands of hair from my forehead, then turns to Noémie and says something brusquely in French I don't catch.

"*Mais non!*" says Noémie angrily, her pouty lips twisting in disgust. "I hate you." She turns away, her arms folded.

The boy frowns. "Forgive my sister," he says. "She has not taken care of you."

"Noémie's your sister?" I say, surprised. And then I realize why he looks so familiar: it's Raphael, the Sorbonne student whose photos I've been admiring for months.

"But of course." That charming smile again. "Didn't she say I was coming today?"

"No."

Noémie turns around just far enough to interject. "You are an asshole, Raffi. Maman is

65

expecting you Sunday. She will lose her mind."

He smiles back sweetly at her. "But, dearest sister, my college term has ended, and I heard from Maman there was a nice new American exchange staying all summer, so I thought I'd come entertain her." He winks at me.

We ignore Noémie as she pretends to vomit.

"Are *you* staying all summer?" I want to kick myself for my obviousness.

He shrugs. "Well, maybe, if I find something fun to do. Otherwise, I will go back to Paris. It can get quite boring here, you know?"

"Yeah, really."

When Raphael tells me that he is nineteen and at college in Paris studying film, I try to pretend I don't already know everything about him. He finds out where I'm from in the States and seems really interested, asking about Boston and my college plans and what music I like. All the while, just at the edge of my vision, I see where Noémie sits scowling. Freddie is sitting next to her on her towel and every so often he just stares in my direction.

It makes me shiver under the shade of the olive tree, so that I find it hard to focus on what Raphael's saying, about how he's seen everything by Tarkovsky ever, and loves the Beastie Boys for their irony, and worships Tom Waits because he is God. I try to hold up my end of the conversation, but my mind keeps circling back to the bad things that have happened. I mean, come on. The texts have been weird. The video was megaweird and scary. But this near-drowning incident makes three.

Three weird, scary things in two days. And Freddie is starting to seem like he just might be stalker suspect number one. Maybe he dunked me like that because he wanted to scare me? Well, he's succeeded.

Molly Swift

JULY 31, 2015

Back in my room, I dragged off my wet clothes with a sigh, lay back on the bed in my underwear, and looked at my phone. Three A.M. *Jesus.* There was a message from Bill that just said, *Call me.* I texted him back saying I had pay dirt for him and tried to send him some of the photos. When I couldn't get them to send with the spotty Wi-Fi, I threw my phone down in disgust and lit another cigarette. Hanging out the window, I looked down at the street below, its potholes and drift of trash, the occasional tourist or bum shuffling by.

I held my phone all the way out the window, as far out as I could manage, attempting to catch a few rays of their three-star internet. As if Bill sensed my moment of vulnerability through the transatlantic airwaves, my phone burred into life, "Jolene" playing on the ring tone. My partner-in-crime's raddled face smiled at me under his name and number. I answered, immediately noticing a shifty tone to his voice when he said hello.

Bill was a journalistic giant in his day, a hero

of the Watergate era, and he likes a good exposé as much as he did when he was my media studies lecturer. I was in night school then, a last-ditch attempt to salvage an education after years of expulsions and reform schools and ultimately dropping out of college to attend the School of Life. Bill was one of that institution's most curmudgeonly alumni, so we hit it off. I wanted to be him; he saw a chance to work again by using me as his eyes and ears, his proxy out in the world. He'd be right at home in this era of whistle-blowers and WikiLeaks if his wife would ever let him out of the house; but he has strict instructions from both his old lady and his doctor to cut back on work, booze, and cigarettes. The fact that he's done none of these might escape his doctor, but not his eagle-eyed wife, Nina, who by the sound of his voice when he spoke to me was sitting in the room.

"What's up, Swift?" he asked, trying to sound jovial.

"Nothing much. Enjoying the red wine and all that jazz."

But just as I know Bill's voice, he knows mine. Knows for certain when I'm holding something back. It's not just the journalist in him—it's the dad.

"Rough day at work?"

"Well . . ." I took a swig of whiskey, toyed with a cigarette. "There's good news and bad news. First the good: I went to see the girl in the hospital, like you said. While I was there, I found out some stuff about the Blavettes . . ."

I started telling him about the police putting a bulletin out on the Blavette family, about going to their house, meeting Valentin. I could tell I'd grabbed his interest by the way he tip-tapped on his laptop as I spoke, probably Googling the news item.

You see, the main idea for *American Confessional* is that we take on stories of police incompetence or just general corruption, and find the real story. One day after he was retired and I'd just lost a job, we met for a drink and came up with the idea of a talking heads show based on old-fashioned undercover work and pavement-pounding. Our first series was a long haul and probably the hardest work we ever did on a case: a miscarriage-of-justice story about Manatee Mack, a poor, black guy from Florida who we argued had been framed by the police for his white teenage girlfriend's murder. We came close to clearing his name, got the Innocence Project on board, garnered support from millions of listeners, only to see the story end in the death chamber at Florida State. Both of us wanted to quit after that and did for a while. It was just too sad.

Maybe that was the reason the second series dealt with the opposite kind of injustice: Mindy

Kaufman, a wealthy old lady who rented apartments on the Upper East Side and who everyone knew had poisoned her husband and housekeeper after she caught them together. Most of what we pulled together was gossip and hearsay, but we had a theory Mindy had used a slow-acting pesticide called Victor Cockroach Gel. The police had either been paid off or scared off, though: they wouldn't pursue it. In a marvelous piece of dumb luck, we got Mindy on tape chatting about the murder to her pet mynah bird. Our listeners devoured that one.

In the end, what started out as a nostalgia piece became a popular show, not to mention a good earner because of paid ads and keen fans. I'm the anonymous roving ear who records the footage and sends it to Bill. He shapes and edits cleverly and generally protects my secret identity. He really knows how to pitch a story.

Finally, I told him about the whole mistaken-for-a-relative thing.

"You mean, they think you're the aunt or something?"

"I guess. At first I only said that to the receptionist to get in for a minute, then when I was sitting in the girl's room . . . a nun came. She was so thrilled that a family member had visited I started to feel pretty weird."

"So you haven't 'fessed up?"

In the background of the call, like echolalia,

I heard Nina's commentary. " ' 'Fessed up,' Bill? What has she gotten into this time? Should you be involved, in your condition?"

"Yeah, I guess I should, really," I said, talking more to myself than Bill, who was now busy bickering, "though I don't have to go back to the hospital, since—"

"Don't you have a casserole to heat up, Nina? Leave me alone," Bill shouted, "and, Molly, for God's sake. You meet the inspector in charge of the case in a parking lot. He opens a goddamn door for you and I'm sure you all but castrated the guy. You have an in with the Holy Sisters at the hospital and you're too moral to play aunt all of a sudden?"

"Not too moral, but . . . I mean, would it be fair to the girl?"

"Fair to her? She's in a goddamn coma and none of her own family is straining themselves. Buy her some flowers if you feel guilty, but use it, Molly. Use it to find the story here. Use Valentin, too. Go to the police station and find something real."

"Okay, okay. I'll do what I can. You don't need to shout."

"Oh, don't mind me. Nina's getting on my case and my sciatica's raging and my prostate . . . never mind. All I'm saying is you have a talent, Molly, if only the one, and that's getting people to open up to you. Your vocation is to pry under the carpet of life and find the god-damn dirt underneath. Don't get—"

"—squeamish. I know. The story comes first. I attended all of your lectures."

"So you're gonna use it?"

I took a deep breath, already feeling guilty. "They'll be onto me in seconds, but yeah . . ."

"I'm not saying you should become a sociopath, Molly," he said in a kinder voice. "I'm just saying, do what those other journalists don't have the balls to do. Make a difference."

Molly Swift

JULY 31, 2015

I crossed the road to the gendarmerie, pulling my baseball cap down over my eyes. I was abreast with the flagpole that marked the entrance, the tricolor on top fluttering serenely in the breeze, when I remembered Bill's words. If I was going to make this work, there was no point being shamefaced about it. I pulled off my cap and shook my hair out, checking it in the glass on the door. A pair of uniformed officers walked past me just as I was licking lipstick off my teeth. I flashed them my most wholesome girl-next-door grin. I was now Molly Perkins, a single continuing education teacher from Connecticut, who loved cats and yarn bombing and, most of all, her favorite niece, Quinn.

Inside the gendarmerie, I took a moment to size up the shabby front desk, the bedraggled receptionist sitting behind it, and the general air of ennui. Behind her a gendarme poured coffee from a percolator into a chipped cup.

"May I speak with Inspector Valentin?" I didn't even bother with French.

"He is over there," the woman said, frowning uncertainly, "eating his breakfast." She pointed to the café across the road, La Grande Bouche.

"I can see why he's solving this case so quickly," I said.

"*Comment?*" asked the receptionist in puzzlement, while the gendarme behind her glared at me over his coffee.

If St. Roch were some place in the Midwest instead of the South of France, it would be what you'd call a one-horse town. One gas station. One supermarket. One clinic. One of everything. What it has lots of, though, is cafés. La Grande Bouche was a smaller and friendlier affair than the boho tourist cafés I'd visited so far. Since it was packed with gendarmes drinking black coffee, keeping an eye on crime from a distance, I gathered that it was a police café. I couldn't see Valentin through the crowd of uniforms eating fried beignets and bacon sandwiches, so I sat at a table near the door and picked up the plastic menu.

Within seconds, a woman with whitish hair tied in a loose bun came to take my order. The badge pinned to her baby blue cardigan told me that her name was Marlene Weiss, the manager.

"Wow, the service is fast in here," I said.

"Keeping a low profile from all these . . . *journalists,* are you?" Marlene tapped her nose.

For a minute I thought she'd guessed my profession. Then I realized that she'd picked up

75

the gossip from the hospital and, hearing my American accent, must have assumed I was Quinn's aunt. Ironically, she now imagined me in flight from the press.

"Just waiting for visiting hours so I can go see my niece," I said with a sigh.

"Well, if there's anything I can do for the dear auntie, please do let me know."

"A coffee would be nice."

"I'm sure we could rustle up a coffee. Georges!" Like a Sherman tank rumbling over a battlefield, she charged towards the cowering kitchen boy.

She brought the coffee back herself and settled into the opposite side of the booth, sliding her intimidating bosom across the Formica tabletop and resting her chin on her hands. "Mind if I join you?"

"I think you already have," I said, smiling a little too brightly.

Marlene leaned over confidentially. "This place is a hellhole, no?"

"Are you kidding?" I said, surprised. "It seems like paradise here. The beach. The mountains. The wine. I love it . . . I mean, I would if I weren't busy worrying about my niece."

"You are mistaking me," she said with a disgruntled frown. "The landscape is satisfactory. But the people . . ." With that, she plunged into all the local gossip. I listened happily enough for a while, hoping she would drop a nugget or two about the Blavettes in there, but no such luck. As she talked, I peered around her, hoping that Valentin hadn't left yet.

I must have been more obvious than I imagined, because the flood of words stopped and, as if she could read my mind, Marlene said, "Yes, that's him. That's Inspector Valentin. He is in charge of your niece's accident and the missing-persons case. I'll introduce you because we're old friends. Ever since his wife left him he is always happy to meet new women."

Before I had time to answer, she was halfway across the room, sliding her arm through Valentin's and steering him over, cup and saucer in hand. He sat down across from me and Marlene squeezed into the seat after him.

Valentin looked me up and down across the table and, after a moment, appeared to recognize me. "Ah, the woman who told me I was . . . what did you call me? A look-alike of Jean-Paul Belmondo?"

"It was a compliment," I said. In the daylight, I saw that, in fact, he was not quite Belmondo-esque, but a debonair blown dandelion of a man, the kind who would once have made an angelic choirboy. "If you'd radioed in about my car like a normal policeman, perhaps I would have known who you were."

"I saw you go inside the gendarmerie earlier," he said mischievously. "Have you reported it?"

"Not yet—" I began.

"Give her some break at least, Bertrand," said Marlene, nudging Valentin with her elbow. "The poor woman has a niece in a coma. Where's your bedside manner?"

"You are the aunt of Quinn Perkins?" Valentin's blue eyes widened. I couldn't help but think he seemed a little skeptical.

"Molly Perkins," I said hurriedly, and then to distract him, I added, "Any leads on what happened to my niece?"

"We searched the woods near the house last night," he said wearily, "and we have been making a list of anyone who might have had a grudge with the family."

"Such a list would be very long," Marlene tutted, "beginning with Stella Birch and ending with the parents of that poor pupil of Émilie's who died—"

Valentin dropped his cup abruptly, spilling most of the coffee into the saucer. "Marlene, I've told you before about spreading these rumors!"

Marlene didn't even flinch. She just raised a sardonic eyebrow and, when he got up to leave, said, "See you tomorrow, Bertrand."

After he'd gone, she wiped the table absent-mindedly with the sleeve of her cardigan, which seemed to double as a dishcloth.

"Someone died at the school? How awful."
I sipped my tepid coffee to hide my curiosity.

"Before it closed down, yes. The poor girl suffocated. They said it was some sort of game that went wrong. The other staff were busy teaching classes to the younger pupils and Émilie was the only one in charge of that unfortunate school trip. She became diverted and did not see who was responsible, so—" she drew her finger across her throat "—fired."

"All I heard was that there'd been 'an incident involving a student' that made them close the old schoolhouse," I said, casting my mind back to my stolen printouts.

"Ah, well," she said, looking at me shrewdly. "Some things happen in St. Roch that are not shared with the rest of the world."

Quinn Perkins

JULY 14, 2015

Blog Entry

There's a weird feature to this house that I'm both creeped out by and obsessing over: out in the hallway is a locked door that once led to the dilapidated building adjoining this place, and I'm not allowed to open it.

The Old Schoolhouse—so called because it was built in the nineteenth century or whatever—*was* the St. Roch school until it shut down a couple years ago. Momma Blavette was the headmistress there (convenient since she lived next door). There's an old photo downstairs from when it opened in 1882: the pupils are lined up in front of the newly built school in a stiff row, unsmiling in their clean white smocks and shiny boots and suspenders, an austere schoolmarm keeping the boys and girls separate.

Not much has changed about the building since those stern and sepia-tinted days, from the outside at least. But on the inside? I'm guessing p-r-e-t-t-y-d-a-r-n-c-r-e-e-p-y, especially since there've been quite a few break-ins there in the meantime. Not to mention the reason it shut down: some incident with the death of a student. Émilie was suspiciously vague on the exact circumstances, but on one subject she was very firm: I am *never* to open the door and go in there.

Naturally this makes me want to see inside there even more. *Who knows?* I thought when she told me. *Maybe one day when they're all out, I'll go take some pics for the blog.*

Today I woke to an empty house. I saw that hussy of a day through half-open shutters, stretching out coyly in front of me, purring its delicious summertime possibility. I thought today could just be the day for urb-exing like I do back home in search of the Rockport Devil, the Fall River Witch. But my plan was derailed by a weird little episode, involving . . . you guessed it: the hot older brother.

The silence of the house tells me nobody's home, so I pad downstairs in my underwear. On the kitchen table I find a piece of baguette with butter and jam in it, a mug of cold coffee, and a Post-it saying Émilie and Noémie have gone to the weekday market in the village. Being an ex-headmistress, Émilie is the kind of mom who makes your food three days ahead, plastic-wraps it, and then writes you instructions on how to eat it, plus some career advice and a mini guilt trip. Kinda nice, though, being mommed like that again.

I mooch onto the patio, where Mme B's violets

are slowly wilting. The paving stones burn the soles of my feet so much they freeze. I jump, treading cartoon water in the thick air before racing onto the sharp bed of nails that's the fried-out grass and doing a little *Sound of Music* spin, taking in the blue, blue cloudless sky, the woods stretching out for miles, cloaking the house in mysterious silence. There's a David Lynch vibe to the creaking swing set the children used to play on, the sand pit, the empty football field. But the house, with its robin's egg shutters and white trellis wound with dog roses, is so perfect it looks like something out of an insurance ad.

A noise behind me makes me jump. Turning around, I see Raphael on the shady side of the patio. I do a little double take, a triple take actually, since I'm now acutely aware that I'm wearing nothing more than a T-shirt and underwear. No bra even. Meanwhile, Raphael's lying on a yoga mat in nothing but a kind of Indian yogi loincloth folded around his groin like a man-diaper. He's doing stomach crunches, his stomach glistening with sweat. Now he's rising from his yoga mat like a gleaming god and he's beckoning to me and smiling, not that blinding Colgate grin of his, but a subtle half smile, inviting me over.

And so I go, crossing hot patio stones to get to him and feeling a little freaked to be walking towards a near-naked man I barely know, in the brazen light of day. As soon as I reach him, he lies back down on his mat, beckoning me to some weird exercise headspace he's in where our near nudity is in no way embarrassing.

"Come," he pants.

I stand over him shyly. "Where?"

"Here." He gestures to his exquisitely muscled thighs and grins the Colgate grin.

"Um, you're kidding, right?" A blush creeps over my throat, along my breastbone, making my skin glow—I imagine—the red of irradiated apples.

He shakes his head, grinning away. "I've been working so hard, my *abdos* are nothing. I look female almost. No *muscles de l'estomac* at all. It's disgusting, no?"

"Oh yeah, totally gross." I avoid looking down at his perfect six-pack in case I get vertigo. "Um, so how am I, um . . ."

"I need a little weight on my quads to stop me tipping up when I crunch, *tu sais*? It would be a big help for me." He leans up on his elbows. I find myself thinking he is too cute, too obviously gorgeous, and he knows it. I don't even *like* guys like this. I'm from the East Coast. I like dark and wounded. And clothed.

But I don't want to be rude, so I sit down obediently on his thighs, trying not to let my whole weight fall on him, holding myself taut as he pulls his torso up easily and silently, an oiled piston pumping away in the heat. Sweat drips from his neck, runs down his smooth chest. It pools under my butt, forming a salty film that joins us together. Is this a way of flirting?

Stop it. Stop it, I tell myself. *Don't think. Don't try to work out what's going on. Just imagine it's some surreal carnival ride.* I do, just letting him rock me, watching the clouds. Even still, I keep thinking the ride will stop, that Raphael will tire, or at least take a break. But he doesn't even get out of breath. A butterfly goes past, a huge blue one with tattered wings, seeking out a blown golden poppy inches from Raphael's face. I smile at the weirdness of my life.

The weirdness makes me think of yesterday, of Freddie, the text. "Hey, you know that Freddie guy. Is he kind of a weirdo?"

Raphael doesn't break from his sit-ups. He just says, "Oh no, he's a great guy, not very cool with the girls. But you know, I've known him since I was two."

"It's just that yesterday he nearly drowned me."

He laughs. "No, it was not serious. He only meant fun . . . to play."

"It didn't feel like playing," I say.

He says nothing, keeps going, and I suddenly have this weird sensation that we're being watched. Seconds more and something catches at the corner of my vision. I look up to see a dark shape flit behind an upstairs window, then turn, pale face to the glass. Noémie. She scowls down as if she wishes we would die. I almost tumble off my precarious flesh-perch. I mean, she's been bitchy before, but I've never seen that look on her face. That kind of homicidal look . . . who knew she was even here?

I stumble up, sweat slick, mumbling an apology to Raphael, who stops all of a sudden and grunts some reply. Later, as I shower, I hear voices raised in anger and can't tell whose, though I'm sure one is a man. They echo through the rickety pipes, gurgle up from the green-stained plughole as if some dark well hidden under the house has just begun to erupt.

Molly Swift

JULY 31, 2015

After the announcement about the Blavettes, the hacks camped outside the Hôpital Sainte-Thérèse seemed to breed. I arrived in the parking lot to see new little ones had popped through the tarmac like mushrooms, including a glamorous Italian foreign correspondent with long, red hair like something out of an info-mercial, and a bored-looking British tabloid news crew. I parked my broken car and locked it—though this seemed a bit futile, since the passenger door was now held on with gaffer tape—slipped on my aviators, and prepared to run the gauntlet.

The Italian reporter took me at a gallop, mike in hand, sound and lights trailing behind her. "Aurelia Perla, *La Stampa*. How do you feel about what is happening to your niece?"

I held up my hand to shield my face and made a run for the reception area.

Aurelia ran after me. "Was Quinn enjoying her exchange before the accident?"

Desperate not to be filmed, I flung myself through the doors and didn't stop until I got to reception. There Sister Agnès, the receptionist who had gazed at me so cynically over half-moon specs the day before, was all sympathy.

"Really these journalists should not do that, but—" she sighed, patting my hand "—the best we can do is to keep them outside of here."

Sister Agnès introduced me to Sister Eglantine, the other nun from the previous day. Ever since the conversation with Bill, I'd been dreading the inevitable moment of discovery: a tap on the shoulder, an unmarked police car pulling up alongside me, a rogue tweet trending, Quinn's real family showing up. The nuns were so kind to me, so pleased that I was there for Quinn, that I began to feel something I hadn't anticipated: guilty. Their faith in me made me uneasy. Maybe in this world of paranoia and Google, unques-tioning acceptance was the weirdest experience of all.

In her little room, Quinn lay unmoving, tucked under starched sheets, looking more than ever like a fairy tale princess under a curse. Sister Eglantine bustled around, opening the blinds, placing a stack of cardboard bedpans in a drawer. I held Quinn's hand and kept half an eye on Eglantine. One of the drawers she opened contained a plastic tray full of personal effects: a scatter of coins, a hair band, and a pair of earrings shaped like bats. An iPhone with a broken screen.

She must have felt me watching her, because

she turned to me and explained in her usual delicate English, "The things she had with her, when . . ." As if the thought of this had upset her, she abruptly left the room.

I sat for a while, staring at the pale arms of birches waving in the hospital grounds, pure blue sky spilling between their branches like paint. I wondered how these nuns got to be so nice, when the ones in my high school were witches. Turning my attention to the bed, I looked at Quinn's hand lying in mine, the groove of her lifeline casting a faint shadow. Her skin felt so new, as if it had just been made. If she never woke and the truth never came to light, what would happen? Would the nuns just keep her here sleeping forever, like Snow White in her glass case?

Make a difference, Bill had said. That's what all this was about. It was why I let Quinn's hand rest on the sheets and crossed the room to the chest of drawers. It was why I reached into the plastic tray until my fingertips found the rough lifeline in the glass of the broken phone. It was why I slipped it into my purse.

Molly Swift

JULY 31, 2015

The phone was charging, the battery percentage nudging slowly up. I'd found an outlet under Quinn's bed and plugged it in with my charger, arranging my bag and feet on the floor to hide it from view. Every time a trolley squeaked past the doorway, I twitched around, trying not to look too suspicious and reasoning that if someone did come in I would just say the phone was mine.

As soon as the battery looked more green than red, I unplugged it and went to the bathroom, latching the door with unsteady hands. I sat on the toilet and clicked the phone on, feeling a passing moment of triumph that there was no passcode. I studied the wallpaper photo, of Quinn and Raphael Blavette huddled under a towel. They were beaded with water, grinning, his arm slung over her shoulders, her head half on his chest. They looked more than close—intimate. I wondered if they'd been an item, before whatever went wrong went wrong.

The big discovery was her blog on the Blogger app, which I glanced at with the same blushing fascination with which I read my older sister's diary when I was a nerdy middle schooler and she was a popular senior, navigating the world of crushes and boys and Shakespearean friendship dramas. The blog's title—*Sympathy for the Devil*—revealed an unexpected side to Quinn Perkins, one kept invisible in her Facebook account.

I made a note of the url and flicked through the phone's other apps, cryptic emblems of the mysterious life of the teenager—Tumblr and Spotify, Tinder and Snapchat. The photos were much like her Instagram account—snaps of the sunny beach and hunks at the pool, though there were quite a few more of Raphael, including some glowing selfies of the two of them together that only confirmed my sense that they were involved.

The time caught my eye—I'd been in the cubicle for nearly twenty minutes, though it had felt like five. I hurried out of the cubicle and back to the room, glancing up and down the corridor before I went in. I didn't see anyone, so it seemed safe to go to the chest of drawers and slip the phone back into the plastic tray. As I did, I noticed a pink iPod shuffle lying tangled in the hair band. I remembered reading an article about how familiar music stimulates the brains of comatose patients. Some patients who were thought beyond hope had woken after hearing their favorite songs.

No sooner had I taken the shuffle out than I heard Sister Eglantine's voice from behind me. "I'm afraid visiting time is almost over," she said apologetically.

"No worries," I said, turning around slowly and trying not to look guilty.

"Look at her sleeping," she said, putting her head to one side. "The poor angel. Anything you need—truly—you must inform us. We are here to hold you up in your necessity."

"Well, there is one thing," I said.

Eglantine hovered nervously while I pushed the earbuds into her patient's ears, noting how their delicate folds looked translucent in the light streaming in from the window. As if she was carved from wax, not flesh. I tried to explain the coma theory. Embarrassed at not understanding me, she smiled and nodded and drifted away, reminding me one last time about visiting hours.

I pressed Play on the shuffle. Some Tom Waits song or other started up, sounding tinny and warped. I don't know how long I stood over her, but my strongest impression from the whisper of the songs was that she had music taste a lot like my dad.

After a while, I had to sit down because my legs were shaking. I'd been standing so still, worried that she would move and I'd miss it. I don't know if it was because I'd looked through her photos, her blog, but something had changed. I felt as if I belonged there somehow, with her. I noticed new things about her—the pale purple shadows under her eyes, the scars on her face knitting together, the new growth of hair on the shaved part of her head. I held her hand, and this time it wasn't a lie.

I was just unplugging the charge from under the bed when I saw something out of the corner of my eye: a tiny movement, just like before. I looked up. Nothing. She was as still as a waxen effigy or a statue carved on a tomb. Perhaps it was wishful thinking or a trick of the mind or something. I dropped the charger in my bag.

As soon as I did, there it was again. And this time I saw it clearly: a twitch of her littlest finger, tiny, but definitely a movement. And then a twitch of all of her fingers, as if she were clutching at the sheets.

"Sister Eglantine," I called.

She didn't answer, so I called louder, my voice hoarse with excitement. It had worked. Her P300 wave or whatever was responding to meaningful stimulus, which meant she could wake up.

Sister Eglantine came in and I hurriedly explained. She summoned the doctor. They prodded and poked and checked the machines, but when they saw nothing, the mood turned into one of vague disappointment. Eglantine smiled apologetically. The doctor cautioned me not to feel too hopeful.

Like all relatives, of course I did secretly feel hopeful: that she would wake. And unlike relatives, I secretly worried: that she would wake.

Quinn Perkins

Blog Entry

This morning Émilie announced that it was a beautiful day and we were going to the beach. All fine and well, except that Noémie hadn't spoken a word to me since she saw me with her brother yesterday. That, and I got to the car to find that Freddie was coming, too. Far from being considered a creep by everyone, he turns out to be some sort of universal family favorite, like the sex-pest equivalent of a Disney movie. Needless to say, it was the car trip from hell.

It wasn't just that Freddie's thigh was pressed into mine the whole time. His actual breathing made me to want to barf. I refused to look at him, even when he asked me something nice like did I want the window open or closed. I kept trying to move further across the seat, but how could I when beach towels and sun cream and plastic-wrapped sandwiches were packed in around us like Styrofoam peanuts? And despite how I felt, I didn't want to seem or even be a bitch. So the whole time I just played nervously with my phone, avoiding the Snapchat app, but at the same time wanting to ward off anything that might've crept up behind me while I wasn't looking, virtually speaking.

"*Merde*, Quinn. You look at it every one second," says Noémie in disgust.

"I'm checking for messages," I say lamely, ashamed to be caught out.

"Why? Nobody ever calls you. Do you have friends at home?" She wipes away pretend crybaby tears with her fists.

"Noé! Leave her alone," says Raphael, sitting shotgun next to his mom. He smiles into the little mirror on his sunshade, catching my eye.

I smile back. At least he's on my side.

"Maman, tell him to stop picking on me," Noémie whines.

"Noé. Raffi. Quinn. All of you can stop it," says Mme B brightly. "I need to focus, children." She launches into a cheery round of "Joe le Taxi" and insists that we all sing along.

A graphic image of Émilie chaperoning a zillion saggy school bus trips fills my head. I crane my neck, trying to look out the window, embarrassed to have caused more conflict. When I look past Freddie to get a view of the white-powder-dust road, the blue zipper of sea just out of reach, Freddie grins goofily and blocks my view. I stare straight ahead to where Raphael is playing air guitar to "Hotel California" and I notice some new things about him—the little silver scar on the tanned nape of his neck, how he smiles to himself sometimes and his cheeks dimple. I tell myself to pack it in. Of all people to have a crush on, my French exchange's brother is clearly the worst.

Madame Blavette swerves into the half-empty parking lot of a river beach we've been to before. She disapproves of sandy beaches, with their turning tide of tanned flesh—"like a roasted chicken on a spit," she says. A pebble-filled clamshell at the foot of an aqueduct, this beach has pretensions, is within a hollering distance of culture. People read on it, quote Latin on it. Noémie hates it. She throws open the door with a disgusted sigh and steps out. I un-peel my bare thigh from Freddie's and head out after her, standing for a dazed moment in the pure midmorning light to taste the salt air and let the heat drench me in a new slick of sweat.

Mme B fusses around happily, singing under her breath, flapping the beach towels out in a neat square of faded tropical colors, laying out her picnic of crackers and homemade pâté and cold 7UP and petits fours. When she unfolds her deck chair, a paperback falls out.

She picks it up, smiling fondly. "Have you read this, Quinn?"

I shrug. "What is it?"

"It is a romance novel by my dear friend Stella, racy in places," she says with a giggle.

"It's written so simply, though. It is not so interesting. I could lend it to you later if you want to practice your French comprehension?" She hands me the book.

I look at the illustration on the well-thumbed cover: a kneeling woman, naked save for a choke collar. "Um, my mom always said romance novels were the opium of the domestic slam-hound, one of the tools of patriarchal subjugation. I'm pretty sure it's one of the few issues my parents agreed on, so, um, no thanks."

Frowning, Émilie strips off her floral halter dress, revealing a pink one-piece. "You know, Quinn, I may be in my forties, but I still get looks from guys, very young men sometimes, younger than Raphael. Probably more than you do, in actuality. Ah, what a beautiful day at the beach with my babies!" Smiling, she settles into her deck chair and puts the book over her face.

Okay, well . . . awkward. Her kids seem to think so, too. In order to avoid the moment, Freddie and Raphael break the volleyball out and start punting it around. Noémie, having basted every inch of herself, lies facedown to roast where no familial eye contact can harm her. In the midst of everything, I am alone, like Camus or something. I find myself missing Mom, who couldn't have been more different from Émilie.

When I was little, Mom was always aiming

her old Leica at me, calling me into the under-stairs cupboard she'd fitted with two big Belfast sinks for developing photos to watch ghostly reflections of myself appear under the flicker of red lights. Or she'd be baking bread, her hands callused with drying dough. When I hugged her, she'd smell of garlic and thyme from the garden and her long hair and fragile features reminded me of the pictures of Joni Mitchell on the vinyl albums she always played. Dad wasn't there much and I didn't like it when he was. He made fun of her photographs, her cooking, never letting her forget he was the important one. I know she wanted to get back to selling her art, maybe after I went to college.

I wish I could have a final memory of her happy at the opening of her very own exhibition instead of the one I do have: my dad's book launch, the glasses of champagne clinking, the New England literati circulating. Mom in the corner with bandaged wrists, avoiding talking to any of Dad's guests because he'd already made her feel ashamed of what she'd tried to do.

My nostalgia soured, I snap back to the present. Freddie's phone is lying on the towel right next to my hand. I pick it up, all sleight of hand. I mean, wouldn't you look? Come on. Be honest. It's a fucking BlackBerry. God, I hate those things. No password, though. I look at his apps. Snapchat? Bingo! Username? Hmm,

Lapinchaude. Well, that could still come up as "unknown" if he hid it somehow, some clever little hack. I have that feeling again—someone watching. Looking up, I see him staring straight at me. He even misses the ball because of it.

I drop the phone and walk to the water to hide my blushes. In the shallows, my feet slap angrily on the soft, sucking sand under the blue, walking faster, harder against the weight of water. It pushes me towards the beach. I push back, fingers skimming the playful licks of wavelets angrily. And when I'm deep enough, I dive, swim hard and fast for the aqueduct, wanting to get away from all of them, have some space for once.

I swim butterfly, half underwater. As it deepens, it changes from the color of pale sea glass to a murky, dark green. One time I surface inches from the orange fiberglass prow of a canoe that speeds past my head, the canoeist never seeing me at all. Today, I don't give a fuck. I just plunge back into the cool green murk and head for the aqueduct, coming up for air at the rocky base of the middle foot. Rolling on my back, I scull idly between clumps of white rock, watching water shadows dance on the concave belly of the bridge. My sulk ebbs away. Everything falls away. I am nothing more than the fierce blood in my ears.

Something touches my hand. Not just

touches. Grabs hold of. I panic, lurching upright, swallowing about a pint of water, choking. Through the red haze, I see Freddie's pale face, smirking.

"I gave you a shock, *hein*?"

"Fuck!" I splutter.

"It is time *pour manger.*"

He scoops his hand to his mouth, miming eating. "Émilie she has made *le petit déjeuner.*"

He keeps grinning widely. I've decided that his face annoys me. "Couldn't you just have called me instead of . . . creeping up on me?" The last words come out with a splutter of river bile. My chest burns. I don't even bother trying to hide my annoyance. It's the imbecile way he keeps smiling. It's the fact that he came to get me for lunch instead of Raphael.

As we swim back, I keep my distance, but he keeps swimming into me. It's like he's bumping into me on purpose. And there's no reason for it, because he's a strong swimmer, a swim-team-type swimmer. He can only be doing it on purpose, the big stalker. The more I try to wriggle away from him, the more he torpedoes me, knocking into my ribs one time so hard I know I'll bruise.

"Stop it!" I hiss.

He just grins wider than ever until all I can see is the gap in his teeth and the gleaming wet pallor of his high forehead, his bony nose. And then when we're just near enough to shore to stand, he grabs my waist.

"Get off!" I shriek, slapping him, kicking him.

"I know you like me because you check my phone. Are you stalking me a bit, Quinn?"

"Are you fucking serious? Put me down," I say in the voice I use on bad dogs and pollsters.

"If you say so." He does, but in the same movement, he whips me around to face him and kisses me, his tongue squirming between my lips.

I push him away and run to shore. My face pulses. I want to be sick. I expect everyone to be staring, to look horrified and tell Freddie off. But no one seems to care. Noémie's just lying with her sunglasses on, plugged into her iPod. Émilie is fanning flies from her sunbaked picnic. Only Raphael is looking at the water, his arms crossed over his sinewy chest, eyes studiously unfocused.

I've begun to think Freddie is some kind of sociopath, who kissed me for no other reason than to humiliate me. Who tried to drown me. Who's definitely the person text-stalking me. When he walks up and kneels in front of me and pinches my cheek, I slap his face, hard.

He falls back into the sand with a surprised little cry.

"*Mon Dieu!*" says Émilie. "Quinn, what have you done?" She stands up suddenly, glaring down at me.

Her anger is shocking. I've only seen her face look passive and happy. Now it is dark. Crumpled next to her, Freddie sobs like a child while Noémie and Raphael stay right where they are, staring as the scene unfolds.

"He pinched my cheek," I say. "He shouldn't do that. And before, he grabbed me in the water and kissed me. And I think that he's—"

"What do you expect when you dress like that?" she says, looking me up and down. "You are asking for it *un petit peu, n'est-ce pas?*"

"Are you kidding? Everyone's in a bikini . . ."

She leans over me and takes the skin of my wrist and pinches it with her nails. "There," she says, her eyes mean and narrow. "Now you know how it feels."

Behind her, Freddie smiles through his tears.

Molly Swift

JULY 31, 2015

I sipped my Jack Daniel's, my reflection vanishing by degrees as I eked out the last drops. I needed every last drop after my phone call to Quinn's father, the great Professor Perkins. I'd called him to head off someone else telling him that there was an aunt type hanging around his daughter. To cover my ass, I'd pretended to be one Mademoiselle le Mesurier, the local contact for Quinn's study abroad program, crossing my fingers that no one from the program had been in touch with him already.

"*Bonjour*, Professor Perkins," I began in my best impression of a French accent. I explained my "role" and expressed my condolences for what had happened as well as my assurance that we were providing all the support we could.

"While I thank you for your call, I must inquire as to what it pertains?" he asked, his voice charmingly polite and yet so unconcerned it sent a chill through me.

Surely he must be devastated about all this, I thought; even if Quinn wasn't a daddy's girl, she was his daughter.

"And what day do you plan to come for Quinn,

monsieur? I ask because, of course, we shall send someone to ze *aéroport.*"

Huffy silence on the other end of the line. Then—

"Well, of course . . . ahem . . . I'm grateful for the offer. So helpful of you. I just don't know when I can be there, because, you see, my wife is very pregnant, so not until after the baby's born at the least and even then . . ."

I put him out of his misery by thanking him for his time and expressing my hope that he would contact the program if he needed anything. I even gave him Mademoiselle le Mesurier's real phone number, because by now I was sure he wouldn't bother. I'd been worried about Leo flying to his daughter's side and blowing my cover in the process, but I needn't have been. He was a cold fish, that much was clear—one that wouldn't swim over here any-time soon. But instead of being relieved, I just felt sad for Quinn, so lonely in her hospital bed. I wished I could go back to the hospital to sit with her.

I comforted myself with the company of Mr. Daniel's and the contents of Quinn's blog. There I read about the ups and downs you might expect on a teenager's first stay far from home: tension with her host; a rocky relationship with her French exchange; unwelcome advances from the local lothario, a kid named Freddie. And then there was something darker:

threatening messages from an anonymous stranger, apparently including footage of someone being suffocated.

I'd taken a look at her Snapchat app and found zip, just as she said. The messages erased themselves, hence the appeal to teens. Reading further on in the blog, it was clear she'd had her own suspicions about whoever might be stalking her. These seemed to circle around Freddie, beginning on a day at the pool. As I looked through the comments section, her online friends seemed to agree:

Update: Just looked at my blog and saw that all you guys came to the rescue on the stalking front!

loserguy38: That guy Freddie has got to be the stalker. Sounds like a loser. Avoid.

gothgurl: Maybe he did send you that snuff text, Q, then try to snuff you, too, but fight back: refuse to be scared.

malady_g: Just checked this, the law can't help with stalkers. Unless he threatens you explicitly, police can't do jack. Sorry, Q ☹

dr_kennedy: Noémie's brother sounds supercute. Pics please!

Qriosity_cat: Thank you, wonderful people ☺. I'll do my best.

Qriosity_cat was Quinn apparently. Her reply to the comments made me sad. She'd put so much trust in these virtual acquaintances and not one of them had thought to call the police or do much of anything when she vanished.

Her story—what I'd read of it so far—gave me an uneasy sense that there was an awful lot going on under the surface of life in the Blavette household, and none of it had made it into the papers. Reading the description of the girl being smothered in the video, I remembered what Marlene had told me about why the school shut down. *The poor girl suffocated. They said it was some sort of game that went wrong.* It was too much of a coincidence. I had to go talk to Marlene again, and find this Freddie, too.

The chair next to me screeched. "How's the aunt?" Aurelia Perla asked sweetly as she sat down and handed me her business card. Up close, I could see that she was very pretty in a put-together sort of way, her beige suit crisply dry-cleaned, the outline of her lipstick so neatly applied it looked machine-tooled.

"Holding up." I smiled awkwardly.

I looked around the bar for a companion, but saw only the same journalists as when I came in, slouching on tables in groups of fours, smoking e-cigarettes and blending into the surroundings like oil blends into water. One table held a couple of hacks and a photographer.

Judging from the amount of gear the cameraman was carrying, he was one of those mercenary mutant paparazzi that feed off of stories like this. I wondered if I'd missed a press release or something, if new details were about to emerge. Else why would the meat flies be swarming around me? It freaked me out.

"Excuse me." Pushing my chair back, I started to get up.

"How are you coping?" Aurelia asked, the American word *coping* sounding labored in her accent. "It must be so hard."

"Do you want something?" I asked, trying to sound naive and bewildered.

"It must be a very hard time waiting for your niece to be well again, not knowing . . ." She frowned sadly. "But the sisters say she has every chance of being well. If she . . . when she wakes, what will be your first words to her?" She smiled expectantly.

I sat half on, half off the chair. I couldn't believe I was so slow to see what was going on—she had an audio recorder hidden on her somewhere and she was baiting me for a quote. Once I knew that, looking sideways at her was like looking at some weird, ghoulish, really well-dressed reflection of myself. This is what I did, sneaking up on people, asking sympathetic questions designed to pry revelations from them. Being on the other side of the questions made me realize how icky it felt to be soft-soaped. *Jeez,* I thought, *I hope I'm more convincing than this woman.*

"Look . . ." I began in a firmer voice.

"Stop that!" A man stepped between us. He was beautifully dressed, in a dark suit and fedora. Inspector Valentin. He glared at our reflections in the mirror. "Get out."

"Sorry," I said, stumbling up. I knew it was only a matter of time before I would be rumbled. And here it was, flung from the hotel, never to be allowed back in the hospital.

"No, not you, Mademoiselle Perkins," said Valentin. He turned to the journalist, glowering, and said something angry in French.

She retorted just as angrily, her glossy red lips spread in a defiant grin. Valentin took out a piece of paper and flashed it at her. Whatever it said made Aurelia get up and move at speed from the bar. She hurried back to the table where the other hacks slumped with their beers, almost breaking a kitten heel. When she was out of earshot, Valentin climbed into the chair she'd vacated.

He took off his hat and laid it on the bar. "I am sorry about that." He smiled apologetically.

"Don't worry, I'm getting used to it," I said, gulping down the last few drops of whiskey, suspicious that he had changed his tune so much since we met in the café.

He ran a hand through his hair. "Journalists in the case are behaving reprehensibly—sneaking into the hospital, telling lies to the nuns to get information, and worse, sneaking in here to bother the girl's relatives. I have told this woman she will face jail time if she pushes this further. *Terrible, n'est-ce pas?*"

"The worst," I said, gulping. There was something about him that made me nervous. I didn't know if it was my justified fear that he was onto me, or his annoying gallantry.

As if to underscore that point, he summoned the barman and ordered two more whiskeys.

"Is one of those for me?" I asked.

"It's the least I can do," he said, patting my arm.

Back to that again. I just wanted to go up to my room and take a shower and dream up my next move on the case, but I remembered Bill saying I should press my advantage wherever I could. When the Jack Daniel's came, I chinked my glass on his.

"To . . . this place," I said, for want of a better toast.

He stopped midchink. "The Napoléon? St. Roch? Be more specific."

"To St. Roch, your beautiful town."

He rolled his eyes and downed the whiskey in one. "*Mon Dieu.* If you only knew the reality. This town is nothing but trouble."

Quinn Perkins

JULY 16, 2015

Blog Entry

There's a sense of dread that settles on a house; not just houses with creaking roof beams and forbidden Bluebeard doors, or even houses where you get pinched on the wrist for sticking up for yourself with guys. You know what I mean. *The fear:* that weird foreboding, the *plinky-plink* of horror movie sound effects, the camera zooming out giddily as you realize how bad things are.

I remember it from the days after Dad left, watching my mom drift around with her bandaged wrists, her eyes blank as the windows of a derelict house. She tried to protect me, never crying where I could see. She reorganized the things in their bedroom over and over as if it would bring Dad back, or hide him away. Later, in group therapy, I found that was one of the signs that someone was planning to kill themselves: putting their affairs in order. She gave Dad's suits away to a neighbor and, in a moment of sheer eccentricity, repotted all our houseplants in the park across the street with his Louis Vuitton shoes buried underneath.

I'd ask if she was okay; she'd say she was *so tired*. I knew what she meant, even if I didn't yet know the word to explain the endless creep of her fatigue, or mine, or our shared need to sleep hours into the day; the secret cutting we both resorted to, a little slice on the inner thigh to relieve the pain inside and a SpongeBob SquarePants Band-Aid to cover our tracks.

If I blamed my dad for leaving us, he blamed me for inheriting the shame of Mom's illness. Worse than that: he blamed me for watching her slide down into the darkness and doing nothing to stop it. Or maybe he was just projecting his guilt onto me—at least, that's what the therapist said to make me feel better. The day Mom died, the air was so thick with fear I couldn't see straight, and every moment leading up to the one in which I found her was a little car crash: the world slowing down for the collision as if it wants to watch just a bit more carefully. The shards of glass hitting you so gradually you don't notice that you are bleeding until later. Like when your guilt-stricken dad has slung you in the nuthouse for six months to "get well." If there's one thing you get in a psychiatric hospital, it's time to dwell.

Whether because of the weird texts, or what happened yesterday (and the day before and the day before that), or just my meds not working, the fear has come to visit me once more, falling fine and plentiful as dust in an abandoned building. I lie in bed. It settles on me. I get up in the morning and it clouds my vision.

Today someone left a book on my bed. A weird kind of bloodthirsty guidebook about some local caves called Les Yeux. When I went to take my turn in the bathroom, there was nothing on my bed except for rumpled-up covers, my iPod, and earbuds. When I came back, there was the book.

Flipping through it, I don't really grasp a lot of the French. But I get the gist. There were murders there long ago. Witches walled into the rock. All the illustrations inside are really disturbing. I mean, I know I watch horror movies by the fuck-ton, but this is like a how-to guide for Spanish Inquisition wannabes. I stand spellbound for I don't know how long, clutching the book with sweaty hands, hearing the *plinky-plink* music, feeling the shaky zoom-out camera.

A knock on my door. I drop the book. Noémie pokes her head around.

I bite it off. "You put this here?" I hold up the book.

She shrugs. "No."

I take a step towards her, hands shaking. "Know who did?"

"No. Are you . . . okay?" She swallows nervously.

"Yeah . . . I just feel like. I don't know. Some-one put this here to freak me out or something."

She closes the door behind her. "Listen. What happened yesterday—"

"You going to tell me off, too? Because Freddie's an ass-hat and I'm glad I slapped him. I mean, you know that creep sent me texts and this awful video. And then he kissed me and the other day he almost drowned me . . ."

Noémie puts her hand on my arm. Her eyes are soft. "Hey. I know. I know. He is always like that with every exchange that comes here," she says, shaking her head, and rubs her hands over her face. "Like touching them in the pool, *quoi*. It's gross. I have no reason why Maman is not stopping him."

I swipe angrily at a tear running down my cheek. "Then why do you invite him along to everything?"

She shrugs. "St. Roch is small small. Everyone knows everyone and there are not always other young people to hang with. Maman asks someone like Freddie so there will be young people for you to meet."

"You serious? He's—"

"Hey, look, let's have fun today. Just us!" She smiles wide, suddenly throwing everything into being cheerful. "We may take the bus to the town and go shop."

It melts my heart a little to see her work so hard to distract me. Maybe she feels like we got off on the wrong foot, too, though I still have my doubts. "Won't your mom mind? She seems pretty strict . . ."

Noémie rolls her eyes. "She's the worst. I know.

But she's not here today and tonight she's staying with her boyfriend. Raffi is in charge, *en fait*. And he is not here either. So I say we do what we want. Go wild, *quoi!*"

It turns out Noémie doesn't go wild by halves. In St. Roch, we shop and we eat ice cream. We tie up our T-shirts to show our midriffs and compete to see who gets the most wolf whistles. We take in zero tourist attractions and many bars where guys keep buying us beer. I never do this back home. I mean, I've maybe used a fake ID once, but it didn't look like me, and the second a doorman confronted me, I freaked and ran away. Somehow Noé makes me bold and I no longer care if what I'm doing is wrong. Boys ask for our numbers and names and we give them fake ones, laughing behind our hands. We drink demand shots. Red Bull and vodka, Jägermeister, Sambuca. Every time I slow down or get sleepy, Noé starts her Little Miss Crazy routine again.

Night falls. Somehow we end up at a nightclub known as La Gorda, on what Noé gigglingly informs me is the wrong side of town. I can see what she means: there's a pest control joint on every corner, a hookup Hilton over the crosswalk from a Mickey D's. According to her, every night, regular as acne, this place turns on its neon and draws in new blood, pulsing hot and intimate as soon as dusk settles. Luckily I'm too drunk to feel fear anymore.

Inside, it's packed out with punks, headbangers with dreads sweeping the floor, and tall, pale chicks with cat's eyes and nose-rings. Atmosphere gushes from the band, burning the air with electric crazy.

Noé's arm steals around my waist. "Let's dance."

"You're so drunk," I say admiringly.

"So are you," she screams, and laughs raucously.

Arms linked, tossing our hair, we push towards the back of the club, to a stage that's not a stage, so tight to the wall it's in the toilets, drawn forward by punk band pheromones. The music kicks off again and people gather in the tiny space pogoing or just standing as still as statues, soaking it in. Noémie and I thrust our bare-bellied bodies into the fray and shake our hips and whip our hair alongside the chicks with blue bangs and the angry guys with gelled black hair, that guy with the leather vest and cop hat who's going wild in the corner.

Noé grabs my hips and grinds against me. We dance pressed close, our sweat making us cling. There are men watching. Leering. We lap it up. Halfway through the set, it gets rough at the front, where two young punks dance like bumper cars, their studded jackets bruising our flesh, splitting us up.

I suddenly feel like I've had enough. When the

growling stops, I look for Noé and can't see her. Everyone's pressed in too tight. I can't find her anywhere. Standing on tiptoes to see above the crowd, I scan the bar. She's not there. A ripple of panic goes through me, thinking how drunk she is. How drunk I am. My head spins. The band starts up and the fray sucks me in, but my heart's not in it anymore. I watch the lead singer growl his lyrics, lips glued to the microphone, pushing his face against it with all he has, screeching words I can't make out.

A hand clamps my wrist and a pale face hovers before me, glassy with sweat. "Come on," says Noé. "We need to get out of here right now. It is fucked up." Her lipstick is smeared over her chin like she's been making out with someone and her bottom lip is bleeding.

I touch her cheek. "Someone hurt you?" I look around. "Where is he? Want me to talk to him?"

She grabs me, holding me close. "No," she whispers in my ear, "you must not. He is a very bad man." Then she starts out across the dance floor as if borne on the angst of the crowd, and all I can do is follow.

Molly Swift

AUGUST 1, 2015

Inspector Bertrand Valentin first met his wife, Lucie, one crisp March morning at l'Église Sainte-Thérèse, the medieval church in the middle of St. Roch. His family had built the walls centuries ago, dragging the stones from the cliffs near the beach and half killing themselves in the process. He and Lucie were married there. His son, Jan, was christened there. Life was good for a while.

Now Lucie hates him. She and Jan live in Lyon and he sees his son about three times a year. They used to play basketball every day. Now they never play. He can't even walk past a basketball court and yet he finds himself in his car at three in the morning parked by his old house, staring at the scarred cement on the garage where the basketball hoop used to be.

Inspector Bertrand Valentin got lost when he was six. A policeman found him and took him home and ever since that day he's known he would be a policeman. And the job's always there. It never bitches and moans or up and moves to Lyon on a whim. God, though, sometimes he hates this line of work: the violence, the sad stories, the relentless paperwork. He just wants to listen to the Eagles and catch some fish and cook them on the barbecue, enjoy a lazy Sunday in bed, daydream. Anything instead of being stuck in this damned job.

Inspector Bertrand Valentin is an old-fashioned charmer: debonaire, irreverent, and obsessed with cheese. It's hard not to like a man composed of so many contradictions: a workaholic who irons his underwear, an easygoing dude who likes playing basketball, a loner who spends his spare time watching cooking shows. After two solid hours of drinking copiously, flirting shamelessly, and lying badly, I was an expert on the inspector and little the wiser about the Blavette case. There we were, staring down the bottom of a bottle of Jack Daniel's, closing up the bar, leaning ever closer as we slurred our words.

When we first started talking, I could feel the eyes of the wolf pack boring into my back, hungry to know what we were talking about. I thought, if only they knew they were watching a scoop in progress. When I started talking to him, I was feeling cocky: *This is how it's done, boys. Learn from a pro.* But try as I might to charm details from Valentin, all I'd gotten was the story of his midlife crisis. Even the wolves loped off hours ago out of boredom.

"Well, I think it's probably time for bed," I finally said, struggling to stand.

"It's been a pleasure, Molly Perkins. I don't know when was the last time I spoke to a woman like this." His hand moved up from my arm slowly and in a dreamlike way he touched my face. "I've told you things I think I have told no one else."

Just not the right things, I thought, caught between the chair and Valentin. I didn't know why I wasn't moving to the door, or at least breaking the awkward eye contact that had started. I mean he was attractive, no question, but I shouldn't be . . . no, no, definitely not. I cleared my throat, laughing at some pretend joke.

Valentin stared at me as if I'd gone a bit crazy and quickly composed himself, saying fumblingly, "As the detective in charge of this case, your safety and Quinn's are paramount." He turned scarlet and stared into his glass.

I took pity on him then, for spending his evening opening his heart to me when all I'd been after was information. In fact, I felt guilty. That must have been why I leaned up on tiptoes and kissed him on the cheek. Or perhaps it was the effects of the whiskey. Yes, that must have been it. I don't usually kiss my sources.

Molly Swift

AUGUST 1, 2015

I've had hangovers. Some were the mother and father of all hangovers, as they say. The one I had today felt like all my previous hangovers got together and started the International Hangover Society, and then decided to host their annual planning meeting inside my brain. And argue. And then have a disco.

Walking from the parking lot to Sainte-Thérèse, I convinced myself I had actual liver failure. When the resident hacks approached me for a quote outside the hospital, I didn't even try to think of some polite way of telling them to scoot; I just told them to talk to the hand. But it didn't seem to be enough today. Everyone was . . . febrile, manic. They buzzed around me like flies, flinging questions I didn't understand as I tottered towards the door in my dark glasses. I started to feel panicky, like I wouldn't get away. A hand landed on my arm. I tried to push it away.

A voice in my ear said, "It's okay." Steered me towards the door. Valentin.

There were more gendarmes on the door than I remembered.

"Has something else happened?" I asked.

"Haven't they told you?" Valentin held the door for me and guided me through with a hand on the small of my back. I guess he remembered the previous night.

Inside, I stood for a moment in the familiar space with its smells of antiseptic, air freshener, and floor cleaner and breathed a sigh of relief to be away from the press. Whatever news there was about the investigation, whatever had gone wrong, the thought of sitting quietly with Quinn actually seemed really nice today. Just sharing that bubble of calm and medical orderliness with someone I'd begun to feel I know a little bit. Getting away from all those nuns running around the foyer like headless chickens.

I turned to Valentin, trying to retain that brief moment of prospective calm inside myself. "So what's up?" I asked.

"Well, I think you should talk to the doctors . . ."

Panic flooded through me. "What's happened? Is Quinn okay?" It surprised me how horrible the thought of anything happening to her felt.

"Don't be stressed." Valentin smiled his best charming smile. "It's actually great news. She's better than okay. She woke up."

I heard the rest as if underwater, filtered through the sound of my blood rushing in my ears. Eglantine rushed up to repeat the good news because she was the one who was there. This morning at precisely five thirty A.M., Quinn woke briefly and asked for water before falling asleep again. The doctors say she's in a normal sleep state now. It's early days yet, but it seems the coma is over.

Everyone was even nicer and more solicitous than ever, because they've come to see us as family, because this was happy news, because they didn't know the thoughts racing through my head: mainly genuine happiness, but one little part total dread at what was sure to come next.

There was no option but to sit in the café and sip coffee and try not to look too shell-shocked. Valentin talked and smiled and touched my arm, but all I could think about was how in a little while those same overly familiar hands would be slapping cuffs on my wrists. I wanted to text Bill and get his advice, but no one would give me the space. And so it happened that when a young envoy nurse came down to summon me and tell me that the miracle had happened once again, I must come see, I had no script, no excuses, no fallback stance. I had to wing it.

I walked to her room like a prisoner walking to the gallows, came to the door ready to faint from holding my breath. Valentin was there to witness the moment along with several nurses and a doctor, all crowded into the little room. And across that crowded room, as they say, I met the eyes of Quinn Perkins.

Quinn Perkins

JULY 17, 2015

Blog Entry

By the time Raphael came to get us, he was pretty pissed off, particularly since he got out of the car to see Noémie's head lolling on her chest and me trying to stop her from choking on her own vomit. Between bouts of puking, I told him what I knew: that we sunk a few beers, danced a bit. And then bam! Someone basically assaulted Noémie in there, and before she passed out I was trying to find out who so I could go punch their lights out.

"The person who hurt her, was his name Séverin?" he asked.

I shrugged. "I didn't see. She wouldn't say."

"I know this was him," he said, rubbing his hand over his eyes. "*Putain.*"

He said nothing more and neither advocated going back into the club to pick a fight nor led the way. He just rolled his eyes like, *I thought you were smarter than that,* and scooped his sister off the sidewalk. As I climbed into his mom's car, I realized I was now officially on the bad side of 66.6 percent of the Blavette family—a whole

124

different 66.6 percent from the side that hated me yesterday.

In the car, all was silent save for the crickets out in the bushes and the movement of the tires on the gravelly road. I sat in the back with Noémie, stroking her hair while she puked out the window. Up front, Raphael's neck was straight as a telegraph pole.

When we got home, we carried Noémie upstairs and laid her carefully on her side in case she was sick again.

As he closed the door, Raphael said, "At least Maman is not here. If she knew about this she would be furious."

"Yeah?"

"She's not in a great mood."

"I guess that's my fault, too," I shot back. " 'Night." And I turned from him before he could say any more.

Needless to say, I can't sleep. I blog, check Facebook, delete the worst of my photos from the day with Noémie, and zoom in on others (here's one)—from the club—to see if anyone looks like they might attack her. But they're all pretty blurry and actually everyone looks kind of suspicious, don't you think?

As soon as I do get to sleep, a text noise wakes me. My phone tells me it's 3:11 in the A.M., and before I even look, somehow I know.

There's no video this time. Just French words

that when I type them into Google Translate come out as, *You will be the next.*

I fling the phone on the bed, run to the bathroom, and retch until clear strings of part-digested vodka glisten between my lips and chin. My skin shakes.

I tiptoe downstairs to get a glass of water, hearing the timbers of the house tick and creak around me. Even the hum of cicadas outside freaks me out. I turn all the downstairs lights on and stand in the kitchen, taking little sips.

Through the kitchen window, I glimpse something silhouetted against the moonlight. A man. From the glint of his eyes, I can see he's watching me. I let out a little shriek and drop the glass. Its contents spill down my T-shirt before it shatters on the floor.

"Quinn!" Raphael's face moves into the light.

"Shit. You scared me."

"It's okay," he says with exaggerated calmness. "I'll get the brush."

"I'll . . ."

"No, don't move," he says. "You have bare feet. You'll hurt yourself."

He sweeps up the glass and goes to the porch door to tip it in the trash. Not wanting to be alone for even a second, I follow him out into the dark garden. As I watch his tanned legs move through the grass in front of me, a little shiver goes through me. Around the back of the house, the trash cans nestle in a little sort of hidden space with a bench and a trellis and dog roses climbing up. The petals of the roses are closed against the night but their scent is heavy and sweet.

"You smoke?" he asks.

"Sometimes." Like earlier tonight, I think, when I was out-of-control drunk.

He takes out a pack of Gauloises and hands me one and we sit on the bench, shivering in the night air. Above us the moon has bloomed an angry orange.

"'Bad Moon Rising,'" I quip. "Blood moon, even."

"Something has frightened you," he says. "You want to talk?"

I take a drag of my cigarette, trying to think where to start, shifting from thigh to sticky bare thigh on the metal bench. My stomach is full of pins.

"I've been getting these weird texts. Videos and shit from a withheld number," I say, going for my usual jokey tone. Instead, it comes out sounding forced. All of a sudden I feel horribly homesick.

But he's leaning in now, eyes wide, as if I've sparked his interest. "What do they say, the texts?"

"Bad stuff." The lump in my throat grows bigger. I'm about to spill my guts. Should I be spilling my guts? "First the video. God, it was horrible, like a snuff movie. And then the texts saying, *You're next . . .*" I tell him all of it.

"You think it was a bad joke, maybe?" he says slowly. His voice sounds completely calm, as if everyone gets texts like this in France every single day.

"Um . . ." I don't know what to say. "I guess I hadn't even thought of that."

His cigarette has gone out and he leans towards me, pressing the pale tip of the paper cylinder to my glowing cherry, sucking in, lighting up.

He exhales in slow rings. "I mean it probably is, right? You're, like, how old?"

"Seventeen."

"Exactly. So who would really want to hurt you?"

"I don't know."

"So probably, the likeliest answer is someone just wants to make you freak out and shake you up. And now it's worked. So probably if you want to win against that person, you should just forget about it, *hein*?"

I take a drag and hold it in, the smoke burning my tongue when I exhale. My eyes prickle. "I've got to go," I say, standing up suddenly.

My head spins, the moon whirling around me. My face is turned from him, so I let the tears fall. I know I need to go to my room, to bury my face in the pillows and cry and cry. I don't know whether it's the texts, the stress of the last few days, or the fact that he seems to think it's no big deal how I feel about it all.

I'm about to run off when I feel his fingers touching mine, taking them. "Hey, don't cry." He pulls me back down onto the bench, turning my face so that I'm looking into his eyes. The moonlight catches the curve of his lips.

His fingers graze mine. "Listen," he says, "if you are stressed you can talk to me. You can. I am here." His arm moves behind my back on the bench. "All I'm saying is, don't be stressed."

I swipe away the tears. "Don't you think it's—"

"Weird? Mean? *Ouais*, but the worst thing when people bully you is to let them hurt you." He stretches out his spare hand—the one not lolling behind my back—and puts his finger almost to my lips to shush me before I can say any more. I can smell the salt of his hand.

"I know it can be hard here . . ." he says, taking a long drag on his cigarette. "There's drama, and it always has been so. My mother, she needs the money from these exchanges. It is hard for her since my father left and she is not always good with the people who come. She tries, though."

I raise my eyebrows. "There've been others, like me?"

"*Bien sûr.* A lot, all through my childhood, there were. Always girls. And Maman can be, you know . . . a bitch. I mean, really, watch out for her."

"Really?"

He nods, matter-of-fact. "And then there's Noé.

She has struggled the most since Papa went. She cuts herself sometimes, makes herself sick. She has always been fragile. She tried to kill herself when she was only twelve."

"Jesus, I'm so sorry."

"*Ouais*. My mother found her that time. That was . . . Now she just does idiot things, like going to that stupid club tonight. She gets in trouble and then, boom!" He snaps his fingers. "Drama. Shouting. That is usually when I take off."

"So I guess you're going to take off soon?" I ask, swallowing smoke, trying not to sound like I care.

"You want me to?" His voice is gravelly, his pupils so big a girl could go skinny-dipping in them.

I shake my head. Something tumbles down inside me, plummeting into free-fall. I lean back and his arm warms my shoulder blades. His head turns towards me, his breath on my cheek.

"You're so much nicer than the others," he murmurs, almost too quiet to hear. Our faces are so close our noses touch. Suddenly all I can think about is that I can smell his skin, his breath, hear the click of his tongue in his mouth. Owls are calling through the cricket noise. I have the ridiculous urge to tell him some endearment even though I don't know him at all. But then I don't have to because his lips are on mine, his tongue pushing between my lips, our mouths merging. He drinks me in. We kiss and kiss and I don't want it to ever end, then our lips part and he's pulling away, his thumb stroking my cheek.

"*Ah, comme tu est belle. Oui, tu est belle et tu le sais.*" He smiles his sweet smile. "And now it is past your bedtime."

"Why?" My voice comes out soft and kissed-sounding.

"Because it's late and you are my sister's American exchange and I absolutely must not be kissing you."

Molly Swift

AUGUST 1, 2015

Quinn didn't remember me, but then she didn't remember anyone. Retrograde amnesia, the doctors said. As a consequence of her head injury, not only could she not remember the days leading up to the accident, she couldn't really remember much of anything about her past, her family, or where she came from. They said they thought this was a transient symptom and that over the coming days and weeks she would recover her memories, at least in part. They told me this anxiously, as if it were their fault somehow, as if I might make a scene.

A therapist came to see us and Quinn gazed at him, blearily, her head weighing heavy on her neck like a small child up past her bedtime. His plan for treatment was that Quinn make a record of the new memories she'd made on a particular day as well as anything she recalled from the past. He also said a bunch of stuff about hippocampal damage and neuronal loss that I wasn't really following. He had a dinky little phone-size video camera and showed Quinn the buttons on it, the functions, and I thought, This is either a genius strategy to distract her from her amnesia, or crazy.

"Excuse me, but how is she supposed to get hold of all this? I mean, she's just woken up from a coma." The words spilled out of my mouth before I really thought about them. God, it was like something my mom would say.

The therapist seemed to think so, too. He shot me an irritated look. "It is really a good tool in cases like these." He turned back to Quinn. "It is simple actually. When you remember some new thing, you can press this red button here and look into the lens and then tell the camera . . . *comme ça*. That way I will be able to check up your recordings and make a sense of the progress you are having. Shall we try it?"

"Sure," said Quinn, though she didn't sound sure at all. She took the camera from him with slow hands, as if her limbs were moving against an unseen current. With clumsy fingers, she pressed the red button and pointed the camera at herself, then she looked up blankly, like a robot that had lost its programming.

"Talk to it," said the therapist. "Say your name, the most recent thing you remember." He was not one of the more patient therapists I'd ever met.

Quinn cleared her throat and I saw a blush creep up it. I felt sorry for her then, newly awoken in a room full of strangers, in pain, alone, and yet suffering every teen's worst nightmare—public embarrassment.

"Don't you think—" I began.

The therapist held up his hand and I fell silent.

Quinn cleared her throat again and aimed the camera at her face. "My name is Quinn Perkins. Um, this is what I remember. I remember, um. I . . . Nothing, I don't . . . I can't do this. Aunt Molly?" Her eyes filled with tears and she dropped the camera. One skinny arm stretched in my direction.

For a moment I thought she was pointing at something behind me, then I realized with a soft shock that she wanted a hug. I went to her, pulling her close a little awkwardly and she whispered in my ear, "Please make him go."

I turned and in a perfect imitation of my mother, I said, "Thank you, but I think she's had enough for now, don't you?"

The therapist coughed and adjusted his glasses. He looked annoyed in that way that suggested he knew there was nothing he could do. I turned back to Quinn, who was still clinging to me.

"It's okay," I said. "It's all going to be okay."

"No, it won't," she said, sobbing.

In shock, I thought, *She accepts me. I am now her aunt from Connecticut, Molly Perkins. You couldn't make it up.*

A flash went off and I heard a snarky-sounding comment in French. I spun around to see a photographer with a huge flash capturing the moment.

Without thinking, I rounded on him. "How dare you? You delete that image right this minute or the next thing you'll be photographing is the inside of your ass."

Sister Eglantine, passing by in the corridor, appeared to overhear this and looked in on us a bit strangely. I summoned her in, pointing out the intruder. Together we stood over him until he deleted the image.

"I don't want anyone in here taking photographs, okay? It's not fair to my niece."

Eglantine tremulously agreed.

I shut the door on them and settled back down in the chair by the bed.

"That was awesome." Quinn grinned. She reached into the covers and pulled out the iPod shuffle. "Is this mine?"

I nodded. "It's got a bit of charge left on it, I think."

"Cool," she said, plugging herself in. I sat for a while, watching her with a certain satisfaction. However bad a person I might be, in a small way I had helped her. For a start, I was here for her when the rest of her family obviously couldn't be bothered. I sat reading my book until she drifted off to sleep, her iPod still buzzing in her ears. I watched her for a little while, her flushed cheeks, her soft breathing, and then I tucked the covers around her. She looked so vulnerable. *Am I using her?* I thought guiltily. *Tomorrow is another day. For now I'm her aunt.* Until she remembers the truth, that is.

Quinn Perkins

AUGUST 1, 2015

Video Diary: Session 1

[In the darkness, Quinn's face is just visible, but the footage is grainy and hard to see. She wears a hospital gown]

My name is Quinn Perkins and this is what I know . . . Uh, not much, as it happens. Woke up when it was still dark and I didn't know where I was.

Only, well, I was in this room. It was dark . . . really dark. My head—God—it felt like it was about to crack open. And . . .

[Long pause. Quinn starts to cry. Her fingers reach tentatively for the stitches on her head]

I felt my hair on this side. It's, like, totally shaved. See?

[She leans in to show the stubbly side of her head with staples pinching the skin together]

Shit, I can't do this.

[Camera switches off]

[Camera switches on]

Yeah, so, I stood up before and fell out of bed. My gown fell around my armpits. I was butt naked underneath. Nice, right? And I was struggling to get up. Then this nun came. God, I thought I was hallucinating.

"Stop screaming," she said, "you'll wake everyone."

Thing is, I didn't even know I was . . . screaming. *[Long pause]*

More nuns came. A doctor. They were talking some language. Couldn't work out what they were saying. And I was trying to speak, but I couldn't even find the words for what I wanted to say. I started to freak out, I think. This doctor stuck a needle in me.

So I was, like, out cold. I don't know how long for. Next time I woke, there were these total strangers crowded around—a man in a panama hat, like someone out of an old movie, and a woman with bright red lipstick and shaggy yellow hair. Another doctor, who said he was my "therapist" or whatever. It was all just . . . confusing . . . like people's words and their mouths were going at different rates.

Therapist gave me this *[taps the camera]* . . . I'm, uh, meant to talk to it. Talk to *you*. Well, so here I am, telling you what I saw today, what I can remember.

[Pause]

Well, what *do* I remember? The dark. Running in the woods. Feeling something sharp on my feet . . . and a smell . . . a wet kind of smell. Reminds me of . . .

[Wipes eyes]

And, um, moonlight. A man's face near mine.

I wish I could, like, reach in my brain and shake the memories out.

[Long pause]

They say that blond woman is my aunt. She seems kind. I mean, how do you know when everyone feels like a stranger? I was glad she was there, 'cause there was someone to tell the doctors to leave me alone for a bit. Thing is . . . I don't remember her.

I don't remember any of the things they're telling me.

Molly Swift

AUGUST 1, 2015

Your typical recidivist relapses into criminal behavior in less than three years, despite experiencing negative consequences for said behavior. Well, I had that record beat. It was a mere three days since my last episode of B and E and there I was, breaking the law again. A quick coffee at Marlene's had supplied me with the name of the student who suffocated at the school, as well as juicy stories about an octogenarian couple that broke into their friends' houses to watch pay-per-view porn, and a local erotica author called Stella, who was a preening narcissist (according to Marlene). Now I was headed for the Old Schoolhouse to see if any records of the dead girl remained there. At least it would be a break from the manic media who were now hunting me down for interviews.

As soon as I was behind the wheel, a text pinged into my phone. *Strong stuff so far. Running it asap. Need more audio. Bx*

Thanks, Bill. Normally I'd have been thrilled at even this obviously lame Perry White–style pat on the head. But right now, I had more important things on my mind.

I parked the car around the back of some olive grove near the Blavette house. It was dark and the moon had come out, big and yellow and ominous. I climbed out of the car to the sound of the crickets. Night drew around me, keeping me invisible from prying eyes as I made my way to the old school building. It was a long, narrow stone structure with very few windows that looked like it might have been a barn before it became a rural school. Even from the outside, I felt its vibe—the squared notepaper, the farts, the ache of boredom during algebra lessons. Same the world over.

At first it was hard to find a way in, and I trudged the undergrowth trying doors and tugging at padlocks. Then I caught a lucky break. Almost too lucky, if I'd paused to think about it—a low window left open a crack. It swung down easily with only a mild groan of resistance and I half clambered, half tumbled in, my sneakers landing on a sloping desk, my torch shining on stacked chairs and dust motes thick in the lonely air.

I jumped down, skimming the torch beam over a glass cabinet full of sports medals, that classic tool of passive-aggressive governance, dividing the heroes from the zeros since always. This particular cabinet seemed to be the story of Raphael Blavette in trophy form. The gleaming cups and medallions framed a smiling picture of sixteen-year-old Raphael, the local sporting hero: golden and confident, a bit on the cocky side. I could see why the girls liked him. Next to the cabinet were hung a neat column of school photographs. I identified Raphael, Noémie, Freddie, and Nicole Leclair by their captions. Nicole was a small, pale girl, with a worried expression. She looked about as distant from Raphael and Freddie in self-esteem terms as a person could be.

Further down the corridor was a door with *Papeterie* written on it. I couldn't remember what that meant, but it sounded like something to do with paper. I jimmied the lock with my pen-knife and opened the door. It was your standard supply cupboard, stacked full of pencils and erasers, blue notebooks filled with squared paper. I closed it quietly and kept going to the end of the corridor until I found another door with one of those squared glass panels. Peering in, I saw a computer on a desk and file cabinets. This door was open, weirdly, since of the two it would have been the one I'd lock. Either Monsieur Raymond wasn't very reliable about locking things up, or somebody else had been rooting around in here.

It was only once I was rifling through the cabinet that I reflected on how awkward it must have been for the Blavette kids going to a school that was run by their mother. Not only was she the head teacher, but many of the classes seemed to have been taught by her, as evidenced by all the grade sheets and annual reports signed by her. Marlene had given me a vague date for the Nicole Leclair incident that occurred two years before, but nothing in the cabinet was organized chronologically. I looked under *L,* but the report cards for her had been removed, it seemed. I was just about to move on to another folder when I saw the gleam of something hidden under the other files. I fished it out—a piece of paper orphaned from the rest. Scanning over it, I saw that it bore the date July 30, 2013, two months before the school closed down. Whatever was on it was densely hand-written in French and impossible to decipher in the gloom. I stuffed it in my bag and moved on.

In the *B* section, I found recent reports for both Blavette children. I photographed them and used the translator app on my phone to decipher a few lines. The one for Raphael, written by a Monsieur Figal, was predictably glowing: "Raphael speaks with confidence in the lessons and displays a capacity for leadership, guiding the other students in a reflective discussion." The one for Noémie was dismal by comparison: "Noémie tries, but she underperforms in English, as in all subjects. She is a reasonably bright, but finally a second-rate student." Shining my torch on the drab little card, I tried to decipher the signature. When I did, I got a shock. Émilie Blavette was the teacher who had criticized her own daughter so harshly. Not the perfect family, after all.

Molly Swift

AUGUST 2, 2015

I walked through the market square in front of the cathedral, overhearing snatches of talk, some translatable if slow enough. *I heard the American girl has lost her wits. She was like a wild animal when she woke and they had to lock her up. I bet she went crazy and killed that poor family. The aunt looks touched, too. Bet it runs in the family!*

Far-fetched as it was, it made me smile. I guess I'd missed that hum of news-fever you only get in little towns where nothing happens, the rumors spreading like cooties until they're everywhere. I suddenly realized that for all the peace and bonhomie and medieval history and photogenic shop fronts, St. Roch was just like the small Maine town I grew up in. It thrummed with buried jealousies and resentments. It burned with eccentric age-old friendships and the hunger for news. It was a hornet's nest of unspoken secrets, buzzing a warning at all times.

The other thing making me smile was that I had a lead on Freddie. Marlene said he hung at the pool each day, a view that was borne out by Quinn's diary. Walking through its green gates with their art nouveau curlicues of leaves and flowers, I had a flashback to our town pool in summer, so full of frustrated parents and wet dogs and inflatable toys and screaming kids in water wings that you couldn't see the actual water. Though if you could, you wouldn't have wanted to swim in it—that shit was green.

I kicked off my shoes at the entrance and surveyed the clutch of punk kids lounged on the orange grass in stonewashed jorts and baggy shirts. Their floppy hair gleamed with cocoa butter. Mediterranean blond coifs were held back with heart-shaped Lolita glasses. Every one of them was wearing some item of clothing that would have made my teen posse in the nineties fake vomit: tight white Speedos, fluorescent tankinis, Bermuda shorts, and backwards caps pitched hip-hop high. Yet somehow it worked. The French people: stylish all day long, even in Day-Glo and denim.

My eye was caught by the kids closest to me, a boy and a girl. They looked familiar, perhaps from Quinn's Instagram. I approached their stoned circle as self-consciously as if I were a teen myself. They flicked me a couple of irritated glances and the joint they were passing back and forth vanished, leaving only a waft of fragrant smoke. I asked for a light. The boy nodded and absentmindedly flicked his lighter for me, before asking for a cigarette. When I produced one, the girl kneeling behind him leaned towards me. I held a cigarette out to her tentatively. Teens up to no good are as skittish as wild deer.

"Some scary shit happening in this town," I said, blowing a slow smoke ring.

The girl cracked a smile. *"C'est ridicule, ça. I do it better."* She demonstrated a series of perfectly formed rings before showing me her party trick—flint dust flicked from her lighter onto a barely wetted cigarette to make it sparkle.

"Very cool," I said with a smile, knowing nothing I said to these kids could ever be cool.

The girl smiled graciously at my compliment. "Sophie." She pointed to herself.

"Molly," I said, and took out some rolling papers. As I grabbed them from my pocket, I flicked the "on" button of my little camera, then I took out another cigarette and split it open with my thumbnail and sprinkled a bit of tobacco into the paper.

Sophie looked at me with undisguised curiosity. "This is Freddie. We don't come here to swim. That is just for kids."

Freddie. I knew I recognized him. My heart beat a little faster to find the very person I'd been hunting for. He'd been staring at some far-distant spot behind my head, his face pale and impassive, and on hearing his name, he came to with a jolt. His eyes slipped between us suspiciously, as if to discern whether we'd been talking about him while he was spacing out. Finally, his attention came to rest on the cigarette I'd split open, my best imitation of a joint in progress.

"Fucking pig cops everywhere now, man— nowhere to smoke but here and the woods. Anyway, you got any on you . . . ?" He mimed smoking a joint and looked meaningfully at me.

"Don't be stupid," said Sophie. "We only just met her, *mouton*. What if she tells on us?" She slapped the side of his head, made a cute little moue with her purple lips and spit *ptooie*. With those big Betty Boop eyes and tiny twenties lips, she looked like a cartoon character or a kitten.

Freddie looked away sulkily. He was her opposite: tall and plain, all lanky long limbs and big nose, his forehead babyishly huge under a shock of brown hair. He took a drag of his cigarette, shrugging, as nonchalant about the inch of ash hanging over his fingers as about everything else. "*Ça ne fait rien.* Everyone knows everyone's business here now. See the pap-rats taking photos at the hospital."

"Is that where that American girl is now?" I asked, trying to sound unbothered about the answer.

"Did you hear she woke up and went crazy yesterday?" Sophie laughed.

"I heard she was crazy before. I am lucky my girl is not crazy in any ways." Freddie leaned his head on Sophie's shoulder.

Sophie jettisoned her cigarette and scooped his

hulking frame into her tiny arms. They kissed for a while. I looked away, but I could still hear the slurping sounds. I was surprised they were a couple—Quinn's blog made Freddie sound like a single loner, out for what he could get with her. Though I guess, just because he was with Sophie didn't mean he couldn't have been freelancing.

The embrace ended and Sophie addressed me in a smoky voice. "I am looking after Freddie today, *quoi*. You know Raphael Blavette is his best friend from school. None of us know what happened to him. He's gone so long. Wanna get high?"

"Sure thing." I smiled, turning to Freddie. "So you guys went to school together?"

"Yeah, until it shut down," he said, eyeing my tobacco, "which I don't care about that because I hate school."

"Yeah, school's the worst," I said, truthfully. "Mine was all girls, no boys to date or anything."

"Our old school was worse than that!" said Sophie, her eyes bugging out. "Émilie, Raphael's mom, she was our head teacher. We hated her! I put a yogurt on her chair once and when she sat down it went *everywhere*." She smiled proudly at this last statement.

"Sounds liked it sucked." I offered her the paper full of tobacco as if I were holding out crusts of bread to some wild geese.

"*Vraiment*." Sophie took the paper with a nod

and started sprinkling in herb from a Baggie. "It was such a boring little school. And Émilie taught us so many lessons. It was . . . *comment dit-on 'elle me fait chier,'* Freddie?"

"Sophie means that Émilie was annoying," Freddie said, rolling his eyes.

I handed him my lighter. "Not a fan of the head teacher, then?"

He took it from me. "She was a bitch to us," he said bitterly. "Anyway, St. Roch has a shining new school now and that old, dusty school is finished forever."

"How come?"

Sophie lit the joint and took a drag, coughing. "There was a girl in our school called Nicole, a really annoying girl. One of those who is always hanging around, trying to be your friend, but—"

Freddie shot her a warning look.

Sophie stuck her tongue out at him and carried on, her cartoon eyes big and stoned. "What does it matter? She is inside the ground now. She cannot annoy us."

I thought of the plain, vulnerable face in the school photograph. It was all too easy to imagine how a girl like that would struggle to fit in. I waited a minute before asking the next question. I didn't want to sound too interested. We finished the joint and I gave Freddie another rolling paper so he could start skinning up the next.

Finally, I asked, "Were you there the day she died?"

Sophie split one of my cigarettes and sprinkled the tobacco into the paper skin. "I was sick that day, but Freddie saw—"

Freddie broke in. "We were just playing a game, *tu sais*, daring each other to do some things. It was no problem." He stared at the pool, the corner of his mouth twitching angrily. I remembered how Quinn had said he'd dunked her, tried to drown her, all in the name of a "game." I couldn't believe they were still playing it after something so terrible happened.

Sophie leaned towards me, talking confidentially behind her hand. "One of the dares was to hold your breath for a long time. Anyway, Nicole must have had a bad heart or something, because one minute she was fine, the next . . . pah!" She mimed an embolism, holding her breath until her face turned red.

"It was her own fault, *hein*, she did it to herself," Freddie snapped. He got up, walked over to the pool, and sat on the edge, kicking his feet in the water.

"*Merde*, you have made him mad, *quoi*," said Sophie, and hurried to his side to do some relationship healing.

Quinn Perkins

AUGUST 2, 2015

Video Diary: Session 2

[Quinn sits in her hospital bed, propped against pillows. Her hair is tied back]
Woke in the dark again today. Covered in sweat. So gross!
[Turns camera towards window]
The light coming through the curtains is sad. Know what I mean?
[Turns camera back and leans towards it]
I had this dream. I was in the woods. It was really dark. There were trees all around, crowding me. I was trying to get home, but there was only, uh, this little bit of moonlight. So I was counting the trees going by—one . . . two . . . three . . . But the moon kept moving between the trees, jumping onto the wrong side of me so I couldn't find the way. Anyway . . . weird, right?

It was hard to breathe when I woke up. Like I couldn't move. The shadows in that corner over there *[points]* kept changing like the moon in my nightmare. I kicked off the covers to try and just . . . breathe. I lay there, just gasping. Till it got cold.

And then—and I was, like, totally nude by this point—I opened my eyes. These two nuns were leaning over me, talking in the strange language, which I now know is French!

"You were having a fit," said this one nun. "Hyper . . . ventilating."

But I couldn't move my mouth to say anything.

"Take these," said the other nun, and pushed two pills between my lips. "You will breathe easier."

It made me cough so hard I had to lie still for a long time afterwards. Don't know how doing nothing can make you so . . . tired.

[Pause]

And everything . . . my skin . . . my eyes . . . are just so icky, you know? So sensitive to every sound, every smell. The lights burn my eyes. When the nuns bring food in, it makes me want to be sick. Every sound basically bursts my eardrums.

So, um, the police came into my room to chat (they said). The guy in uniform was smiling, young. Said his name was Didier. The man in the panama hat—the one from before—never said who he was, but when he went out of the room, Didier said, "That's Inspector Valentin. He's in charge of your case."

I was, like, "What happened?" And Didier was all, "They found you wandering in the woods outside of town or whatever. A car hit you! And now they're searching for the people you were staying with. The Blavettes, who happen to be missing."

So, uh, anyway . . . the therapist already told me those things—the accident, the Blavettes, that I came here for some kind of study abroad thing. It was superweird having strangers explain my life to me.

Not that I don't trust them . . . exactly . . . just, um, when I think about what I can remember, there's, uh, there's nothing there. Just a blank feeling, y'know . . . like staring at a wall.

[Long pause]

I think I cried a bit 'cause I couldn't remember any of it. Made me feel like I was going crazy. Didier was nice. He said amnesia wasn't the same as being crazy. He gave me some tissues. The inspector came back and took out a big notepad, just like the therapist. I told him my memory about the woods, trying to escape, the dark, and the crickets chirping. Feeling scared.

The inspector asked lots of questions—if I remembered my home and my parents, or traveling to France, or what I was doing the night I got lost.

"A disco, maybe," he asked, "a bit of dancing?" He did a little jiggle then, dancing with his hands.

[Quinn demonstrates]

I burst out laughing. I laughed and laughed. There they were just staring at me. I couldn't help myself! The inspector was all . . . like . . . frowning and stuff. I think he was mad at me, like I wasn't taking it seriously.

"Is there nothing else at all?" he said. "It could help save lives. It is important."

So, um, I squeezed my eyes shut and thought about the woods and the moon and the trees . . .

It was no good. I told them I felt really bad about it. Didier smiled and said it didn't matter. But if that was true, the inspector wouldn't have asked the same question like a gazillion times! It must matter, mustn't it?

[Long pause]

If I could make myself remember, maybe it would help them find the people they were looking for. I keep closing my eyes and trying to see them—the Blavettes. I was staying in the house with them for weeks, they say. I must have had dinner with them all the time. I close my eyes and try picturing a dinner table and food . . . people around it. But all I see are these, uh, these three featureless faces. Smooth. No noses, eyes, ears, mouths . . . Like moons of just . . . skin . . .

[Quinn stares into the camera]

. . . pointing at me as if I've done something wrong.

Molly Swift

AUGUST 2, 2015

The shouting was audible from the hospital reception area and as I walked down the corridor, it grew louder. Some of the nuns were running towards me. When they ducked inside Quinn's room, my stomach plummeted.

Hovering in the doorway, I got a front row view of Quinn's tantrum. It was like a scene from *The Exorcist*. Her face was red and contorted with anger. The mattress and sheets were on the floor. As I went in, a bedpan hit the wall inches from my face and fell with a clatter—thankfully empty. Didier, the poor gendarme assigned to her door, was trying to grab one arm without hurting her, while Sister Eglantine grabbed the other.

Quinn broke away from them both, clawing now at the bare bedsprings, flinging open a drawer with bed linens in it. The fragile bird of yesterday was now wild and fierce and frankly insane, muttering the same words over and over. "Ivan." Or maybe, "My phone." *iPhone.* Of course! I crossed to the drawer I'd rifled through two days before and reached into the plastic tray for the phone, now long since run out of charge. I went to the bed and gave it to Quinn.

She froze midsnarl and dropped the pillow she was shredding. "My phone." She took it from me, her thumb running over the cracked surface, calm once more.

Sister Eglantine sagged with relief.

"She seems to have access to some very recent memories," the therapist was saying.

"Really?" I said, feeling both nervous and intrigued. On the one hand it was fantastic that she was remembering more, both for her own sake and for mine. On the other hand, I wondered how long it would be until she tore into me the way she'd torn into that bed.

"Some of her video entries. Well—" his gray eyes flicked nervously behind his glasses "—they are so recent that they are quite disturbing."

"What sort of thing?" I asked, scratching nervously.

"She remembers the woods, running through them before the accident. She remembers terrible fear. Her brain is still healing, though, and as it stands her memories are more like strong emotions than actual narrative memory."

"Have you told Inspector Valentin?"

He nodded. "He has spoken to her at some length by now. But really there was nothing concrete for his missing-persons investigations. I have informed him, though, that Quinn's memory is likely to be jolted by objects or photographs . . ."

I peered at Quinn, who sat wrapped around her

dead phone, miles away. The possibilities opened up like some ancient grimoire, as fearful as it was wonderful. I could show her photos of people—Émilie, Noémie, Freddie, Nicole—and watch her reaction. Or would that make her worse? "So you're saying that if I showed her, like, her Instagram or old family photos or something, she might remember more?"

"Yes," he said. I thought he would leave then, but before he did, he leaned closer to me, his mouth a grim line. "A caution, Miss Perkins. Your niece is evidently traumatized. She will have other symptoms: paranoia, aggression, and, as we've seen, violent behavior. However you decide to help her, you must tread very carefully."

When I told Bill what had happened, he seemed a bit too interested. I got the uneasy feeling that he was mulling over using it as some sort of angle on the story—as if Quinn were a suspect. I hadn't had a chance to turn off my hidden camera before I ran into Quinn's room and saw what was happening, but I didn't want anyone else to get a look at her in that vulnerable state. I tried to undo my slipup by telling Bill that there was no way he was using any of the hospital scenes. He was so irritated with me I half expected him to have an aggressive episode. I panicked a bit then: all my video automatically uploads to a shared area so that I don't have to risk storing it. I woke up in the early hours sweating and went to remove the file from the index on the site. I was in a cold sweat, convinced I never should have turned the camera on in the first place. But by the time I found the folder where the clip should be, it seemed Bill had already deleted it.

Quinn Perkins

JULY 17, 2015

Blog Entry

I wake up to someone shaking my shoulders.

"Get up," says the voice.

Dark eyes stare into mine and hands clasp my arms. For a feverish moment, I think Raphael has come to kiss me again. Last night, after we kissed, he lent me his T-shirt to sleep in instead of my soaking-wet one and kissed me good night. I still haven't come down from the high of it. Wanting him closer, I raise my hand to his pale face and stroke his cheek, my thumb lingering on his lower lip as full and soft as a girl's.

The hands push me gently back against the pillow. "Quinn, *qu'est-ce-que tu fais*?" It's Noémie, sounding both anxious and annoyed. "We must go from here. Maman is not well . . . not happy. Raphael has gone off somewhere on his bike and we don't know if he will come back. Did something happen last night?"

"No," I say, hoping she can't tell from my face that I'm lying. The thought that Raphael has run off after what happened last night is too upsetting to think about.

She shakes me again. "Please, we need to get ready. We are going for lunch at a house of a friend of Maman's."

"Fine. But seriously stop shaking me. Else I'm gonna puke."

"I know, but I need this T-shirt . . ." she says, and to my amazement, she lifts the shirt over my head a little roughly, as if she were undressing a naughty child. The fabric rakes my eyes.

"Noémie, stop," I say, annoyed. "I'll do it myself, but why?"

Noémie rubs her eyes with her hand and I realize she's crying. "You do not understand. It is so bad for her sometimes. Ever since Papa left, we are always in trouble to pay the bills."

All of a sudden, it clicks. "That's why you joined the exchange program, isn't it? I'm not here so you can improve your English. I'm like some kind of cash cow, paying the bills." I fling Raphael's shirt on the bed, mad at all of them.

Noémie shrugs wearily. "We have had many exchanges. They are staying always. From Russia, India, China, UK. You are not the first that has come."

I get up, shaking with anger, wanting to go confront Émilie now. "And I bet this happens every time. It starts out fine and then she gets mad and starts being mean."

She doesn't say anything, looking past me at the sun outside the window. I notice how pale she is. On the tops of her arms are the faintest bruises, like finger marks, as if someone grabbed her by the arms and shook her.

The emotion drains out of me. I sit down on the bed, feeling weak, remembering how Raphael said Noémie hurts herself, tried to kill herself when she was only twelve; how *Maman can be, you know . . . a bitch. Watch out for her.* "I should go home," I say. "I'm just causing trouble here."

Noémie looks startled. "Please don't go," she says fervently. "Maybe it will be fine today. Maman will be happy, I know, and you'll want to stay."

Her sudden enthusiasm for my staying surprises me. She looks so fragile. My anger fades and I remember that I am topless. I grope for a shirt and pull it on hastily.

"Come on, then, let's go," I say, even though I feel the bad mojo rising. I take her hand, so thin it feels like a silk glove full of twigs, and we sneak out onto the landing on tiptoes. I almost giggle at this, remembering how Kennedy and I would plan sleepovers at each other's house, then sneak downstairs after our folks were in bed and do a taste test of some of the more exotic drinks in the liquor cabinet. Blue curaçao, crème de menthe. It would be all the more thrilling because of the constant fear of discovery, a punishment—being grounded, or in her case actually being spanked. Yes, back when we were twelve, that's how life was.

That's how life still is for Noémie. That's how scared she is of her mom.

The lunch turns out to be with a very proper family friend of the Blavettes, the very British Ms. Stella Birch, a wealthy writer of kinky erotica novels and fan of all things cucumber-related. It is, as the British like to say, fucking awkward, from the moment we walk in and Stella greets us, to the second course (after the cucumber soup, before the Eton Mess) when something Émilie says makes Noémie burst into tears and run from the table. Émilie makes excuses and follows her out and they're gone awhile.

The atmosphere plummets from medium awkward to mega-awkward until Stella saves the day by unexpectedly breaking out a decanter of single-malt whiskey and a pack of Virginia Slims and offering me both with a kind of freewheeling flappy hand gesture that suggests she doesn't really give a fuck how much I smoke or drink in her house. I can suit myself. And I do. We sit on her immaculate patio getting quietly drunk. I watch her from the corner of my eye, trying to puzzle her out: late thirties, childless, husbandless, fancy-free, her freckled porcelain skin a little roughened by the sun, her auburn curls beginning to silver, her blue eyes tending to look away when she speaks in that crisp British accent, as if she has secrets to keep or sorrows to hide.

"So," she says, breaking the long silence. "Enjoying life *chez Blavette?*" There's a mischievous twinkle in her eye that tells me she already knows the score.

"Yeah," I say, looking around nervously and seeing that Émilie's nowhere in sight. "I mean, no. Not exactly. The vibe's kind of—"

"Highly strung?" She inhales a delicate puff of smoke from her Virginia Slim. "I imagine it's a little cramped for Émilie and co., disagreeably shoehorned into the schoolhouse annex. They used to live here, you know, at Mas d'Or."

I look around at the gleaming marble walls, the golden dragon things and cherubs spewing mineral water, the gleaming pool. "No shit."

She snorts a polite little laugh. "Yes shit. Marc—Noémie's father—vanished a couple of years ago. The school closed at roughly the same time and they fell into a spot of trouble, money-wise. I took the place off their hands as a matter of fact."

She says it as if it was a charitable act, but knowing Émilie, I can imagine how it went down. "Um, that was nice of you."

"Yes, just imagine. For centuries, really, their

family had the best of everything. Houses. Vineyards. Land. Most important of all, their status as the greatest family in the region. In two short years, it was gone. Every whit. And then there's you, a young American, brash and nouveau riche. How do you imagine that makes them feel?"

"They probably hate me," I say. "Émilie probably . . ." I'm just about to finish that thought when an Émilie-shaped shadow falls across the pale stones of the patio. I don't know how long she'd been standing there. I catch a strange look in her eyes, a hurt look, as if whatever she heard peeled away a layer of her and left a wound open to the air.

Without meeting my eye, she says, "Stella, Noémie is quite unwell. It was a delightful dinner but we must now take our leave."

"Of course, darling. I do hope everything's fine," says Stella, getting up with marvelous elegance for a drunk girl, "torrid day and all. Do hope everyone pulls 'round. Do hope poor Noémie . . . speak of the devil!"

Noémie stands in the patio doorway like a hollow-eyed ghost from a Japanese horror film. She stares, glazed, as if something terrible has happened in the depths of that mansion between her and Maman, something darker than I can imagine.

We leave in haste, as if rain clouds have gathered

over us, although actually the sky's so blue it makes me ache. In the back of the car, Noémie cries silent tears. The dusk swells, darkening the air, and I let my hand creep along the passenger seat and slip inside hers. She holds it tight all the way back to the house. There, a new message awaits me and another video, actually the same video. The woman's face, distorted and terrified. A text that simply says, *Help me.*

Molly Swift

AUGUST 2, 2015

I was sitting outside La Grande Bouche drinking black coffee and taking a break from my duties at the hospital. Until you've been a fake aunt to a recently woken coma patient with amnesia, you don't properly appreciate alone time.

Still, alone time isn't what it used to be. I'd managed—with a combination of hard graft and Google Translate—to get a sense of the report from July 30, 2013, I'd taken from the school. It didn't say much more than what I already knew. It mentioned the unfortunate death of a student by suffocation. It listed the students present that day, including Freddie, Raphael, and Noémie. The report censured Émilie Blavette for "poor making of decisions" and being "slow to react to the series of consequent tragedies." It concluded that there were "conspicuous inconsistencies" in the testimony of the various witnesses that suggested "an absence of management that appeared chaotic" in the school and a "culture of intimidation," but it didn't say who was bullying whom.

Given the negative contents, I was surprised I'd found it at all. Maybe Émilie had meant to get rid of it and it had fallen down in the filing cabinet before she had a chance. Based on its contents, I'd been digging a bit deeper, but for all my boring internet research (and even a trawl through the microfiche newspaper archives for 2013 in the town library) I'd found nothing further on Nicole Leclair, which seemed pretty strange. You'd think the death of a local teen would be a major story.

I remembered Marlene saying, "Things happen in St. Roch that are not shared with the rest of the world"; but a cover-up on such a scale would take connections in high places, surely. It would also make great material for *American Confessional*, if I could find some evidence to back the theory up. Nicole's parents seemed like a good starting point for that: there must be some reason they hadn't sued or kicked up a fuss. Could they have been paid off or frightened away from St. Roch somehow? Regional paper *Sud Ouest* had run a dry little obituary for Nicole that gave more details of the Leclairs, but a Google search told me they'd moved to New Zealand a year after her death. Their number was ex-directory. I managed to find an email address for the mom and dropped her a tactful line in the hope that the parallels with Quinn's story might draw them out.

I had a theory: that Freddie was involved and for some reason Émilie had shielded him. But it seemed as hard to prove that as to prove that

Freddie-the-stalker had anything to do with Quinn's accident or the Blavettes' disappearance, or even that he was a stalker.

The only concrete thing I had actually found was a weird coincidence. Marc Blavette had walked out of his family's life in the same week as the Leclair incident, leaving Émilie about as messed up and broke as a person could be. However mean she might be, I couldn't help but feel a bit sorry for her. I decided to pump Marlene for more details on the mysterious Marc.

I was just about to finish up my coffee and go back to the hospital when a shadow fell over my table. "You look ghoulish, Fräulein Perkins. Are the beds at the Napoléon still made from rock?" Her waxed eyebrows twitched.

I smiled up wearily. Without spelling anything out, Marlene and I had reached a tacit understanding. We would trade one of her tall tales for a piece of my hearsay on a fair, individual basis. She didn't seem to speculate about why a devoted aunt like me would need to know these things. In her view, scandal was lifeblood, the best—indeed the only—currency. Ours was the kind of forthright turkey-talking that could only be had between a pair of accomplished rumormongers. When she slid onto a chair and leaned her bosom towards me, I knew what she needed.

"There are bedbugs," I said, leaning close, "and

the breakfast room serves the same pastries three days in a row."

"How do you know?" asked Marlene in a hushed voice.

"Because I left myself a message in a croissant and I found it this morning."

She grunted. "This is just fantasy. I can't do anything with this."

"Why did Marc Blavette leave his wife?" I asked suddenly. "It was the same week as that accident at the school."

"Yes, indeed, that was not Émilie's week." As I'd hoped, it caught Marlene off guard. She looked away, her lower lip twitching at the dilemma. It was beneath her to trade what she knew for so paltry a price, but on the other hand whatever it was must be too good not to share. To sweeten the deal, I offered her one of my Gauloises.

She countered with a pack of Marlboros. "I smoke American," she said in her gravelly accent that made me think of my mother's crackly collection of Kurt Weill songs.

"You told me you hated Americans," I said, lighting up.

"The people, not the cigarettes." She bummed a light.

"You're a complex person, Marlene. There are layers."

"Complex! Layers! This is exactly one of the reasons I hate Americans. These words you

have invented. This psychobabble. It's all—"
she gestured with her cigarette "—meaningless.
It does nothing but encourage people to
blame everyone else but themselves for their
problems."

"Yeah, well, you may be right about that." I
laughed. "And the French never do that, I guess?"

Marlene looked disgusted. "The French! Don't
speak to me of the French with their affairs and
their snobbishness and their secrets. *Scheiße*, I
have lived with the French for too long. And you
know they will never accept you completely.
Even in a place like this where there are barely
any French at all and it is basically just the
English and the Germans running the place. Yes,
yes, basically little Germany here." She dragged
deep, eyeing me skeptically as if she expected
me to disagree.

"So do people mix here—English, German,
French? Or do they stick to their own nationalities?"

"Oh no, of course. People are friendly. Very
friendly here. There are very many events here.
The Ceramics Expo. The stupid Strawberry
Parade. The Sauerkraut Festival—now that is an
extraordinarily boring event."

"And did you ever used to see Marc and Émilie
Blavette at these events?"

"Well, of course. Émilie was positively the
Queen Bee of these things back when she was
wealthy. She has always loved to boss the people

around, organizing this and that. She and Stella are unstoppable . . ."

"Stella Birch, the porn writer you mentioned?"

Marlene scowled. She could see what I was doing. Nothing was ever lost on her. But gossip was like salted caramels. One was never enough. "They are joined at the hip," she said, almost angrily. "Those two would run the whole town if they could, though why I don't know, given their history."

I didn't even need to interject. I just kept smoking and she kept going.

"Even though—" she leaned closer, mouthing the words with barely a sound "—it was plain to me that Stella was having it off with Marc Blavette before he disappeared. I felt sure he would run off with her actually."

I took a long drag to hide my expression of surprise.

Marlene still caught a whiff of shock, though, and it clearly gratified her. "The thing you must know about Stella, though, is that she is an awful hypocrite. Marc vanished without a word and no one could find or contact him. When Émilie became poor and had her little nervous break-down, many people expected her to blame Stella, cast her aside. Especially when Stella moved into Mas d'Or, which had been the family home for centuries. But Stella was so cunning. She paid for the children's clothes and music lessons, made sure there was food on the table. By the end of the day everyone thought she was an angel really, she had shown so much charity."

Marlene's story was beginning to seem just a bit too one-sided, perhaps one of those long-buried grudges small towns are so good at nurturing. "You make her sound evil, Marlene," I exclaimed. "No one's that bad!"

"Bah! She is British, you know. And the British . . . well . . . I will organize a lunch and you will see for yourself. It will distract you from all your troubles at the hospital." Her eyes shone. I could see she was desperate to find out the details of Quinn's condition.

I was just as keen not to discuss them, though. "I have to admit I'm curious now," I said, steering her back to her favorite topic, Stella Birch.

"She knows where the bodies are buried," Marlene whispered, "quite literally."

I laughed. "Okay, you persuaded me. And so you're saying that in all this time, no one ever found out what happened to Marc Blavette?"

"I told you, there are things that happen in St. Roch—"

"—that no one ever finds out about. I'm getting that vibe."

"Besides, solving cases is not poor Bertrand's forté as you may have seen. But the strange thing is . . . there have been sightings many times."

"Sightings?" I asked, wondering if we'd strayed onto weirder territory than usual.

"Oh yes, people swearing they've seen Marc in the flesh. In the woods by the Old Schoolhouse, near to the caves, even once at that church over there."

I gazed skeptically at her over the rim of my coffee cup. "And what was he doing in these sightings?"

"Searching," she said, looking spooked, "as if he had lost something."

Quinn Perkins

AUGUST 2, 2015

Video Diary: Session 3

[Quinn sits cross-legged on the bed, the sheets kicked off, the pillows pushed to one side]

Um, I reckon French people don't like sleeping much. I keep turning around in this bed, but I can't settle because of the way it's been tucked—see what I mean? The pillow's all hard and also a really dumb shape like a tube of mints. The sheets basically sand your skin off if you move and the springs . . .

[She bounces on bed]

Hear them? Also, I keep hearing funny noises: boards creaking, wood stretching, floorboards moving. Like someone was walking outside my room. Must be one of the nuns doing night rounds, I guess. I've tried counting sheep, counting nuns . . . but nothing works. I'd better get on it, though, 'cause Sister does not approve of insomnia.

Don't think she approves of me either. I heard her talking to one of the other nurses today and I know enough French to know what they were saying, because they were saying it yesterday, too, as they handed out the trays and emptied bedpans. How no one has come to visit me except my aunt—police and therapists and journalists, sure—but not my family. It's sad, apparently, that my dad doesn't care enough. They keep showing me pictures of him, as if they're trying to make me even sadder. But I still can't remember him, so I'm not.

[Turns the camera off]

[The camera is on again. Quinn is lying under the sheets]

Okay, I definitely cannot sleep. Plus *[speaking more quietly]* noises are getting creepier. So, yeah . . . There are shoe-leather-squeaking sounds again. Heavy sounds. Either Sister Eglantine has gained a lot of weight in the last few hours, or she's turned into a man, right? Weird. Still it could be my imagination, I guess. Everything's so damn loud.

[Quinn turns the camera off]

[The camera is on again. Quinn is lying in the dark under her bed. She is whispering]

Okay, so things got way weirder after that. It was dark—I dunno, about two A.M. I kept hearing the footsteps, so I just lay still, trying not to breathe too loud. The steps kept coming, but, uh, muffled or something.

[She pulls the camera right up to her face]

They came into the room. Someone . . . came into the room. And when they were almost at my bed, they stopped.

It got really quiet.

There was this noise and I just . . . *knew* someone was standing over me. There was this smell like cigarettes and a wet smell, like the woods. I kept my eyes squeezed shut. I heard . . . like . . . breathing, the drawers opening, stuff getting moved around, then the footsteps again, but this time they were walking away.

[Pause]

When I was sure I was alone, I pushed the covers down. I, uh, I could still smell the damp smell. The cigarettes. I had this crazy itch on the tip of my nose and I didn't even want to scratch just in case he was out there waiting . . .

I waited ages. Then I groped around for the cord next to the bed. The light came on and I sneaked over to the chest of drawers. I slid the drawer open and felt around for the things inside the plastic tray. None were missing, but each one was in a different place from where I'd left it. Weird, right?

[Quinn draws further back into the darkness. She's hardly visible now]

So I slammed the door. Hid under the bed, under here. Then I slipped my hand up between the mattress and the bed until I could feel the edges of my phone.

[She shows the iPhone to the camera. The screen is cracked]

Is that what they were looking for? Something in my head told me to hide it.

How did I know that?

Molly Swift

AUGUST 3, 2015

After my visit to La Grande Bouche, I went to walk Quinn around the hospital grounds. It was the first time the doctors had allowed her out and seemed to me a sign that they thought she was improving. She was still weak enough to need a wheelchair, though, and she had to wear my aviators because the brightness of the blue sky hurt her. When we got past the line of trees shielding the hospital from view, I lit a cigarette.

"You're smoking?" she asked, sniffing the air.

"Yep," I said unapologetically.

"Aren't I sick and in the hospital?"

"Smart-ass. Are you kidding? This is what aunts do."

"Model poor life choices?"

"Yeah," I said, and laughed, surprised by her snarky turn of phrase. "As a deterrent."

"Obviously," she said.

I suddenly thought of my own little niece, my big sister's kid. What was she now, four? Maybe I could store up this type of aunt wisdom for her one day. When we walked back, past the line of birch trees, Quinn shivered.

"You cold?" I asked, reaching to adjust her blanket.

She shook her head. "It's just those trees. They give me the creeps. Last night I thought I heard . . ."

"What?"

"It's . . . never mind."

I looked up at the trees she was avoiding, their spectral shapes clawing the blue sky. They *were* a bit spooky, reminding me of the woods around the Blavette house, the woods she walked out of screaming.

"Sometimes I dream about being in them," she said, "those trees. And in my dreams, I feel like someone's coming—" She broke off, pulling the blanket around her.

I hesitated a moment before saying, as neutrally as possible, "The doctor says you've been remembering some stuff. Do you remember what they looked like, this person in your dreams?"

She looked away from the trees. "Can you stop for a minute?"

"Sure."

She took off the sunglasses and turned around to me, her eyes running over my face, my hair, as if she was searching for something. After a few moments, she said, "We don't look much alike, do we?"

It was the moment I'd been dreading, a bullet I'd hoped I'd dodge somehow. I could feel the sweat breaking out in my pits, the squawking lies coming home to roost. What should I say? *You take after your mother's side of the family. Um, actually, I'm your dad's adopted sister. We do look alike! Everyone always says . . .*

Before I could think of some neat way to sidestep her first question, she asked two more. "Anyway, why has my dad not visited yet? Why is it just *you?*" She sounded angry, as if she'd had enough of me, or worse, as if she saw through me.

"Your dad's on vacation," I said, smiling lamely. "He'll come soon, I bet." *Not too soon, though,* I thought to myself.

She put the aviators back on and turned to face the trees again. "I don't remember him, anyway," she said, and that was that.

I think I'd expected her to cry or shout, but in the end, it was the flatness of her voice that made my heart break a little, as if she was one of those orphans that haven't been hugged enough and doesn't know how to love. It was hard not to feel how alone in the world she was then, with me, a total stranger, as her closest relative.

"Well, you've got retrograde amnesia or whatever," I said, by way of comfort. "The docs say your memories will come back gradually and stuff."

"Mainly, all I remember is being in the woods," she said suddenly, before adding in the same flat voice, "Can we go back now?"

I wheeled her back to her room and she got up and walked to the bed. Watching the way her knees knocked as she stumbled into bed, wiped out after ten minutes of fresh air, I realized I'd pretty much never felt this guilty in my life. I wanted to fix things somehow, to give Quinn something real to hold on to, not just the fake and not-very-reassuring reassurance of my company. I rummaged in my bag for my spare iPhone charger and plug adapter.

"Here," I said, "maybe we can charge your phone, and then we could see if you had any family photos on there to look at or something." After all, it was what the therapist had suggested.

"Give it to me," she half growled, grabbing the charger out of my hands. "That technology isn't designed for old people."

Her change of tone gave me a chill. "Excuse me?" I asked, my voice sounding too much like my mother's again.

"Um." She looked up, embarrassed, as if her aside was something I wasn't meant to hear. "Anyway, thanks."

Within seconds, she'd scooted under the bed and plugged the phone into the outlet. Feeble no more, she pressed and held a button down. After a second, the little red battery image popped up on the broken screen. She looked up smugly, like, *See?* A few moments more and the screensaver picture popped up. I felt another pang of guilt at knowing so much about what lay beyond it.

She rubbed her thumb over the screen. "I think I would like to look at photos, but I'd rather do it alone. Do you mind if I do it alone?"

I shook my head, trying not to feel too disappointed. "Bye, Quinn."

I turned back to the door with a little shiver. Perhaps after she'd been through the images on the phone, her memories really would start returning, like a Pandora's box opening. That was the whole idea, to use that key to open the closed door of her mind and let the truth out. I didn't know whether to feel more happy for her or more fearful.

Valentin was waiting for me in reception. In fact, he was pacing, a bouquet of red roses held behind his back.

"For Quinn," he said, thrusting the flowers at me.

"Thanks," I said, oddly embarrassed to take them from him.

He took off his hat, revealing his fluffed-up hair. "Might I take this opportunity to apologize for my drunkenness the other night? I enjoyed our conversation very much. But I didn't mean . . ."

"It's all right." I smiled. "I enjoyed it, too."

He tipped his hat. "I'm glad." And then he gave

me that little half smile he knew was appealing. "I thought that perhaps you seemed to be hiding."

"I've just been a bit preoccupied," I said, but I couldn't help smiling back. Even though there was something about him that made me uneasy—his chivalry perhaps, or his too-easy charm—I couldn't help liking him. I wanted to ask him about Nicole Leclair and Marc Blavette's mysterious disappearance and reappearances, but there was no way to do it without being obvious.

"How's the Blavette case going?" I asked instead. "Any leads?"

"Oh!" he exclaimed, taking off his hat and rubbing his hand through his curls. "It is really very stressing. We have had so many hundred tips by phone and it is really killing the girls handling these call lines. Each one tip we must look at and yet nothing is leading us to the family. I wish we had something more that could help."

I stared down at my espadrilles, feeling more than a little guilty about Quinn's phone. What if there were things on there that might help? I didn't want to betray her trust, but I didn't want to actively impede Valentin's investigation either. I was about to say something when he touched my arm.

"Listen, it would be nice . . . to have a drink again sometime perhaps." He looked away shyly, pulling his hand away as if I might bite.

I was getting the feeling that Valentin had a crush on me and in fact it wasn't just a drink he was suggesting. It was a date. At any other time, I actually wouldn't have minded going on a date with him. After all, he was hot, he was French, and he was a complete emotional train wreck—in other words, my type. It was just that, right about then, I felt like I'd become about the worst person I could be.

"Well . . ." I began, trying to think of some kindly form of letdown. Then I remembered Bill's words about *using it* and making a difference. "Okay. I guess."

He looked at me uncertainly. "Really? You don't sound as if you are so keen, but . . . tomorrow night, then, at the hotel bar?"

"Sure," I said, rubbing my hand over my face. "That sounds . . . classy."

"And if Quinn tells you anything," he said, his mouth creasing into a sad little frown, "anything of any kind, please ring my phone at once. Your niece's memories are the keys to breaking this case, and time, as they like to say, she is running out."

Quinn Perkins

AUGUST 3, 2015

Video Diary: Session 4

[Quinn lies on her bed in fetal position, the sheets pulled over her]

Aunt Molly wheeled me around the hospital grounds today . . . like I was a total invalid. I could've walked around with her, but she wouldn't let me. So I just sat like a baby in a stroller with her sunglasses on, while she smoked and checked her iPhone.

And then, um, on the way back . . . we walked by some trees. White, skinny ones, like the trees in my dreams. They gave me the creeps, those trees. I could remember running through them . . . from them, someone chasing behind me, trying to get away.

[Pause]

Then the car hit. They say that's why I'm in here. Hang on—

[Quinn pokes her head out of the covers and talks to someone off-camera]

"No, no. I'm fine. *Bien.* Yeah, bye."

[She settles back on the pillows]

So anyhow . . . it's pretty cool hanging out with

my aunt. Don't know what the rest of my family are like, but judging by her, I'm guessing pretty laid-back. A hippie family who get high a lot . . . ha ha!

[Quinn holds her iPhone up to camera]

Oh yeah, well, I've got new tech to play with now . . . in my hours of boredom. Aunt Molly gave me a charger for this iPhone, though she was too clueless to work out which end of an iPhone is which. As soon as it charged, I, um, well, I kinda wanted her to go, because it gave me butterflies to see this picture come up on the screen.

[She shows the camera an iPhone cover picture of herself with Raphael Blavette]

It's weird actually, because I didn't remember Molly, and when she showed me a photo of my dad, I didn't remember him either. But I remembered the guy in the photo: Raphael. Though maybe that's only because his face is on TV all the time, his and his sister's and his mom's. Whenever the nuns catch me sneaking off to the lobby to watch it, they order me back to bed. I think they don't want me to know the tabloid version of the story or the fact that I'm in the middle of it. My therapist is supposed to guide me through that process step-by-step.

[A long pause as Quinn flips through photos on her iPhone]

So . . . I spent ages lying in bed, doing this,

taking a look at what everything was like before the accident. My TV-soaked brain put names to the faces: Raphael, Noémie, Émilie. Looks like we were having an awesome time, on the beach, at the pool, in a nightclub. There was one image that I couldn't have taken, that kind of freaked me out a bit: a screenshot of a woman screaming with a man's hands around her neck, like a still from a horror movie or something.

[She shows the photograph to the camera]

This is freaky, right? Really freaky. Maybe it's from TV, like a film still or something. I took the same picture four times, see? Weird.

So, later, I woke up *[yawns]*. Oh yeah! I, um, I totally remembered something new: Noémie and Raphael in the woods with me. At a party, I think. I remembered those freaky trees, the darkness, and music, loud music shaking the ground under our feet. We were dancing. In the firelight, maybe, or like someone was swinging a flashlight around. I remembered Raphael, you know, not just a face . . . more . . . a feeling.

[She leans back in the pillows and closes her eyes]

And when I close my eyes . . . I can feel the boards creaking under my feet in that house, uh, the Blavette house, I think. I can see myself, creeping past Émilie's door to get to Raphael's room, past Noémie's door, the purple sign hanging on the handle with flowers and French words that roughly translate as *Go Fuck Yourself*. Ha ha! Then Raphael's door with its map of the Paris subway and some kind of pretentious film poster and a sketch of the night sky he made when he was twelve years old and wanted to go into space on a moon mission and leave all of this behind. Like it's a picture, that's how I remember this moment.

[Pause]

And then . . . I push his door open. God . . . and . . . my stomach just has, like, butterflies, when I see how he's sleeping on his side, his hair falling onto the pillow.

[Quinn stares at her phone]

You see this?

[Shows photo]

He's not in this one, just his rumpled bed. If you look closer *[zooms in]*, there are these two little hearts torn out of pink tissue. Did I put them there? Am I that corny? And there, on his bedside table, there are some tattoo transfers of skulls with roses in their teeth, a little pink tube of Love Hearts candy, a seaside postcard in bad French. *Je t'aime.* I love you . . .

I know it's my writing 'cause of all the consent forms I've been signing. *I love you.* Eww, was I really that obsessed?

[Quinn throws herself back on pillows]

I keep pushing my brain, you know, like a really tough workout. I want to remember the rest, but the memories just get tangled up like a nightmare. My mind goes to a dark place and my heartbeat gets so loud. There's water dripping in this night-mare. I call out and, uh, nobody answers. All I know is, this is a place where bad things happen. I'm alone there.

[She hides her face until it's hard to hear her muffled voice]

And there are footsteps, following me.

Molly Swift

AUGUST 4, 2015

It was just past noon when Marlene piled into my cramped rental, casting a skeptical eye over the cardboard repair work. True to her word, she had engineered a lunch invitation at Mas d'Or and dressed for battle accordingly, very latter-day Bardot in a black plunge-neck dress and tortoise-shell shades. I decided not to dwell on my fashion choice of jean shorts and flip-flops.

"The turnoff is on the left at the cliff edge," she said, gesturing dramatically. "I don't know why that whole *mas* is not just sliding pompously into the ocean."

The seascape moved beyond the hot tinderbox of the car in blue and gold ribbons, towards a golden house poised like a dancer on the edge of a cliff.

"It's like a fairy tale castle," I said, trying to sound suitably impressed.

Marlene rolled her eyes sarcastically, but underneath, her face lit up with the prospect of fresh gossip. "She bought the place from Émilie for *pennies*."

I pulled the car to a juddering halt in front of the grandiose gates, and got out to press the button. After a moment, the intercom crackled and the gates creaked open.

"They did a *French deal,*" said Marlene significantly when I got back in. "The new owner, she does not buy the house outright or make a mortgage, she places a bet."

"On the cost of the house?"

"On when the owners will die," she said in a macabre tone.

"Shut up! Seriously? Isn't that kind of . . . morbid?" I pulled the car up in between a gorgeous E-type Jag and a gleaming vintage Buick, hoping my parking wasn't too obviously insane.

Marlene threw open the door, panting in the heat that swamped the car. "It makes sense to me. The owners receive some pocket monies for their house and then the buyer, she pays them a rent each month. If they live a long time, until one hundred years old, say, the buyer might pay millions, much more than the worth of the house."

"And if they die quickly, the buyer gets a mansion dirt cheap," I said, climbing out.

"*Exactement.* And now the poor Blavettes have disappeared." She slipped on her shades and headed for the Grecian temple of a front porch as if she was going to a funeral. I could see where she was going with this one; but the fact that Stella was her social nemesis made it all a little less plausible. She pulled the bell. "At least it is no longer a moldy old *mas* with the wallpaper on the ceilings and the doors." The delicate chime echoed down some distant hallway inside the house.

"Wallpaper on the doors?" I eyed the clean neoclassical lines of the porch.

"These old *paysans* like the Blavette family, they love flock wallpaper. They put it everywhere except the floors. When you go in it is like snow blindness with this wallpaper everywhere. Wallpaper blindness."

I started to laugh, but was interrupted by a solemn butler ushering us into an immaculate foyer with a sweep of stone staircase and minimalist white walls. "Well, Stella may be a murderess," I whispered, "but she's got fabulous taste."

We followed the butler through to an elegant living room where there was no television and not a piece of lavender or local art in sight. It was a little spooky in its clinical whiteness. When Stella herself appeared in a tailored orange dress, it seemed as if the house had sent out a human avatar of itself. Her face under its dark chignon and her yoga-toned arms were beautiful in the same cold, white way as Mas d'Or. Together they formed a single sculpted marble organism, which I soon found spoke in the voice of Mary Poppins.

After Marlene introduced us, Stella announced, "We're lunching on the patio, ladies. Follow me."

Under the wisteria-twined pergola, we sipped Prosecco and chitchatted. All lunch long, the butler served up cold soup that tasted of vinegar, and there seemed no opportunity to move the conversation on from the title of Stella's latest novel and how the last two were selling. Once or twice, she asked me solicitous questions about Quinn's recovery and I gave vague answers, which she listened to without seeming especially interested. I had given up on discovering anything when, with a little wink to me, Marlene asked how Stella was managing without her best friend.

Stella's reply surprised me. "I'm sure Émilie is fine," she said with complete confidence.

"Really?" I asked, watching, in the corner of my eye, a lizard crawling in and out of cracks in the wall around the patio. "Seems like the police are taking it seriously."

She shot me a polite little frown and drained her Prosecco. "Noémie, poor thing, is quite unwell. Anorexic. Bulimic. And Raphael has his troubles, too. Émilie does her best, always, but she'd be the first to admit she's not a natural mother. Perhaps she's whisked them off for one of those American-style interventions."

"Leaving the exchange student to roam the

woods?" I asked, feeling as perturbed as I probably sounded.

"Well," Stella sighed. "Émilie means well with all these exchanges she takes under her wing, but she overloads herself and sometimes she struggles with the children in her charge—"

"Such as that girl at the school who died," said Marlene darkly.

"Well, that one wasn't quite Émilie's fault." Stella gave Marlene an odd look. "It was Marc who took the children on the trip to Les Yeux that day, after all."

"Les Yeux?" I asked. The name sounded familiar.

Stella turned back to me with a patient smile, holding her glass out for a refill. The butler silently obeyed. "Les Yeux are the local caves— *the eyes,* don't you know—positively the jewel in the crown of the regional heritage foundation. Marc's first love. Oh yes, he was an expert on all things Les Yeux," she said bitterly. "He adored taking hapless groups of children there, a captive audience for his lectures on local history."

"And family history," Marlene added, "don't forget that."

"Oh yes," Stella said, sipping fervently, her lips, bereft of rouge, now gleaming white. "The Blavettes *are* the region's history, really, the number one family. As I remember it, there's some dreadful family secret locked deep in those caves he liked terrifying the children with. Sounds as if it worked a treat that day . . ." She let out a manic little giggle and Marlene and I exchanged looks.

"You think the girl from the school died in there?" I asked quietly. I couldn't help thinking of poor Nicole, her death swept under the carpet somehow, forgotten.

"Oh, something like that." Stella took a most unladylike swig. "There was a big stink, I seem to recall, but Marc's disappearance rather eclipsed it for everyone, y'know. To tell the truth, I'm pretty hazy on the details."

The butler refilled my glass without me asking him. I pressed it to my mouth, not really wanting to get any drunker, but not wanting to be rude either, despite how crazy my hostess seemed to be. "And what was the deep dark secret hidden in the caves?"

"Oh—" Stella drained her glass "—some hidden chamber of horrors or other they all used to visit. Truly, I can't remember. I'm a claustrophobe, y'know. Never even let him take me into the first chamber."

"Perhaps he became lost in there, wandered off, Stella," Marlene suggested.

"Oh no, not Marc!" Stella retorted with irritation.

"He knew that place like the back of his hand. They all did, those Blavettes. Surprised they didn't all just move in there, really, y'know, when I pried this place from their grip."

Quinn Perkins

JULY 18, 2015

Blog Entry

I wake up to the sound of what I think is crows calling from the roof, but as I come to, I realize those rackety sounds are someone retching air in the bathroom on the other side of the wall from my bed. I hear Émilie's voice then, soothing, and Noémie sobbing pitifully before being sick again.

I imagine her concave belly lurching with each spasm, her greyhound ribs pressing the cold rim of the bowl, her skin rough with goose pimples, suddenly pale, her lips dry, dark stings of burst capillaries freckling the soft flesh above her eyes. I pull the sheets into me, feeling a coward for not helping her somehow.

Later, Émilie pokes her head around the door and says could I find something to do on my own today, because Noémie has food poisoning or something and doesn't feel up to going to the glass-blowing thing we had planned.

I peer over the sheets guiltily. "Maybe I could put a video on, cheer her up?"

"No thank you, Quinn," she says firmly. "I think she really just needs her mom today." She turns away, her face as closed as my shutters.

I remember what Raphael said about his sister: *She makes herself sick.* And what he said about his mom: *Watch out for her.* Later, as if to underscore the point, I hear their voices rising and sharpening just like the crows on the roof. I'm beginning to get the feeling that they have a pretty toxic relationship—the way some people get trapped in a vortex of blame and fear . . . and love, I guess, just like Mom and Dad did before they split. I put Howlin' Wolf on repeat and turn him up loud.

The heat is too much, pressing in on me. It makes me drowsy. I wake to a hand on my shoulder. I open my eyes and my stomach flips over. It's Raphael. He's back! Back! I didn't scare him off, after all. ☺

He reaches over and pulls the buds out of my ears. "Come with me," he says.

"Okay." I get up, shaking the pins and needles from my feet. Dazed, I hunt for flip-flops, lip gloss.

"Quickly," he beckons, sounding hassled.

When we reach the stairs I see the unfallen tears in his eyes. In my pocket, the iPod I never switched off sings tinny through the earless earbuds. *That spoon, that spoon, that spoonful.*

We climb on Raphael's bike and neither of us wears helmets. If my mom were alive and she saw me doing this—if my dad saw me doing this, even . . . Jesus, for once they'd agree on something. Oh God, the thrill of the road unspooling fast as tape, carrying us . . . to where? Raphael was cryptic to say the least. All I know is that we are getting away from the Blavette house and its lightning storms. I don't look at the road or the ruffle of his hair in the wind, or the sky or the sea. I just close my eyes and feel the bike's hum, feel it skim the road so low I know we will crash.

After a while, I open my eyes, startled to be alive. Green is all around us, surreally lush. The bike grumbles itself quiet. We leave it to sleep against a great oak. Raphael takes my hand and rests it on the far side of his hips.

"As a child I always would come here when I wanted to be alone. It is the best place, really." He jumps up, pulls down a young twig, and rips it from the bough, turning it into a switch to beat the ground with.

I look up to the great stained-glass dome of green leaves and blue sky. "It's beautiful."

"It's dark," Raphael whispers in my ear, "and it has many secrets, just like me."

"Ah, the mystery man!" I laugh.

He frowns and throws the twig away, lets go of my waist. I can see I've offended him and, for a while, follow awkwardly behind, feeling a blush creep along my throat. I look at the ground, the pattern of red and yellow leaves broken with green shoots, white flowers. I wonder what the forest's secrets are. Raphael's, too, for that matter. Or if either of them is worth the trek up and up over the dry land, the earth's hot pulse on our feet.

Looking up, I find the scenery has shifted, the forest's curtain parting to reveal darkness. Two eyes stare at us, the great black eyes of a double cave. Their appearance is so dramatic, so unexpected, it's more like a scene out of *Twin Peaks* than real life.

I stop dead. "Wow."

Raphael turns and grins.

"I told you it would be good. We have come to Les Yeux. The Eyes. We call them the Devil's Caves."

Molly Swift

AUGUST 4, 2015

When I arrived at the hospital after my strange, drunken lunch, I found Quinn in an edgy mood. She barely looked up when I came in, except to cast a look of exquisite disdain at the bag of pastries I dropped on her over-bed table.

"Hey," I said. "Feeling okay?"

She did a grunt-snarl combo, the corners of her mouth turning down.

"I'll take that as a yes," I said.

She shrugged.

We sat in silence for a while. A thought struck me. What if those iPhone photos *had* jogged her memory, perhaps throwing up some childhood memory or other without me in it? I'd been planning to ask her to show her phone to Valentin. He didn't know about what was on it. In fact, he seemed too unobservant to have even noticed it. You'd think it would have been his first port of call when they found it on the scene. Though I suppose a phone with a smashed screen and a dead battery would have appeared as far beyond hope as Quinn did. Since she woke, she'd been hiding it under her bed or in her pillows, almost as if there was some secret on there she didn't want found. Whatever it was, I felt sure it could help the case. But I didn't dare push her about it, not when she was in this state of mind. Instead, I stared out at the blue day sheared in tender sushi slices by the plastic blinds. My hands twitched in my lap. I had to do something, not just sit here feeling nervous.

"Well, I better get going." I started up, avoiding her eyes.

"Wait," she said. "I need to . . . show you something." She beckoned me near and with a strained look she pulled the phone out from under the sheets, flicking it past the smiling picture to the videos section. She tapped on a file and it opened up.

It wasn't easy to see with the light streaming in the windows behind us, but as far as I could discern, there was dancing, laughter, loud music, some sort of wild party in a dark place that was hard to make out because the quality was so grainy. The perspective swiveled around. I saw a pale flash of Quinn's grinning face, looking utterly different from what I'd become used to. Wild and confident and happy, she planted a kiss on the gleaming, tanned face of the man beside her. Raphael. The camera swung around again, this time showing the slim frame of Noémie Blavette. She wasn't dancing or laughing, just standing and looking fearfully in their direction. The video ended.

Quinn gulped audibly. "I think it has something to do with what happened that night, the night they went missing. I know we were in the woods or something. I remember . . . flashes of it. I . . . maybe if I went back there, I might remember more."

I looked at her uncertainly. "When you're stronger, Quinn. But right now, I think maybe we should just tell Inspector Valentin what you remember so far? Has he seen this phone even?"

"No," she snapped, and shoved the phone under the covers, as if that was a great way of hiding it.

"Quinn," I said gently, "that could be evidence. I mean, it must have phone calls, photos. It could be their best chance of finding . . ."

"Are you on my side?" she asked sharply. "I mean, sometimes I wonder if you're even really my aunt. After all, I have amnesia, you could be anyone. You could be an imposter. And if I screamed loud enough . . ."

The hate in her eyes shocked me. I got up off the bed. "Jesus, Quinn."

As suddenly as it appeared, her hateful look vanished. She shook her head. I remembered what the therapist said, about how her condition might make her aggressive at times, even violent.

"I'm sorry," she said, looking droopy again. "I'm just . . . going crazy here. I have to get out of here before I lose it."

I perched on the edge of the bed a little

nervously. "You've been through a terrible trauma. I mean, you're supposed to have doctors around, and nurses, around-the-clock medical care or whatever."

Her eyes got that defiant look again. "I've already spoken to the doctor and the therapist. I can walk and I can talk and I can piss straight, can't I? They say if you take me, I could go. They say it's only you and the police keeping me here."

"What the . . . what . . . ?" I didn't know what to believe, or where she even came up with all this. *Paranoia,* the therapist said. Maybe this was it.

"Please, Aunt Molly," she said. "Please get me away, take me back to your hotel. I can't sleep. I hate it here." She whined the words, like an upset toddler.

The cogs in my head jammed fast. I was in this up to my neck as it was. I couldn't imagine getting any deeper, looking after a sick teenager, taking responsibility for all this. "It's dangerous," I protested. "There won't be police to protect you like there are here. Sweetheart, you should just show the police the video and let them—"

"No!" Quinn said. "I thought I could trust you. But now I'm not sure."

"Quinn . . ." I said pleadingly. I felt I'd drawn on all my child and teen knowledge, used up all my experience, and now I was hitting the bumpers.

She took hold of my arms, pulling them around her, burying her head in my shirt. "If you get me out, if you take me to your hotel, I'll show the inspector my phone. I'll be good, I promise. But I have to get out of here. I have to."

Patting her head, I let out a sigh. "I'll do what I can."

Molly Swift

AUGUST 4, 2015

I returned to the Napoléon feeling thoroughly guilty about Quinn, and more than that, really weirded out by her odd behavior at the hospital, the way she'd blackmailed and bullied me. As little as I wanted to give in to her, I felt that I had to do something to help her. It seemed like the wrong kind of coincidence that my next date was with Valentin.

I walked into the hotel bar feeling a shameful little thrill of reassurance to see the barman's eyes swivel to look at me. Well, not at me exactly—at my tits cantilevered in a tight red bandage dress my sister gave me for my thirtieth birthday because, in her subtle way, she's working against my certain future as a lonely, single freak who embarrasses her at family gatherings. Valentin was already propped on the bar, double Jack Daniel's in hand, straight up, one ice cube. He looked mussed and a little bit lost, even from the back: his hunched shoulders in yesterday's shirt, his thinning blond hair a rumpled haystack. I knew that he knew: that he was losing, that everyone thought the Blavettes were past all hope. My heart—as they say—went out to him.

I sat down and said I wanted one of what Valentin had. The barman laughed and winked. I watched the reflections of the media circus behind us in the mirrored bar until Valentin turned to look at me. His face was pouchy and red, his eyes tired, his breath positively intoxicating. He was so far gone he was barely able to stay on the barstool. The dress, the lipstick, was wasted on him.

"*Ça va, Molly?*" He shot me a sad half smile.

"*Ouais, ça va.*"

Valentin chuckled. "*Bon.* You are picking up a better French."

"You think so?"

"*Vraiment.* You even say *ouais*, like yeah, like you're a spotty teenager or something."

"When you do compliments, you really go to town." I lifted my glass.

He lifted his. "*Ouais, c'est ça. Bon santé.* To mother tongues!"

"To mother tongues," I said, laughing and clinking glasses with him, aware out of the corner of my eye of the other hacks watching us like hawks. The fact that we were laughing and toasting wouldn't be lost on them. They would be thinking that either there was a break in the case they didn't know about or that we were a couple of delusional psychos. The latter, clearly, was true.

We drank, the laugh dying away just a bit too soon.

Valentin sighed and rubbed his hand over his nose, a now familiar gesture.

"You okay?" I patted him on the back as I said it, trying not to feel too ashamed of myself for playing the seductress so obviously.

He shrugged. "It's just . . . for all the talk and press conferences and paperwork and forensics . . . in the end it is real people who are affected by our work. If we succeed. If we fail. Real lives. It's hard to sleep at night, you know?"

"Yeah." I nodded, wishing I had a solid lead I could anonymously slip him.

He touched my shoulder gently. "Apologies, Molly. Of course you know. You must have lost nights of sleep worrying over Quinn. Truly, I apologize."

"No, don't." I smiled, not minding that he was groping me this time. But then it reminded me of the last time someone touched my arm: Quinn's desperate pleas, her mad promises. "No one's lost as much sleep as Quinn, you know. She's trying so hard to remember something . . . anything. I worry she'll get worse."

I had his whole attention now. "And has she . . . remembered anything more?"

I swallowed hard, thinking about the phone, the deal we cut. "Little bits . . . about the woods. It's coming back to her in fragments."

"Yes." His hand was on my arm again, whether prompting me or holding on for steadiness, it was hard to tell.

"I think that she might remember more if she was out of the hospital."

He shrugged, frowned. "But I mean . . . her head injuries . . ."

"Are minor . . . are healing."

"And her other contusions."

"Scrapes and bruises."

"But her psychological state—"

"Is best when she's with me. It's hard for her when we're apart."

Valentin closed his eyes, as if trying to clear his mind and think straight. When he opened them again, their bloodshot blueness surprised me. "Okay, Molly. If the hospital agrees, I agree. On the condition that one of my men watches over your hotel door. Be warned, Molly, you may both be at risk now."

I nodded, swallowing nervously, less about the risk than about the enormity of it all. From fake aunt to real au pair.

He raised an eyebrow. "Remember the break-in to your car? That could be the tip of the iceberg. We still have no clue who is behind all this."

I thought that deserved another kiss on the cheek, and he didn't seem to mind.

Quinn Perkins

JULY 18, 2015

Blog Entry

I stare at the blank eyes of the caves, remembering the book on my bed, the horrible pictures and the morbid passages underlined in red. Did Raphael put it there? Gazing into the gloom barely visible from where we stand, I hear the drip of water coming from the cave roof. "It's a bit *Blair Witch Project*," I say, trying to sound cool.

"Oh, it's much better than that," he breathes, and there's something new in his face, a ripple. "The stories about this place go back to the Middle Ages. Witch hunts. Bad things."

Another shiver, that anticipation, the opening credits of a horror movie, the ghost story told around a campfire before bed. "What kind of things?"

He leans close, hamming it up. "A man lived in St. Roch in the 1600s, during the great witch hunts. He killed many and the king honored him, made him Witchfinder General. He heard a story that there were dark rituals happening in the caves, prayers to Satan, sacrifices, murders even.

And so he came here with a group of men and they searched the chambers with torches, and found that his wife and children were inside one of them."

The image he creates of claustrophobia—worse, of familial anger—is so stifling I turn my eyes to the ground. "What were they doing there?"

I hear the flick of his lighter, the gasp of his inhale. "Who can say? Blavette did not pause to find out."

"Blavette . . . like your Blavette?"

"Yup." He exhales smoke, which hangs around my face. "My great-great-great-great-great-grandfather or something."

"So what did he do with his wife and kids?"

"He ordered his men to block up the entrance to the chamber they were in, so there was no way for them to get out. And soon afterwards he married the young girl who was his mistress."

I shiver again, feeling the force of the story rattle my bones. "Your great-great-great-great-great-grandmother or something like that?"

Raphael nods. "*Exactement.* Come on, let's go."

In the cave, the shock of the sudden temperature change makes me dizzy. I can hear Raphael, smell him, but the light is so low now I can no longer see him. I start to panic a little, my hands out in front of me, feeling for walls, for cobwebs that might catch my face, ears straining at every drip-drip, every whisper of wind through the dark tunnels I cannot see. My fingers brush something warm. Before I can stop myself I let out a little shriek.

A hand grabs my wrist. "Shhh. It's me."

I hear the flint-grind of a lighter, smell fuel. A flame casts shadows on the ragged walls around us, glinting off fleshy chandeliers of stalactites hanging from the ceiling. Raphael stares at me across the bluish flame, his eyes black in the dim light. "Some say that the mother and children suffocated in the next chamber to this one. On a still day you can hear them scream to be freed, their nails scraping at the walls." He crosses to the wall, his light making shadow beasts on the yellow stone. "Some say that the children ate the mother. That they lived, bred, stayed in the caves, that they remain here . . ." He turns around slowly, holding the lighter under his chin like a kid with a flashlight spinning ghost tales at camp. "Your face is so funny."

I laugh uncertainly. "So if we get eaten in here, it'll be by your cousins a few times removed?"

Raphael shrugs, shucks an American Spirit from the pack, and cups the lighter to his face. "These are stories made up to frighten children. Who knows what is true. Except one thing perhaps . . ."

"What's that?"

"Blavette was an evil man. And I do not believe his evil has died out in our family. Its stain is on us like a curse, maybe, to make us forever unhappy."

The way he says it is sad. I go over to touch his arm. "I'm sure that's not true. Not really."

"Who can say?"

He touches his nose to my nose, his eyelashes to my cheek. The lighter clatters down, its light guttering. I switch off my brain and listen to our breathing echo through the maze of corridors and chambers we cannot see. I don't know how long we are in there, only that I forget time and the world. All I am is lips, hands, skin.

It's only outside in the daylight that I come to, dazed and not myself, as if we'd dropped acid in there or channeled a ghost. We smoke, descending the hill in silence, swapping shy smiles. By the time we find the bike, it is dusk.

"Fuck," says Raphael.

The loudness of this word makes me jump. "What?"

"I forgot to show you the best part." He play-slaps his own cheeks, then catches my wrists and pins them behind my head, kissing my neck. "Beyond that chamber is a door to another chamber. Inside are natural gases, ones that can kill people. It is like a gas chamber carved in the rock, a place of execution. People who have tried to go in there have disappeared . . ."

"Disappeared? What the fuck? We were just in there."

"I know those caves, Quinn. My father took me there all the time, exploring. But other kids, you know, they would go in for a dare or drunk. People started to call Les Yeux 'a keeper.'" He lets my hands drop.

"'A keeper'? Like it kept the people who got lost in there?"

He turns around to face the handlebars. "Every last one."

Molly Swift

AUGUST 5, 2015

The following day, after I'd cut through all the red tape the doctors had wrapped Quinn in, she moved into my hotel room for what may have been the most high-stakes sleepover party of all time. In the end, although the nuns looked on sternly, everyone seemed fine with the move and the therapist actively encouraged immersive family time as an aide-mémoire, his warnings about her violent outbursts seemingly forgotten. As the nuns of Sainte-Thérèse waved us away, I realized they were probably relieved. Now instead of clogging the parking lot and harassing staff, the media would stalk Quinn here. Now she was my problem. I hovered over her anxiously while she picked a bed and a nightstand in the shiny new twin room the hotel ushered us into. I couldn't help but feel that she was fragile: a china cup with a hairline fissure only I could see.

It turned out that this out-of-hospital Quinn clad in jean shorts and a Fall Out Boy T-shirt was reassuringly like an ordinary teenager. After a two-hour shower, she emptied her rucksack onto her bed and within minutes had trailed its contents over the whole room. She plugged the speakers I'd bought her into her iPod and played some god-awful thrash metal band at top volume until a downstairs neighbor banged on the floor. Then, completely without asking, she borrowed my liquid eyeliner.

I countered this performance with what I do best: act like my own kind of old-age teenager. I smoked out the window and stole sips from one of the minibottles of cherry wine I'd picked up at a corner store, staring at the street where people moved happily about their nonweird lives, seemingly feeling no compulsion to be workaholics whose lives literally turn into their jobs every few months. *But, oh,* I told myself cynically, *their carefree lives must be so boring.*

Refreshed by my schadenfreude, I turned back to the room to see that Quinn had discovered the wine and was swigging it from the bottle, in a nest of covers and pillows harvested from both beds. She had also found the remote and some steamy thriller to watch on silent while her music blared. In the gentlest way possible, I wrestled the control from her and flicked past the hard-core danger zone and onto a Road Runner cartoon. She scowled up at me, looking alien now that she was lip-glossed and panda-eyed.

"Playing couch commando already?" New Quinn sneered. "We've only been rooming together five seconds."

I felt as if I'd failed a major auntie test. In my

best cool-aunt voice, I said, "I am when you're watching X-rated movies."

"Prude much?" Her eyes narrowed.

I'd thought she was just acting out, but now it seemed she was doing her best to shock me. I had a belated flash of pity for my mom and the horrors I know I put her through when I was Quinn's age. "Okay, I am when it's a pay channel," I said, trying to break the awkward atmosphere. "That nice film you wanted to watch about the cop and the hooker with a heart of gold cost ten bucks." I laughed uneasily.

"Cheapskate."

I rolled my eyes, handed her the control, and retreated to the window. This was going to be a long day . . . night . . . however long this lasted. I'd heard nothing about Quinn's dad booking her a plane ticket home as yet. He seemed curiously unprotective, uninvolved even, though if he was as detached from reality as my dad, that might explain it. I'd thought this hotel stay would be nice after the way we'd . . . bonded kind of. But as much as she was actually my meal ticket, I guess I was her hall pass out of the hospital. I never really got on with my own sister when we were teens, and I've never wanted kids. So maybe it figured.

A sob from behind me jolted me out of my cynical reverie. "Quinn. Hey, hey . . . what's up?"

I navigated to her over the soft terrain of pillows

and clothes and knelt down. She buried her mascara-streaked face on my shoulder. I hugged her. She mumbled something I didn't catch.

"What's that?"

"Sorry . . . [sob] . . . for being an asshole [sob]."

"Hey, hey. You're not an asshole. You're never an asshole. You're . . ." Words that wouldn't embarrass her failed me.

"Broken?" She looked up at me, her face smeary and blotchy and sad. It was all I could do not to lick a hankie and start dabbing.

"No, no . . . not broken. Anyway, there's nothing broken that doesn't get mended somehow."

"Been watching *Oprah* again?" She raised a Sharpie-lined eyebrow, the hard shell of her cynicism closing over her. She edged away from me again, feral and skittish, teetering on the edge of some deep pit I couldn't imagine.

I sighed, sitting down beside her on the rat's nest of duvets and sheets. "You're right. Things don't get mended so much as they just kind of . . . heal over like broken bones. And you never really forget what happened, because you always feel that lump in the bone. That thing that makes you not the same as you were. How's that?"

"You sound like you know," she said, catching her lip with her teeth in the gesture of futile stoicism I'd come to feel quite fond of. "I mean did you . . . were you . . . ?"

"Not the same as you. Nothing as terrible, I'm

afraid." As I talked, I brushed a hair from her face. She let me and I relaxed a little. "But you know . . . everyone goes through stuff and thinks things will never go back to normal. 'I'll never be normal.' "

She rolled her eyes. "What are you going to say next? Hey, but look at me. I'm normal now!"

It was my turn to give her a cynical look. "Do I seem normal to you?"

She laughed a bit too hard at that. "No!"

"Thanks."

"I mean in a good way. Like you don't seem like a grown-up. It's why I can talk to you, I guess. I don't know if we're always like this . . . close like this . . ."

I thought of the prim single teacher from Connecticut I was impersonating and gulped back the bilious taste of my lies. "Yeah. Always have."

She leaned her head on my shoulder. "It's just so hard to know . . . I mean, I heard from Dad, like, yesterday, a really short call to tell me about how Meghan and the baby were doing. He asked how I was and stuff, but it was . . . really formal, like he didn't even know me."

"You mention me?" I asked, trying to sound casual.

"He never gave me a chance. It was like he was my parole officer or something. And he could have been, because I don't remember him . . . so . . ." She leaned her face on her arm, stifling a half sob, half laugh. I heard the rest of it muffled by tan flesh. "And I've been texting a girl called Kennedy, who messaged me on Snapchat and says she's my best friend, but I don't remember her either! At first I even thought she was some journalist trying to get the inside scoop on me like just about everyone . . ." She looked up, a catlike gleam in her eyes. "They've been on TV, you know, my buddies back home, telling all about me. Did you know that?"

I shook my head, hoping she couldn't really see through me, even if she looked like she did. I remembered the tragic stuff on her blog: her mother's death, her illness, a phrase about how everything was normal, and then one day everything was broken. I wasn't the only one who'd pored through her virtual life either: after Quinn's name was released to the media, it wasn't long before they found the more easily accessed layers of her online presence. They followed up the leads provided by tracking down a bunch of people on her Facebook "Friends" list and interviewing them.

The better papers had given only a vague sense of her history for context, implying that it wasn't the first tragic accident to befall the Perkins family; the tabloids were already drawing crude connections between her obsession with all things horror and what had happened to her, as if writing a couple of ghost stories could cause your life to implode. Her BFFs had given mixed reviews. The Kennedy girl she'd been Snap-chatting with was sweet and a little tearful when she said she hoped "poor Quinny" was coming home soon; a guy named Zeke I assumed was an ex had taken the opportunity to say that "Quinn was always kinda weird." He claimed she'd been obsessed with him their junior year. Yes, she had every right to be angry.

I wished I could make up to her for my spying by being honest about myself in return. I wanted to tell her my real life story. How I came from this cheerful home—dad lawyer, mom paralegal, life peachy—until my dad was sued by a former client for malpractice and lost everything, including his mind. But being her fake aunt, I couldn't tell her anything real and we were both too cool to hug. Instead, we ended up bundled up in blankets drinking Cherry B and watching *Buffy* reruns late into the night. All the lying and trauma and possible murder aside, it was actually nice, as if we'd always known each other, as if the lies I'd told her were true.

By one, she'd fallen asleep half on top of me with Dick Van Dyke from *Diagnosis Murder* murmuring in the background. I woke up dry-mouthed and covered her up with a blanket and tried to stop myself thinking that when the truth came out, it would hurt her in more ways than one. I was just dragging myself to bed when there was a knock on the door. This time, it didn't surprise me too much that it was Valentin.

"*Bonsoir.*" He smiled sheepishly. The day had been too busy for us to exchange anything but a few formal words and the odd awkward glance. I still didn't know if he even remembered the night before.

"*Bonsoir,*" I said solemnly, craning my neck around the door to see Didier perched on a chair playing Sudoku.

"For your security," said Valentin with a chivalrous wave of the hand.

I nodded, letting our embarrassed silence fill the corridor.

"So." Valentin leaned on the wall near the door, an awkward attempt at seeming casual. "May I ask if anything's 'come back' to Quinn?"

I nodded. Down to business. "You may." I peeked inside, where the light of the muted TV flickered over Quinn's sleeping face. I pointed at her silently, indicating that I didn't want her to overhear.

"Well," said Valentin. "Didier is guarding the door. Would you mind debriefing in my room?"

"Um, no." I stifled a smile. "We can debrief if you like."

Valentin said a few words to Didier in French and Didier nodded briskly.

"He has the keycard," said Valentin. "If anything should go wrong."

Before we went, I remembered something: Quinn's iPhone, where she'd left it in the bathroom. I ducked back into the room and slipped it in my pocket for the second time, telling myself it was an intervention and not a betrayal.

Quinn Perkins

JULY 19, 2015

Blog Entry

Last night a badass storm punched a hole in the sky, loosing the trapped heat that was choking us all. So when a loud noise woke me at exactly 3:05 A.M. I thought, at first, it was the thunder calling.

I crept from bed to unbolt the shutters and stuck my head out into the rain. For once there were no cicadas, as if the rain song had pressed their mute button. Eyes closed, mouth open, I soaked my hair and face until the storm eased. I was about to pull them closed again when I heard the noise that must've woken me—a shrill voice, coming from downstairs, then a lower voice, a man's, talking fast and in French. I couldn't hear what either was saying.

For a few moments, the house fell silent. I leaned on the windowsill, my unease growing fresh horns and claws, becoming the same mean-spirited little incubus it had been before. Someone ran out into the rain—Raphael, his white T-shirt soaked, his face a blur. He climbed on his bike and kicked on the engine. I called down to him and for a brief second he looked up at me, his face tight.

He said nothing. His bike sped into the night and the reek of burned rubber and gasoline beat out the scent of the rain-wet world. A woman ran out after him and, seeing him gone, stopped in the middle of the yard and slowly turned back to face the house. Émilie, just staring up at me.

Now it's raining again and I am typing this on my phone under cover of my covers. Raphael's latest Facebook status says: *Paris j'arrive*! I can't lie that it doesn't hurt to feel he's so excited to leave for Paris without saying goodbye. Nothing about me on there, of course, and he's yet to answer my text checking if he was okay. Whatever he and Émilie argued about was bad enough that he had to climb on his bike in a rainstorm and be free. Or maybe it was me he ran from. Or maybe he didn't run; he just never planned to stay.

The gray light sees my fucked-up night and raises it a shitty day, a lover-left-me-without-a-word day, a homesick day, a nowhere-to-go and nothing-to-do day. In short, all the worst times rolled into one. I don't need to get out of bed to tell you in detail that the world has turned one hundred percent crappy overnight. Outside the window, fir trees and burnt-orange grass are smeared by rain. In the mirror, my hair looks greasy, my skin pasty, and a big zit is ripening on my nose, the kind that however much you squeeze it won't quite pop. Down the road, a small town looks depressing in the rain. Down the hall Noémie's retching and Émilie's nagging. So if anyone reading this has a helicopter or a Learjet or something, I'd quite like to be airlifted out of my life and dropped into someone else's for a while, thanks.

As if reading my thoughts (or maybe my depressed Facebook status), Kennedy messages, *Hey bro what Up?*

Mucho of nada ☹

Uh-oh. Boy trouble?

Can I call?

Late for basket weaving class -_-. Wish u were here!

Me too ☹ *Call later?*

Later. Miss ur face. Hang tuff! X :p

Later gater X :p

I knew it. She's made new friends, those kind of intense summer friends that totally eclipse your feelings for your BFF.* I fling myself back on my bed, all the better to reach the depths of self-loathing. To hasten the inevitable meltdown, I flick through photos of Raphael taken on my phone, all two hundred and fifty of them. Lucky he didn't look at my phone by accident, realize I was obsessed and climb on his bike then and there. But who can resist taking photos of him when he's so gorgeous in every single photograph?

*Kennedy, if you're reading this, it's totally cool you've made new friends. I'm stoked for you, srsly ☺

Down in the kitchen, I mooch, stomach growling, yet not hungry somehow. I make Lipton tea with a slice of lemon, missing the Boston Tea Company shop back home where Kennedy and I—fresh from auditing a freshman psychology class—took online personality disorder tests for every single person we knew, starting with guys we liked and continuing with our parents, siblings, and friends, performing postmortem surgery on every last party, class, and date in a Freudian psych-fest that was as hilarious as it was brutally enlightening.

God, Kennedy, I wish you were here with me so we could do an autopsy on this. Or if it's not quite dead yet, at least measure its sputtering pulse. If you were here, I could shake off this mood with some biting sarcasm, then we'd laugh about the Blavettes until we cried, while the huge metal urns of chai farted perfumy steam and our bone cups clicked genteelly on our saucers.

The rumble of another argument breaks my train of thought. I'm so used to this now that I know the chords, riffs, and bridges like I know "Born Under a Bad Sign": Émilie's voice grinding on and on, a monotone lecture delivered in rapid French, kept just low enough that it should be out of earshot (but of course it's not), Noémie's voice chiming in, gravelly with tears, the loud slam of a door and something smashing, more shouting, fists on the wall. I feel so sorry for Noémie. At least Raphael can run away from it when he wants to.

My tea has a greasy skin on it, a baby-oil slick reflecting the day outside. I don't want to be here anymore. I'm actually thinking about cutting my trip short, phoning up Dad and falling on his mercy. Please, Daddy. *Please*. And I do it. I actually dial the number of the hotel room in Tahiti, simultaneously preparing a speech and bracing myself for Meghan to answer. But she doesn't. And he doesn't. The phone rings and rings with no answer.

Footsteps on the stairs. Madame Blavette. She's swathed in a flannel bathrobe, her hair unwashed, in pins, and she looks ten years older. She sets her cup in the sink with the other cups. "I am making chicken escalopes for dinner. Will that be fine with you, Quinn?" Her voice is brisk.

"Of course." I smile the tight fake smile of the terrified.

"Yes, you Americans really like your food." She smiles, flicking her eyes over my tits, my hips, as if to imply I should probably eat less. "I know you like your food even more than the other girls I have hosted."

Let it go. Let it go. Let it go.

"*Bon.* Well, I hope you find things to do in this rain. There are books if you like reading books. Or perhaps you can just play with your phone all day."

Something snaps in me. "I was phoning my dad."

"Why?"

I'm amazed at her tone. She sounds almost paranoid.

"Because I miss him."

"Well, fine, but calling Tahiti? Surely your phone bill will be—" she waves her hands frantically as if the melodramatic word she's searching for is wafting through the air around her "—astronomical!"

"He asked me to keep in touch."

She raises her eyebrows, shrugs, reaches for a heel of stale baguette on the counter behind her, breaks off a dry crust, and sucks on it like a rusk. "You know, Quinn, woman-to-woman. Fathers . . . I mean, they say these things, but they are not like mothers. Chitchatting to their daughters is not high up on their list, especially when they have gone to Tahiti with a young woman barely older than their daughter, *hein.*" She raises a neatly waxed eyebrow.

I hear a smash, feel wet soak through my hiking socks. But it's not until I see Émilie on bended knees with the brush and pan, sweeping up shards of china, that I realize I've broken her mug.

"Sorry," I mutter, kneeling down to help her.

"My hands shake sometimes because of my . . ." I'm about to say "medication," but I stop myself. Because she doesn't need to know about that when she already knows about Meghan. And come to that, how does she know about Meghan? "Dad ignores me in favor of his trophy wife" isn't exactly the kind of thing you list on a cultural exchange application.

"Ouch," says Émilie. She stops brushing and sucks her thumb. When she pulls it from her mouth there's a bead of blood forming around a tiny shard of china. She pulls it out and sucks at the blood, her dark eyes watching my face.

"Sorry," I say, though I don't know why I'm saying sorry over and over.

She straightens and pulls her thumb from her mouth, dabbing it on her dressing gown and making tiny red marks. "It's okay," she says slowly, as if she's trying very hard to keep her voice level. "I have had exchange students here ever since my husband was taken from me. I have them because the school has shut for two years now and a single mother must support her family somehow. And always it is the same. Fine for a week, two. Then they fight with my daughter and they flirt with my son." Her eyes meet mine. "It is a hard thing to understand, perhaps, that a boy like him, with a shining future ahead, would not be interested."

"I think he gets on with *me*," I say weakly,

stopping myself before my voice gives too much away.

"That is funny," she says, "because he told me he was leaving to get away from you following him around like a puppy. I begged him not to, of course . . ." Smiling, she stamps on the pedal bin step and dumps the china shards with a tinkling crash. "After all, he is my baby."

Quinn Perkins

AUGUST 5, 2015

Video Diary: Session 5

[Quinn sits on the edge of a half-made bed in a hotel room. She's dressed in jeans and a T-shirt and seems lucid and alert]

I'm out of the hospital. Yay! I'm in a hotel room now. See?

[Quinn pans the camera around the room]

There's TV, Wi-Fi, and a frickin' minibar for the win. I'm psyched! It was driving me crazy to lie there doing nothing while they came and asked the same questions over and over again. They've left me with this . . .

[She taps the camera]

Why? So I can keep giving the same useless answers, I guess . . .

Yeah, I was really going nuts listening to the bleeping of machines hooked up to me. Staring at four walls painted that shade of green that's meant to be therapeutic, stupid from the drugs they shot into me. If you ask me, there's *nothing* therapeutic about the color green.

[Pause]

Even less therapy value in talking to my friends. That girl Kennedy—she acted nice, but I saw a clip of her on TV saying she thought I was "kinda quiet." As in "it's always the quiet ones." Am I right? Not to mention my other good "friends" who've been chatting with Fox News. I've blocked them all now. And then there's my dad. He called yesterday on the hospital phone and I stood there listening to him, shivering in my gown and slippers while the other patients wheeled their plasma bags by.

He asked me how I was and said sorry for not being there. "The baby's due any day and Meghan's really struggling at Boston West. Inadequate care there if you ask me. Her first child and all . . . unimaginable what she's going through."

Yes, unimaginable, Dad. I mean, I've not been in the hospital after a hit-and-run or anything. He talked and talked about his wife and her problems and him and his summer school marking as if I was someone he'd just met on a train. I felt this anger well up, like I would burst if I heard any more excuses. Wasn't he supposed to be my parent, to care about me, to save me?

In the end, I blurted out, "Have you seen the news? It's a really big deal here, what happened to me." And, um, there was this really long, awkward silence on the other end of the line. I thought maybe it had gone dead.

Then he said, "Are you getting all the *attention* you need, Quincy, after your . . . *accident?*"

Before he could squeeze in another word, I slammed the receiver down as hard as I could. I couldn't breathe or see straight. The way Dad said those words—*attention* and *accident*—it was obvious he meant he thought it wasn't an accident. He was implying I did it on purpose, for attention.

[Quinn hits bed with the flat of her hand]

I don't even like attention! I don't want to be coddled and soothed and patronized anymore, not by the doctors and not by Dad. He's not visiting me here, that much is clear; he didn't even make plans for me to come home yet. Though he did make some small talk about my start date for Bryn Mawr. Does he hate me? Did he always? Is it because I like "attention"? Have I always hated him, too? See, that's the kind of question that keeps me awake at night, trying to jog my memory. It feels like when I was a kid and I had loose teeth I was always trying to push out with my tongue. Twice as frustrating, though.

[Pause]

But those memories are starting to come back. I've been thinking about that dark place I was in, with the dripping water. Remember?

A name finally came into my mind: Les Yeux. I

think it's somewhere near here. Tomorrow I'm going to tell Aunt Molly about it and see if she'll take me. Dad may be a waste of space, but at least my auntie loves me and I feel . . . yeah, I can really trust her. Maybe if I find that place I'll remember the rest. I Googled it on my phone and it's a real place, only a little way away from this hotel. Speaking of my phone, I've left that thing somewhere.

[Searches]

In the covers? No . . . On the floor, maybe? No, that's Aunt Molly's . . .

[Knocking sound outside the door]

"It's me, Didier."

"Hang on, I'll let you in."

[Sound of the door opening]

"Everything okay, Quinn?"

"*Ouais.*"

"I'm thirsty. I think I'll go kick that vending machine downstairs. Want anything?"

"Coke Zero?"

"One Coke Zero coming up."

[Pause]

That cop Didier has a great smile. He sits outside the door of this room playing Sudoku or Flappy Bird or texting his girlfriend or whatever. Being normal, I guess. I don't know where Aunt Molly's gone, seriously. I fell asleep and I thought she maybe had gone out for cigarettes, but she's taking ages.

[She pats the bed, searching for something and growing increasingly frantic]

Where is my phone? Seriously? Where is my fucking phone?

Molly Swift

AUGUST 5, 2015

Valentin's hotel room was reassuringly as I had expected: hospital corners on the double bed, his dry-cleaned suits hanging neatly in plastic—a sand-colored one, a white one, a dark one. An empty Scotch glass and an overflowing ashtray on top of a pile of police files demonstrated how he'd been occupying himself while I was keeping Quinn entertained. God, he was a walking cliché, one too lazy to commute from La Rochelle to St. Roch for this case every day by the looks of things. I wondered if his flat in the city was the same.

When the cliché gestured to the bed, I raised an eyebrow and he laughed. "Let's sit, talk." He offered me a cigarette and a Scotch. Perched on the armchair together, we smoked out the window, watching the rain run off warped old tiles, dyeing them brown, slipping in rivulets down facades of medieval stone tugged crooked by the centuries. It made me think of the book I'd found in Quinn's room at the Blavettes' detailing the dark tangle of secrets that tied the family's ancestors to Les Yeux. I unfolded a scrap of paper on which I'd scribbled down a quote I'd Google Translated.

>> The seventeeth-century history of the region includes the notorious story of Duc Philippe Blavette, a Witchfinder appointed by Louis XIII the Just in 1623. Upon Blavette's land lay the network of caves known locally as Les Yeux and one night a local farmer came with a troubling report of satanic ritual murders committed there. The following day, the duc and his men searched the caves and found a woman and some children hiding in one of the chambers. Despite being informed of the fact that the woman was his wife and the children his own, the Witchfinder was pitiless: he had the chamber blocked up, where it is assumed his family died. Not a twelvemonth later, Duc Philippe was wed before the king to a young hand-maiden in the queen's service. It is a tale of persecution and torture, greed, and betrayal rivaling none.<<

Women trapped in the caves, the machinery of local gossip and prejudice working against the innocent. I shivered. What was it someone said about history repeating itself? Maybe the contra-band phone I had on me, the one hidden in my bathrobe pocket, could help.

I handed it to Valentin. For a moment, he held it nonplussed: the confirmed technophobe holding a piece of random technology. Then he clicked the button and the photo of Raphael and Quinn appeared on the lock screen. Two tanned kids on the beach, smiling and young and in love.

He glanced at me, a kind of sad tenderness on his face. Despite all the drinking and the panama hats and the irritating chauvinism, it was his sentimentality that made me like him. He wrinkled his brow at the passcode screen that had popped up over the picture. In a fit of hospital-bound paranoia, Quinn had added it, but I'd watched her key in the code a dozen times. Guiltily, I keyed it in for him.

"How did you get this?" he asked as the compact rectangle of metal and glass that contained a teenage girl's whole life spun open.

"The old-fashioned way. I took it."

He shot me an odd look.

"Believe me, I don't feel good about it."

He shook his head. "That is not what I was thinking." He took up a little notebook and Biro that seemed quaintly outmoded, and turned back to the phone.

For a long while, he looked through the contents without speaking, occasionally tutting when he couldn't work out how to use an app. When he'd skimmed some of her blog, I helped him unlock the little secrets of her life: the parts of her Instagram and Facebook accounts that the media hadn't been able to access because they were password protected. They were easily seen on her phone. Finally I led him to the little folder of videos. He played one of Quinn and Raphael laughing and whispering, their faces spotlit by the light of the phone.

"You hear that in the background behind their voices?"

I nodded. "Sounds like dripping water."

"A cave perhaps . . ." He scrawled a note. *Les Yeux*. The name sent a chill down my spine, reminding me of what Stella and Marlene had told me.

He tapped another cigarette out of the pack. "How do I keep these photos?"

"I think they're all on here." I clicked on her Instagram. "And here." Her blog. "And probably her Facebook, too."

He made a note of what I'd said and handed the phone back to me, a stern look on his face. "It seems bad that Quinn has not shown us this."

"She probably didn't think it would be useful," I said, sounding more defensive than I meant to. "I mean, it's the last bit she has of her life, her thoughts and feelings. I can understand how she would want to cling on to it."

Valentin took out his own phone and typed out a couple of rapid texts. "Perhaps she doesn't understand that the lives of the Blavettes are at stake. If I can discover the reason Quinn was wandering at night in the woods, I might be able to find the family."

"I'm pretty sure she does understand," I said, surprised at the sharp tone of my voice. I didn't know why his words made me so angry. He wasn't saying anything I hadn't thought myself. Perhaps that was why. In the back of my mind lurked the fear that Quinn was not telling me everything she knew—that she might have more agency in this strange situation than she was letting on—and he'd just made it seem more true.

A text pinged into Valentin's phone, buzzing obnoxiously. He glanced at it, nodded to himself, and switched off the screen before I got a chance to read it.

"*C'est ça*," he said. "It's done. The team at St. Roch are on to this now, looking through her social media still more thoroughly than the papers have already been doing. I have made a flea in their ear, though really I know it is a problem of understaffing in this rural place. And myself, I am too technophobe for this . . . Instagram."

I turned away so he wouldn't see the guilt in my eyes.

Valentin rubbed his nose with a sigh. "I'm sorry, Molly. I didn't mean . . ." He touched my hand. "I know how you love her. You're like a mother to her. When I see you together, it reminds me of my own . . ." He trailed off, looking sad.

I took his hand between my own. "What?"

"My wife. My son." He put his face in his hands and rubbed again. When he looked up his eyes were bleary. "I fucked that up."

I picked up the bottle of supermarket blend whiskey and topped up our glasses. "Here's to fucking things up."

He chinked his glass against mine, smiling wistfully. "It was strange to see that picture of your niece and the Blavette boy. On the beach. Carefree. In love. Remember those days when it was easy?"

"Yeah, those days are long gone, I guess. Anyhow, I should go . . ." The phone was burning a hole in my pocket. I had to get back.

So I don't know why I let him take my hand and turn it and kiss my wrist, or slip my robe back to plant kisses on the inside of my elbow, or unfasten the cord at the waist and push the robe down.

In the afterglow, I stood near the window, my head muzzy with whiskey, my throat smoked raw. The world and its pain seemed far away. I felt unexpected happiness—the elusive satisfaction we all seem to grub around looking for, that kind that feels way too good to last for very long and, reassuringly, never does. *Grab it while you can,* I thought. *Take it now.* Lying near the window, I saw something else I could take—or at least take a look at: Valentin's investigation

242

files. Should I have a quick glance before going back to the bed? I went to the bed and threw myself down next to Valentin's half-covered body, and looked at him instead, listening to the rain outside slowing as it bled its last.

After a while, Valentin sighed and reached for his cigarettes. "Well, Molly, I have not felt like this for a very long time."

With my cliché of a new man, I enjoyed that most clichéd of moments—lying side by side in bed, smoking and looking at our phones. I hoped he wouldn't feel the need to tell me lies or say that he loved me, that he could leave not-quite-felt things unspoken.

But inevitably, after a while, he seemed to give in to some inner rom-com script, and started whispering sweet nothings: that so many bad things happen in life, but sometimes good comes out of them, et cetera. I suppose it was nice to hear this said in his soft-accented voice in the darkness. I heard his expectant silence, and whispered to him that he wasn't so bad himself and that, in fact, I'd had worse evenings.

He almost pushed me off the bed. "Really, you are a terrible woman. Here I am emptying my heart for you and you are mocking me!"

"Sweet nothings aren't my strong suit," I said.

"Clearly." He wound a length of my hair around his hand. "Ah, Molly. *Je crois que je vais tomber amoureux—*"

There was a knock on the door and whoever was knocking didn't pause while we answered. They knocked again while we both scrambled in the darkness for our clothes. Valentin gestured towards the bathroom and I sprinted there, pulling on my robe, shutting one door as he opened the other like something out of a French farce. I couldn't help but smile to myself in the dark mirror, thinking of him tucking his rumpled shirt into his trousers, smoothing his tousled hair for official business. Through the door I could hear a conversation conducted in rapid French. The other voice was muffled, but it sounded like one of his gendarmes reporting to him.

I was slurping a sip from the faucet like a child when I heard the room door close with a bang. I went back into the room. Valentin stood by the window, biting his nails. He looked about ten years older than when I'd laid eyes on him moments before.

"What's wrong?" I said uneasily.

"Molly . . ." He tried to pull me close.

I pushed him away. "Something's wrong and you're not telling me."

He shook his head. "I don't know what to do."

"Tell me."

His face, in profile, was washed yellow by the streetlights. "Quinn's gone."

"Gone where?" In my surprise I laughed, disbelieving.

"We don't know, but it looks like there was a struggle . . ." He took me by the shoulders too gently, the bedside manner look in his eyes, the dealing-with-the-victim's-family look. "We think she's been taken, Molly."

Quinn Perkins

JULY 20, 2015

Blog Entry

One thing I know for certain: Émilie Blavette is a bitch. The second thing? I'm getting out of here before I go insane.

Pacing my room, I'm consumed by a familiar mental toothache that used to be constant but comes more sporadically these days: the yearning to pick up the phone, press speed dial, and hear a familiar voice, a little breathless from running upstairs. *Mom.* I could tell her everything, spill my guts, cry and wail and ask for advice, and be given love and reassurance. She would know what to do. Maybe she does know, wherever she is, up in heaven or reincarnated as a dolphin or whatever.

I try Dad's cell again. The phone rings and rings mournfully. Finally someone picks up, but it's not Dad. It's Meghan, bright and sweet and fucking infuriating as ever.

"Hey, Meghan. Is Dad there?"

"Hey, hang on, I'm multitasking. Omigod, I have *so* much to *do* before we fly tonight! The baby's kicking me like mad and Leo is still wrapping up the summer school. You know how he is."

"Yup," I sigh, deflated. "Um, so you mean you guys aren't in Tahiti yet?"

"No, didn't your dad say?"

"Um, nope. I've been trying to get hold of him for days. I just . . . I'm wondering if I could come home early, or . . ."

"Hang on, hon. Dropped my pen. What was that, sweetie? God, my belly is so huge and I'm sweating bullets. Trying to pack a suitcase and leave notes for the cleaner and the cat-sitter and the gardener and basically the whole neighborhood here, y'know."

When she found out she was pregnant, Meghan decided to start talking to me as if she was my mom. I say "talking" because it's just that, a kind of sweet fake-parental babble, like a Stepford wife might do. It doesn't go any deeper. For all our hours together sipping apple cider at my dad's keynote lectures, we don't know each other at all. I've made sure of that, not because Meghan's an evil stepmom, but because if I befriended the woman who started dating my dad right after we scattered Mom's ashes, it would feel like I'd killed her myself.

"Yeah, I can see you're real busy," I say, sighing. "I guess I just really wish Dad would pick up sometimes. I need to—"

"He's not here, honey. I said."

"It's just, he never is. And I actually need to speak to him . . ."

"Oh, Quinn, I thought we went through all this in family therapy. You *know* you're your father's number one priority, right?"

"Clearly." My sarcasm going unnoticed.

"Well, then, you know he'll call you back, sweetheart. What was the message?"

"Um. The message is, I fucking hate this place and the woman I'm staying with is a total bitch who just basically wants to cut my heart out with a spoon, and I'm a little bit concerned that if I don't leave soon, I'll probably go postal and kill her and her entire family, so I kinda need him to buy me a ticket home."

"Um, okay, got it. Well, I'll definitely pass that on."

I wonder if she's even listening. Meghan usually makes a little more effort to sound concerned. Hanging up the phone, I hear tires on the drive. My heart thumps. I feel an awful pang of hope that it's Raphael, and can't help but imagine him sweeping me off my feet.

But it isn't Raphael and it isn't Noémie or Émilie coming back from town. It's an older, rat-like guy with greasy hair. He is small and skinny and I tower over him. Leaning in the doorway, he coughs a hard, racking death-rattle cough, hocks a loogie into the bushes, and turns to me with unsmiling, watery blue eyes.

"*Raphael, il est là?*"

"*Non.*" I shake my head.

He coughs hard, spits on the ground, and says something angry-sounding in French I don't understand, but that kind of sounds like a curse word. I think the rat man will go then, but he just stands sniffing on the porch. I push my mind to think of some French pleasantry to fill the silence. Maybe a comment on the weather. *Il pleut*? *Il pleuris*? Is it polite to remark on unfavorable weather conditions? Do the French talk about the weather, or is that the British? Normally, faced with this type of situation, I would just beam and say something guilelessly American in my best French accent. I've been told that's almost as good a form of communication as actually speaking a language, but something about the man puts me off. Scares me actually.

So I look at him and he looks at me and the rain drips off the eaves. He sniffs loudly, wipes his nose on the sleeve of his coat. I realize that part of what freaks me is that he looks as sick and downbeat as the rain itself. And yet determined somehow. When he jams his hand in his pocket, I flinch a step back. I can't help it. I don't know what I think will be in there. A knife? A needle?

When he pulls out a wad of paper and a few greasy euros, I let out a sigh and realize I've been holding my breath awhile. He waves it at me, his hand shaking so bad I think he will drop it, but with surprising agility, he slips it into my hand. Then, touching his fingers to his forehead in a strange gesture, as if he were crossing himself, he pulls up his collar and heads out into the storm.

Shivering, I turn my back, too, heading into the house and slamming the door. I gaze down at the damp paper in my hands. It's an envelope addressed to Raphael. I turn it over and find it sealed. Another mystery. What else would you expect, when a rat-like man turns up unannounced to leave money for your vanished not-quite-boyfriend who ran off to Paris in a storm?

I walk upstairs to his room to tuck the envelope inside a book of Baudelaire poetry on his desk, where I know he will one day find it. The doubts about him that have been forming steadily melt away because his room smells so much of him. And how can you know someone better in the end, than by their smell?

I can't resist flinging myself on his bed and burying my face in his pillow, reaching under it for the soft old Nirvana T-shirt I know will be there, taking off my own shirt, and slipping it on. Neither can I resist sending him a helpful little text to let him know that a man dropped by for him and left money.

I lie there a long while watching the screen of my phone as the light fades outside and the daytime moon glows stronger, drifting in and out of an uneasy sleep. I have a dream where someone is pacing on the gravel, up and down, up and down, under Raphael's window. But each time I wake, I can still hear it, the pacing.

Like I said, I'm going insane.

Molly Swift

A new search had begun, no less clueless than the one that had been going on for days through the town and the woods. There was a different feel to this one, though. Panic had replaced methodical investigation and a sticky air of guilt clung to everyone involved, especially me. Valentin suffered from it, too, as did poor Didier. Thirsty and bored, he'd sloped off to get a cold Coke from the bar. When he came back, the room had been turned over and Quinn was gone.

As the next of kin, I had been impounded in a private room next to the bar and was under close supervision. Valentin's minions brought me hot coffee with sugar to curb the hysteria they seemed to feel sure would erupt from me at any moment. I refused their offerings, annoyed that I was being politely detained under the guise of protection. In the process, I was also being denied my clothes and my phone while forensics picked over the remains of our room at a glacial pace. On the plus side, in the four hours it had taken them, I'd had ample time to reflect on how entirely to blame I was for this new turn in events: for taking Quinn out of the hospital, for bringing her here, for leaving her alone while I made bad romantic choices.

The fact that Valentin couldn't seem to meet my eye when he rushed in for a moment told me he felt the same way. "There has been a tip about a possible sighting," he said, brusque and business-like, and then he was off, leaving me to twiddle my thumbs while he charged about.

I had to find a way to escape.

In the end, a little bit of cunning and a good deal of charm was all I needed to evade the security detail slash support group Valentin had apportioned me. It went like this: I spent some quality time with Didier, reassuring him that I in no way blamed him and even helping him beat some deathless game of Words with Friends he was stuck on. Clutching my stomach, I then intimated that I had lady problems. He asked how he could help. I said he couldn't, unless he knew of an all-night pharmacy and was willing to go buy out their supply of Midol plus a jumbo pack of tampons. He looked like his head would explode. I suggested that there was one other option: I could slip to my room for a second. He agreed. Avoiding the elevators, which had become a police thoroughfare, much to the dismay of the hotel staff, I took the stairs two at a time up to the third floor.

The room I had briefly shared with my pretend niece was in ruins. Furniture had been turned over. Sheets and clothes were strewn everywhere. A shattered glass, white with printing powder, lay next to a crime scene label "5." A red stain drying on the carpet freaked me out when I spotted it, though when I leaned close to the carpet and sniffed at it, I reassured myself that it was Cherry B rather than blood. The bathroom was almost as bad. The little pots of creams and powders Quinn had purloined from me were flung on the floor, their glittery contents spilled over towels and smeared on shower tiles. This much I knew—whoever had done this was angry.

I wondered what the intruder could have been searching for that would have made them trash the room, especially since Quinn was right there for the taking, prone on the bed, a sitting duck. They could have taken her quickly and quietly without doing any of this, and what did it achieve?

I turned back to the room, trying to remember how it looked when I left what felt like centuries ago. Squinting my eyes, I could picture the sheets on the floor and pillows strewn every-where, the open bottle of Cherry B on the floor near the TV. In other words, the room was already trashed when I left it and the bathroom had already been a flurry of towels and teenage makeup application. The only thing different, other than the mess left by forensics tramping through, was the overturned chair and the snowfall of broken glass, the spilled Cherry B and the smeared makeup.

Weird: to rip the lids off of lip gloss and eyeliner and spill them, to shatter the sad little glitter cakes of eye shadow and blush and smear them everywhere, almost more like a teenage temper tantrum than a break-in. In fact, the whole thing seemed more aimed at me than at Quinn, almost as if *she'd* wanted to get at me, but why would she? Casting my mind back to my teenage years, I remembered the crushing embarrassments that fueled that kind of meltdown: when your dad grounded you on the eve of a big date, or your big sister read your diary aloud at the dinner table.

Your diary . . .

That's when I understood what had happened. She must have woken fuzzy-drunk and all alone. She was thirsty or needed the can and stumbled into the bathroom. There, she followed the invisible umbilical cord that should've led to her phone, but it wasn't in sight. She hunted under towels, inside tubes of lipstick. When she couldn't find it anywhere, she knew I'd taken it and vented her rage on my kohl. It was dumb luck, probably, that sent her out in the hallway in the moment that Didier was getting his Coke and the coast was clear.

With shaking legs, I staggered over to the Cherry B stain, fell beside it with a thump, forced my ass up, pulled my jeans on. I was on autopilot, ready to go. I patted my back pocket, checking for my own phone. It was gone.

It was my turn to trash the room. I tried to be grown-up and methodical, searching carefully under pillows and sheets, in drawers, but I ended up looking in crazy places—the window ledge, the wardrobe, under the bed. That last place was where I found it.

I snapped it on and found the usual—one message from Mom, one from Bill. My eyes blurred. I flicked past them. No stranger to phones getting hacked, I tend to be a bit more careful than Quinn. I never keep masses of social media apps and notes, not even contacts. Important photos I email to Bill, then delete. It's positively generic with its raindrop wallpaper, almost as dull as when I bought it. Mom's messages come up as *Lillian* because that's her name. I don't save maps or browser history. In other words, there was no clue in my phone that would have let Quinn know I wasn't her aunt. The only thing I'd been careless about was leaving evidence of my own nosiness lying around: the one page open in my internet browser was Quinn's blog.

In other words, she woke up drunk to find that not only had I stolen her phone, but had, in effect, been reading her diary, trespassing on her innermost thoughts, a privilege she carefully saved for a handful of anonymous internet "friends." No wonder she pulled a Lindsay Lohan on the room. When my sister read my diary, did I run away and make everyone lose their minds for a week? You betcha.

Icky with guilt, I sat transfixed in my phone's bluish glow. Quinn's words slid back and forth before my eyes like distant ants, cold somehow now that I was in her bad books. I'd been a mom for precisely a week and now my only child had run away.

"Today was amazing and scary," said Quinn's italicized words at the top of the blog. "The place Raphael took me to is steeped in ancient history. Witch burnings. Murders. Passions running wild and cutting a swathe through generations of families. Les Yeux, a name soaked in blood." The kid needed an editor, seriously. I mean, *a name soaked in blood?* It did make me shiver, though.

Les Yeux . . . I might have had her blog open, but it was days since I'd been on this entry. Which was as much to say, this was the bit she'd last read. I flicked to Maps. Sure enough, she'd been in there, too, looking for a way to walk to the caves. The blue line plotted a circuitous path around the outskirts of St. Roch and up through the same woods she walked out of screaming that day.

Quinn Perkins

JULY 20, 2015

Blog Entry

I'm in Raphael's room again. This is becoming a habit. Prickling with the icky ant bites of my raw nerves, I hunt down a pack of Gauloises he keeps in his sock drawer and light the first in a chain of many intended cigarettes.

Snapchat ate the video again, but I can't get it out of my head: that weird, grainy handheld *Blair Witch Project* shit haunts me. I feel like I should have screen-captured it somehow so I can look more closely. Maybe if I did I would spot some clue, some hint I missed the first time around, and I would be able to work out who keeps texting and what they want from me.

Out of the window, I smoke, hand shaking. In the abandoned sports field the burned grass looks pink. The pines that fringe the house are trembling shadows. Further beyond lie older trees, primeval woods that have lain far longer than the land has been peopled. I know because Raphael told me when he took me there to walk under the darkness of leaves, my feet cracking tree bones under me.

I took off first my shirt, then my skirt, in the belly of that cave and he filmed me smiling and naked. He talked to me so charmingly, teasing me to strip off just a little bit more to show just a little more skin for the camera. I know I should never have done it, but if it happened again, I'd do the same.

I stub out the cigarette and drop the burning tab end onto the patio below, where Émilie will find it later and tut about the fat American girl polluting her household. I turn to the desk, where Raphael's college books and DVDs and cast-off boxers are strewn, picking things up randomly: a Bic pen with a chewed end, a cheapo fake Swiss Army knife, a half-written note on squared paper (a quick glance reveals it to be the first verse of a Wu Tang Clan song, not a love note to me), a textbook on lighting, course notes about François Truffaut in his round French hand. Wherever he's gone, there must be a note, a clue. He'll have his phone with him. So why isn't he answering his texts? There could be something on his computer, maybe. The hard drive blinks on and off, its little blue light strobing as it chats to itself, saving things, updating things. I switch the monitor on. The black screen resolves to blue. Password protected.

I start typing band names, names of loved ones, trying to guess his password like some hacker chick in a cyberpunk film. And then what? I think. Read his private emails, run his college essays through Google Translate for clues? Him not being here doesn't make that seem any better. It makes it seem worse. I reach for the Gauloises, tap out another round of cancer bingo.

I'm just about to give up when a random word pops into my head. Or rather two random words: *Les Yeux.* I type them in and the beach ball spins for a moment before letting me in.

The desktop opens like a treasure chest. A half-finished email sits waiting to be sent. Scanning it, I discover it's an email Raphael was writing to a friend complaining about needing money now that he's been kicked out of uni and lost his scholarship. Looking further, I find more—that nobody knows he's been kicked out yet. That he's lost his Paris digs and doesn't even live where he said. That he's desperate and doesn't know what to do.

As the mystery of where he's disappeared to deepens, I can't help but feel sorry for him. I close the emails I've been reading, carefully covering my tracks by leaving the one that was open exactly where it was, though then I start to worry that when he comes back he'll see the last time the computer was opened. I'm just about to get up when a stray folder on the desktop catches my eye. "Girls," it says. I double-click. It's locked. I try the Les Yeux password. No luck. I try another. Nope. Probably just his porn collection.

A cough makes me turn around.

In the doorway stands Noémie. I wonder how long she's been there, watching me snooping through her brother's things.

A staring contest ensues. Noé is probably thinking that I'm obsessed with her brother (and she'd be right). I'm just hoping she won't run and tell Maman. So far, so standoff.

I start to fidget with my shirt. Then she says, "Wanna go to the pool?"

This surprises me more than anything. It's like she hasn't even noticed I'm in her brother's room, breaking into his computer, like she doesn't remember Émilie designating this house a nuclear test zone yesterday. Maybe she's finally cracked, or maybe Walt Disney came in the night and swapped her with a robot.

"It's kind of a gloomy evening," I say, squinting at the dingy clouds.

She shrugs. "I'm bored and I said I would meet friends there. But if you want to stay here with Maman . . ."

I let out a hard little laugh. "Smooth-talker."

We cycle along the fickle road, oily with rain. Under a darkening sky, the abandoned pool looks sad. I see things I haven't noticed before: the rust on the fence, so far gone that it's a wonder the spikes haven't broken in half; the skin of green algae crusting the water. With no bare-chested boys to loll on it, the burned grass just looks sick.

When we get closer, I see that the gates are shut, a padlock hanging from them on a heavy chain. "Um, I don't think we can get in there," I say.

Noémie shoots me a mischievous look.

"Hey, I'm not trespassing," I say. "I'm in enough trouble and . . ."

But before I can finish my sentence, a busted pickup with a tarp pulled over the back pulls up and a boy leans out, his tanned, pimply face half hidden by aviators. I recognize Romuald, the lifeguard.

"*Salut, Noé!*"

"*Hé là.*" Noémie leans in the window of the truck and slips him some tongue.

I look away.

"Come on, Quinn," she says, beckoning.

"I don't think I should go . . ." I begin.

"Need to go back and look at my brother's emails again?" she says with a giggle.

We sling our bikes in the truck bed and squeeze in the front. Noémie sits in the middle, a long tanned leg straddling either side of the stick shift, Romuald's arm draped over her shoulders.

"Didn't know you two were an item," I say.

"We're not," says Noémie with a bored shrug. "But it's something to do."

"*De quoi parles-tu?*" Romuald scowls.

"*Rien,*" hisses Noémie, turning to me. "He does

speak bad English because he is an idiot." She slaps her forehead—*Doh!*—and laughs and pushes the car lighter button down with her big toe. It's that other side of her again, that wild Jekyll and Hyde side, the one that got us into trouble at La Gorda. "Let's go fast, really fast. Like the wind!" She repeats the words in French, her voice squeaky with excitement.

Romuald shrugs and floors the gas. The pickup lurches into action. Soon we're speeding out of St. Roch, along the dark road through the woods. My stomach flips with each bump of the worn tires over the road. The whole thing feels unreal and I can't work out what devil has slipped inside Noémie, making her whoop with joy as we go faster and faster.

Cars that pass blare their horns in warning.

"Let's go back, Noé. I feel weird," I say, reaching forward to touch her shoulder.

She shrugs off my touch. *"Plus vite alors!"* she shrieks.

Blindly, I hunt for a seat belt and, finding one, disentangle it from the crummy old seat and strap myself in. When the buckle clicks shut, Noé flicks a disgusted look at me in the rearview mirror. Her eyes narrow, as if she's disappointed in my cowardice, my lack of cool. She leans over to Romuald, in one smooth movement nipping his ear with her teeth and flicking the headlights off. I don't know how long we coast like that for:

blind and in free-fall. All I know is that, for some reason, I let go of everything. Fear. Desire. Thoughts of home . . . and Raphael.

The squeal of the brakes and Romuald's panicked shout break the silence. I smell burned rubber as the pickup slows and makes a sharp turn down. *One of those ditches,* I think, *or a cliff edge.* Noé screams. I squeeze my eyes tight shut, though in the darkness it makes no difference. We come to a stop. Not the crash I'd feared, though my neck jerks painfully against the edge of the belt.

"*Merde!*" Romuald shouts. "*Putain quoi!* This truck, he is my brother's." He flicks on the headlights, illuminating the disaster. The truck has fallen face-first into a muddy ditch, the windshield cracked, the back tires suspended in midair. When we get out and stand staring at the wreck, Noé starts to laugh and won't stop until Romuald kicks her shin and says something angry in French I don't catch. Then she cries pitifully into her hands like a child and I have no choice but to gulp back my anger and hug her until she stops shaking.

Molly Swift

AUGUST 6, 2015

I parked as far into the trees as I could manage, my flashlight gripped between my teeth. The first thing I saw was police tape slung between birches, as if the woods had been festooned for some macabre local police investigation festival—signs that Valentin's people had already been here, though how recently it was hard to tell. Unde the tape, you could see the deep gouges where tires had plowed through the mud. The rain now falling filled them in dingy puddles.

I was five steps through the rough dirt parking lot when my flashlight faltered, flickering on and off in a panicky semaphore. I stopped still, hearing the shrill nagging of cicadas, the sarcasm of passing owls. A moth fluttered up into the flashlight, batting at the intermittent light, looking as incompetent as I felt right about then. I banged the flashlight a few times against a tree until the flickering stopped. There, good as new. The sound of voices murmuring low somewhere ahead in the trees made me switch it off again.

I groped my way towards the sound, barely able to see my hand in front of my face. I didn't have to wait long to be illuminated, though. A few steps further and the sweep of a white light blinded me. When my eyes adjusted, I saw the white gleam of a police cruiser. Before I'd even taken in the police van and two local news vans parked next to it, I started to feel sick. They'd found something. Was it related to the "sighting" Valentin had mentioned? I didn't pause long enough to start worrying what that might mean, but plunged on towards the floodlights, the yellow tent, only to be tripped over by the knotty stump of a fallen tree.

I scrabbled up, squinting down at the harsh halogen bulbs. Moving inaudibly and mysterious in their spotlit circle, the police looked tiny. I could just make Valentin out by the outline of his panama hat. The moment I thought that, he looked up at me. I crouched behind the fallen tree, noting where the trail I was on swooped steeply down into the hollow the police were searching.

I inched along the footpath until there were enough trees between me and the crime scene to hide me from view, but there was still no way to go down other than at a run. So I gunned it, speeding through crackling leaves and over the stray roots of trees before grabbing a tree trunk to slow myself. From there, I could see that the discovery was a Renault that had smashed into a tree. The hood had crumpled back like a snarling lip and the windows were smashed, but it was impossible to tell if there was anyone inside it from where I stood.

The doors and trunk were open and forensics people were combing the car and the ground around for evidence. I didn't see any body bags and there was no ambulance, so that was a relief. Maybe it was just a car they'd found and nothing to do with Quinn, after all. As I rubbernecked, a male voice behind me said, "Molly. What are you doing here?"

I turned around to see Freddie. Freddie-the-stalker.

"Fuck," I said. "You scared the . . . anyway, yeah, I was out for a walk and I saw all this. Looks crazy. What d'you think is happening?"

"A night walk . . . in the woods?" His eyebrows beetled together as if he didn't quite believe me. "Got a cigarette?"

"Sure." I fumbled inside my jacket for one, flicking a wary look at him. I didn't like the way he had just appeared here, right in the middle of the fray. "So how'd you hear about this?" I asked, trying to sound casual.

Another boy appeared behind Freddie, joint in mouth.

"This is Romuald." Freddie shucked a thumb in his direction. "We were just hanging here. There's a place in the woods where the kids all go."

"What for?" I asked, creeped out by the way the two of them stood there, staring.

Freddie cracked up. "To get high, of course. It's over there." He pointed back through the trees.

"What is all the confusion there?" Romuald pointed down at the crime scene with his joint, looking nonplussed.

"Looks like a woman driver has been here," Freddie said with a smirk.

"Recognize the car?" I asked nonchalantly.

Freddie craned his neck, cupping his hand over his eyes and squinting against the police lights. "Yeah . . . it looks like . . . Émilie Blavette's. That is weird, man. I have been in that car so many times."

"What is this, Raffi's family, *quoi*?" Romuald asked, his voice throaty with pot. "Are they dead in there or what?"

"Or what," I said, chilled by their unconcern. I looked past his head to where a woman in a white coverall was swabbing the edge of the car door. "Would it bum you out if they *were* dead in there?"

"Yeah," whispered Romuald, looking behind himself as if he was afraid someone would hear us. "It would make me shit on myself."

Freddie wheezed a stoned laugh. "*Putain.* Don't do it." He leaned on Romuald but Romuald pushed him away.

"I mean it, man," said Romuald, sounding annoyed. "Too many bad things happen in St.

Roch already. It is killing my high." As if on cue, his joint went out.

"I guess there is a lot of bad shit going down around here." I nodded, giving Romuald a light. "The Blavette family, that chick that died in the caves."

"She didn't . . ." Freddie piped up, his long face suddenly pale. "It was . . . we went in the caves that day and she just went crazy, man. Les Yeux gets inside your head. And so many people they go in there thinking it is cool, *hein*, and they are lost, then. Monsieur and Madame Blavette, they should not have taken us that day when . . . Those kids only got out safe because me and Raffi knew the way back. The school board should have been thanking us, not discipline and closing the school." He dropped his cigarette and ground it out angrily with his heel.

I thought about Quinn heading to the caves alone, not knowing the way. I had to help her. I held out my pack of cigarettes to them. "Maybe you could take me to the caves, show me around? There's twenty euros in it—" I smiled at them "—for each of you."

Romuald's eyes bugged. "*Jamais*! Only someone fucked inside the head would go there now." He eyeballed Freddie, who was looking more than shaky—sick. "Ever since that girl and Marc Blavette, other people are disappearing in those caves."

"I haven't seen anything about that." I was starting to feel annoyed. "I think you're making this shit up, like, *ooh ghosts in the caves,* because it's dark and you're chicken."

"Bah!" Romuald took the bait, tweaking his jacket on his shoulders to make himself look bigger and tougher. "Ghosts do not scare us. Anyway, there is no ghost at Les Yeux, just some *salauds* who like to hurt people."

"Yeah, everyone knows they use that place," Freddie said darkly. "When Marc Blavette went away, everybody thought it was those guys. That Sicilian boss-man Séverin had everything to gain from him going, since he took over Marc's clubs after that. And Raphael was mixed up with them, just like his father, doing jobs for them. The Séverin gang probably made the Blavette family crash there and took them, too. You are *idiote* if you go."

"Know what?" I said, taking a step closer to Freddie. "I don't believe you, but what I do believe is that you stalked Quinn and saw how that poor girl died. I think you're nothing but a tall bully, but you don't scare me. I'm brave enough to go to those caves, anyway, and soon I'm going to find out exactly what you know."

"Hey, fuck you," said Freddie, glaring down at me. "Go into Les Yeux. See it for yourself. You are such a crazy *salope* probably the caves will make no difference."

Molly Swift

AUGUST 6, 2015

I struck out in the direction of the caves, the police lights fading behind me, along with the muttered insults of the two boys. The faint track through the trees was cluttered with fallen logs and slushy from the rain. Time and again, I pulled out my phone to look at the map. Reception was actually not bad and it reloaded quickly and neatly, telling me I was almost there.

A few steps from the caves, I stopped, some primal instinct telling me not to go any further. Not that I was frightened by the stories those boys had told me—the ghost stories were just ridiculous. I stood listening for the echo of footsteps, hearing nothing but the soughing of the trees. The moon shrugged off its mantle of cloud then and lit up the scene before me: two bottomless pits of eyes staring, the twin doorways of Les Yeux.

When my phone buzzed, I jumped. It was a message from Bill.

See the shit's hit the fan. Call me? Bx

For once, I did as he said.

"Hey, kiddo." Bill's comfortable voice crackled in my ear.

"Hey."

"You at the hotel?"

"The woods actually," I said, looping the earpiece over my ear. "I think Quinn might have gone to the caves. Read the blog link I sent. It kind of explains it."

"Yeah, I did. She had a tryst with Romeo there. So?"

"So she was checking how to get here on my phone."

"She looked through your phone? Jesus, Molly." He sighed.

"Why else do you think the shit's hit the fan?" I said angrily.

"Well . . . I mean, it kind of has in every way possible. The kid's gone, or taken, and it may or may not be your fault. And now I bet your cover's most likely blown."

"I knew you could cheer me up, Bill." I took the last few steps towards the staring eyes without thinking too hard. "It's so comforting the way you always see the glass half empty."

He cleared his throat. "You mean there's a good side to this?"

"Hell to the no."

"But you took it on yourself to go find this girl, anyway," Bill said. "Despite the army of police already looking for her and the fact that she probably hates your guts?"

"I think I owe it to her, don't you?"

There was a long pause in which I could hear the cogs of Bill's mind turning. I walked a few steps inside the first chamber, shining my flashlight on white spears of stalactites aimed at me from the roof of the cave. It smelled wet and tainted, as if something had spoiled.

I sighed. "Quinn's not here. I need to go deeper inside and look for her." As soon as I said the words, I heard how foolhardy they sounded.

"What's that, kiddo? You're breaking up." His voice crackled.

"Reception's fucked."

"Make a video or something?" He sounded a million miles away.

"Okay."

"I can watch it after you come back, see what goes down."

"Just like the *Blair Witch Project*."

"Eh?"

"Never mind."

"If I don't hear from you in a couple hours, I'll call Cave Rescue."

I dropped the call and made sure my little camera was switched on. It wouldn't be able to upload the feed to Bill right away, but at least if I died in here, maybe someone would eventually be able to work out how. Ahead of me was a narrow opening in the rock. I squeezed into it sideways, hearing the echo of my own footsteps as the darkness closed in on the space behind me. Rock scraped my back, pinched my elbows. The wind howled into the cave, high and weird as a cat's scream.

"For reference, this place is creepy as all fuck," I told the camera, my nervous laugh ping-ponging around the tunnel, a rising cackle ushering me into the next chamber.

This tunnel was smaller and staler. Little rivulets ran around my feet, tributaries of some underground stream. Their music should have comforted me, but all it made me think about was how deep the caves went into the belly of the earth. From ahead came a tumble of stones, a sound like footsteps.

"Quinn?" My call echoed into the honeycomb of the next chamber.

The air around fell silent all of a sudden. I edged through the dark space that pushed back at me, scraping and biting. A tiny rockfall crumbled from the ceiling, jarred by my presence. I wiped the dust out of my eyes and pushed on. The rocks on either side caught hold of me. I couldn't move forward or back. I stopped and took a deep breath. *Calm the fuck down, Molly.* Words from Quinn's blog, not to mention my little chat with Freddie and Romuald, echoed in my mind—the cave's local reputation as a "keeper." People who vanished here were rarely found.

From the darkness beyond me, the footsteps sounded again, slower this time, their echo shaking dust from the rocks around me. They moved faster, lighter, scampering towards me, stopping inches away, around the corner where I could not see. My flashlight flickered. I gave it a whack, but it dropped down on the floor and rolled away. I was in total darkness. Shaking, I gripped the rocks in front of me and wiggled my hips, but the more I moved, the more I was trapped.

Something was moving into the tunnel towards me, scratching the walls, knocking off little pellets of rock. I squeezed my eyes tight shut, telling myself it was my imagination.

In the darkness, a hand grabbed mine.

"Fuck!" I tried to pull my hand away.

"Molly." The whispered word echoed eerily. "I've got you."

"Quinn?"

She didn't answer. Instead, she pulled me by the wrists with a strength that surprised me. She wrenched me free and I hurtled out like a greased pig, falling on top of her in a tumble of sweat and dust. For a moment, we just lay there, panting.

"I can see my flashlight."

"Yeah," she said, pushing me off her. She picked it up, screwing the bulb end on more firmly until it stopped flashing. The brightness was blinding.

"Hey, Quinn, I can't see."

"Why are you here?"

"To help you."

"Where's my phone?"

"I think the police have it." I squeezed my eyes shut, shielding them with my hand. "Listen, I'm sorry. I just thought it might help them find the Blavettes."

"Yeah."

"Are you mad?"

"No . . . I just . . . something weird happened, a flashback or something. And then it was like I was sleepwalking. When I opened my eyes I was here."

"Are you okay?"

"Not really." She turned her eyes away.

"Well, can you get the flashlight out of my face?"

"Sorry." She angled it down, casting elongated shadow-Mollys onto the cave wall. They looked like some kind of grotesque cave painting. I struggled up, feeling bruised and old, but relieved that I'd found her and that she didn't seem to hate me.

I held out my hand to her. "Should we get out of here?"

Her mouth trembled at the corners. She blinked her eyes, closed them. "I . . ."

"Quinn?" I took a step nearer, clasping her hand in mine. "You're freezing."

She backed away from me. "I remembered something." The flashlight dropped with a clatter.

She fell to her knees, her hands covering her face. "I think something terrible happened in here."

I knelt in front of her, rescuing the flashlight before it rolled away.

Painted with watery light, she looked out of it, her eyes unfocused, face blank. "There was blood." She scrubbed at her eyes, leaving raw, red tracks on her face.

I put my hand out to stop her. "Don't do that, sweetheart. You'll hurt yourself."

Her hands fell, her eyes staring without seeming to see me. "He's still in here with us. He's still . . ."

"Who?"

She swallowed, a dry, clicking sound. Then, quick as whip, she was up, somehow far ahead of me, snaking into the next tunnel, out of sight.

Stumbling up, I ran after her, pushing through the tunnel ahead, ducking a millisecond before bashing my brains out on a long spoke of rock hanging down. I dodged around it, her footsteps fading ahead of me. I entered the next chamber just in time to see her shadow slipping out of sight around a bend.

"Quinn, stop!" But she didn't stop, or answer me.

I sensed that she was somewhere else, driven by whatever horror movie was flickering in front of her eyes, driving her deeper into the earth. From ahead, I heard her words echoing—*blood, stop, don't*—as if she was narrating the moment of her trauma while she led me from chamber to chamber and into the belly of hell. I had the sick feeling that if she knew where we were before, she wouldn't know now, even if I did manage to catch her.

With every new turn, I tried to remember where we'd just been, blazing the trail like I did with my dad in the Maine woods, way back when. But the chambers, the tunnels, all looked the same to me and none of them were anything like the woods at home.

We came to a different sort of chamber: large and high ceilinged. I heard its dimensions in the echo of my footsteps before I saw them lit by the flashlight. It was a great, red, domed cathedral of a chamber, hung with fine-spun chandeliers of stalactites. I swept the flashlight beam over it. Quinn had stopped in the middle of the chamber, barely seeming to breathe. Her eyes were fixed on something in the corner. It looked like a bundle of pale, dirty rags. I flicked my flashlight over them.

The rags moved—a faint rustling quiver of movement. Under the beam of light, they unfurled like a moth's wings, a pale shape turned upwards, a sliver of moon—a face shrouded by short dark hair, smeared with dirt or blood, so that it was hard to see whether the person was a girl or a boy, a child or an adult. Eyes swiveled towards me, dark orbs bouncing the flashlight's glow back. It was then that I recognized her from the pictures: Noémie Blavette.

Slowly, the dark eyes turned around, taking in me, the flashlight, turning until they came to rest on Quinn. Noémie's mouth dropped open. She screamed. Quinn, jolted from her own trance, moved towards the girl with her hands outstretched, but the closer Quinn moved towards Noémie, the louder she shrieked, until, when they were inches apart, she leaped up, her starved bones of arms outstretched, her mouth wide. She bared her teeth and scratched at Quinn. Quinn grabbed her wrists.

Noémie fought, fierce with rage and fear, her chin juddering senselessly up and down as she screamed the same words over and over again.

"Murderer!"

Quinn Perkins

JULY 21, 2015

Blog Entry

Time for today's traumafest, guys. Worse trauma. *The* actual worst. Like I can't even . . . yada yada. It was déjà vu all over again when I woke to the chimes of the being-shaken-by-someone alarm clock, someone screaming my name, and I was miles away, dreaming about a drama-free day, like fat-free yogurt.

"I'm tired, Noé." I sighed, lids so heavy I'd need to physically pry them open. My neck ached from the place the belt dug in.

"Quinn, get up." The voice was sharp, insistent, and not Noémie.

My eyes opened a crack. Émilie's face hovered over me, skin pale and tight, mouth a ghoulish rictus. "What is happening, Quinn?" At this point, her nails started digging into me.

Sweat flooded my pits like a kid about to get grounded for a zillion years, like the time I smoked pot in the locker room and Mr. Edison found me, like when the police came after Mom . . . My bladder was achingly full. My mouth was dry. Her hands were hurting me. I was scared, then furious. *How dare she wake me this way?*

"Take your hands off me," I said, my voice icy.

Her lips quivered. Close up, I saw her sun-damaged skin, the gray in her hair, the dry white flakes on her lips. "You come here. You sit at my table, sleep under my roof, take trips with my family. You come like any other exchange, care-free, ignorant. And then like a snake, you abuse my own children under my roof."

I caught her wrist just before she could scratch me with her long plastic paste-ons. If I'd sunk to her level, I could've pulled one off. Instead, I gripped her wrists hard and with muscles bulked by years of handstands and volleyball and parallel bars, I twisted the skin just enough to make her let go.

"How dare you manhandle me," she shrieked, leaping up.

"How dare you barge in here and pin me to the bed and make false accusations?" I shouted back. She was blocking my way out of the bed, so I sat up against the bedstead, clutching the covers around my breasts.

"I assure you, they are not *false* accusations," she sneered, her mouth an evil grimace. "Romuald's mother has been to see me about the car crash last night. I have spoken already to my daughter and she has told me all that happened, that it was *all* your fault. She is younger than you by over a year, Quinn. You are a bad influence and I want you out!"

My head reeled. "Bad influence? You've got to be kidding me. Noémie is six months younger than me, and Raphael is eighteen months older. What they do is their business. You may treat them like they're six years old, but—"

The back of her hand stopped me short. My hand flew to my mouth. I tasted metal. My eyes burned. I didn't cry, though, or give in. I can be a bitch, too, sometimes. "You know what Noémie and I did last night? We got away from you! I'm sorry you're lonely and poor, relying on rich visitors to support you. But if people are paying you for the privilege, newsflash, lady, you can't just come into their room and harass them. Also, keeping your kids prisoners won't stop them from running away and leaving you like your husband did."

I expected a bitchy retort, a mean comeback, but when her hand dropped from her face I saw she was crying hard. She spun around, walked into the door, almost fell over, then ran to her room and slammed the door hard.

After a minute, Noémie poked her head around the door, her face red from crying. "Quinn, I'm sorry. I couldn't keep something like that a secret from my own mom. I had to tell her."

"Yeah," I say, "apparently you had to blame it on me, too."

Okay, well, maybe it didn't go down quite as hard-core as that. And maybe I was trying to make myself sound a little tougher to impress you, channeling my inner Philip Marlowe. Maybe I even cried . . . whatever. It's dark by the time thirst gets the better of me and I go downstairs, tiptoeing around the house like a trespasser.

I needn't have worried: no one there. The lights are off and the house is silent except for the cicadas whispering under their breath in the garden. I stumble around, groping for the light, find a tumbler, run myself a glass of water and glug it down, feeling like someone who's just done something actually hard like cross a desert or something, as opposed to hiding in their room all day.

Next, a cigarette. I walk through the porch door, making sure it doesn't slam behind me. The night is tar black, starless. So different from the starry starry night when Raphael first kissed me. I light up and look down at my dusty flip-flops, my toenails with their grown-out blue polish. Anything to not remember how good everything was for a moment, before it got fucked up.

It's when I go inside that I see the envelope on the table with my name on it. My hands shake as I open it up and see the English words written in French handwriting. Before I even read them I know what they say. It's politely worded enough, offering me the name of several local hotels I can arrange to stay in until I manage to book a flight back, as well as the number of the friend's house that Émilie and Noémie have gone to stay in until I do, in case of emergencies.

Kennedy and I text it out and my sense of shivery outrage fades a little. I tell her I'm leaving France. Correction: I've been asked to leave. She texts back, *Yay!* She'll see me that much sooner, adding that for what it's worth, the Blavettes sound majorly douchey and Émilie is clearly a psycho-bitch on wheels. Also that next time (if there is a next time) maybe I should consider not sleeping with a member of the host family three months into my stay. And finally, for the record: three weeks does not true love make. *Don't be blond, Q, Srsly.* Also, she's met a really hot guy called Indigo and he's perfect for me, will be good for me. Plus, major emotional triage session at Boston Tea Company the second my plane lands. When I read that last part, I have a little cry.

So it's all fine and clear in my head. I start packing. I feel strangely calm. Then I hear the front door open, boots striking the stairs. As suddenly as he left, there he is again in my doorway, his dark eyes taking in my tears, my half-packed bag. He's back because he misses me and there's rain in his hair, rain beading his lips and eyelashes. He kisses me and I smell the road on his skin, gasoline, and hot leatherette. We kiss and I think it will go on forever. We undress, not for sex, just so that he can feel me naked against him. He traces his finger over my neck and back in slow circles and writes his name along the bruise on my collarbone.

I tell him what happened, fearing his reaction when I say how I fought with his mom, but he just keeps stroking my neck. For all the strength Kennedy gave me over the phone, for all that she is the one person in the world who loves me for who I am and is one hundred percent right about everything, I forget every word she said, because when his skin is pressed on my skin all I can smell, feel, think is him. The shutters are open and the stars have come out. We hold hands and watch the dog star burn.

"*Quinn, je t'aime*," he says.

"Hmm?" I know perfectly well what he said, but I need to hear it again.

He bites my ear. "I think I'm falling in love with you."

"I love you, too," I whisper, biting my lip.

He pulls me closer into him. "*Dieu*, I love you as much as I hate my mom and sister. Don't worry. We'll find a way to hurt them back for being so mean to you."

Molly Swift

AUGUST 7, 2015

Outside the green curtains of my cubicle I could hear Valentin's Italian shoe leather squeaking on the hospital linoleum. The nurse was taking my blood, checking for something or other I didn't understand because everyone kept gabbing away in really fast French and/or running around like headless chickens. The nice boys from the Charente-Maritime volunteer Cave Rescue Team who found us were still hanging around in the waiting room, poking their heads around occasionally to see how I was. There was altogether too much concern for my welfare. I wasn't used to it. The nurse drew the needle out and handed me a cotton wool ball to hold over it. Valentin poked his head through the curtains, looking stressed, then disappeared.

"Don't you have some paperwork to do?" I asked irritably.

He poked his head in again. "Say something, *chérie*?" He looked so anxious.

I tried to sound a bit gentler. "It's just . . . you're pacing around like an expectant father and you must have stuff to do. How's Quinn? How's Noémie? Have you found the others yet?"

He frowned, rubbing the bridge of his nose, then turned to the nurse and asked her to kindly leave us.

Perched on the edge of the bed, I felt my skin prickle, the bad vibes coming off Valentin mixing with the painkillers and adrenaline in my system. For the first time since the caves, I started to shiver. "Valentin, what's going on?"

He pulled the curtain closed and came to me, putting his arms around me and kissing the top of my head. *"Dieu merci*! I'm so glad nothing happened to you . . . nothing worse. I don't know what I would have done."

In spite of my wholehearted cynicism about love, I let him kiss me. It calmed me a little, and I remembered reading somewhere that male pit sweat has a more relaxing effect on women than Xanax. Bring it on.

After a while, he held me at arm's length, checking out the dressings on all my little cuts and scrapes. "That cave has chewed you."

I rolled my eyes. "It's nothing. I don't know why they won't let me go and check on Quinn."

He looked away. "Quinn is helping some colleagues of mine with their inquiries and there's a lot to get through. I mean, she's remembered things, important things, and we need a full statement."

I pushed him away. "You mean they're questioning her."

"I don't really know," he said wearily. "My colleagues are handling it."

"Okay," I said, deciding not to push him too much just yet. "How about Noémie? I mean, she seemed in pretty bad shape."

His body sagged a bit. "They had to sedate her. One of her ankles is badly sprained, which is why she could not move from there. She was—"

"Hysterical." Closing my eyes, I remembered the way she screamed.

"She's been saying a lot of things, but she is not in a state to respond to questions about the rest of her family. The doctors had to calm her in order to treat her."

I nodded, trying to take it all in. "Are they searching the caves for the others?"

"Yes." His face was grim.

"They could be in different chambers further on. I mean—that place is vast. It's so easy to get lost in it." A shiver ran through me.

He took my wrists and kissed them. "I'm so glad you are not lost, Molly. Truly you have been brave. If you had not gone after your niece, if you had not found Noémie, they might both be dead."

I shrugged. "It was the Cave Rescue guys really. I know Bill called them, but they did well to find us. It was weird, though. The second they got us out, we were separated . . ." I looked at him, hoping for an answer to my implied question and feeling all the while a twinge in the pit of my stomach about how Bill's call could have blown my cover.

He just nodded absently, stroking his thumb over the edges of a sticky dressing on my arm. "How did you get that one?"

"Scraped it on some rocks when my hips were stuck in a fucking tunnel. I'm not a whip-thin teen with Mick Jagger hips, you know," I said, going for a laugh.

"Hmm." He frowned. "Are you sure it is only the cave that has made you hurt? I mean . . . that nothing else has attacked you in the darkness?"

"Attacked me? What, like a cave monster? I've already given my statement . . . this isn't *The Descent* or something."

His hands tapped nervously at his pockets. "Oh, Molly, I don't know . . ." He rubbed his nose again.

"I can see you're gasping for a smoke. So am I. Why don't we get out of here?"

He nodded very slowly, as if he'd suddenly started feeling his age.

"Mind going out a minute while I dress?" I gestured to my filthy clothes.

I expected him to make some lecherous comment, but he just nodded slowly again and disappeared through the curtains.

Quinn Perkins

AUGUST 7, 2015

Video Transcript of Police Interview

*Here follows the transcript of a police inter-
view with Quincy Jane Perkins, conducted by
Detective Inspector Thierry Desjardins (TD) of
the Commissariat de police de St. Roch on 7
August, 2015.*

TD: Could you repeat your name for the record?
QP: Quinn Jane Perkins.
TD: Do you understand why we are detaining
you?
QP: Am I under arrest?
TD: No, but we have brought you here to talk
to you about the whereabouts of Émilie and
Raphael Blavette. We are at present attempting to
locate them. As we are interviewing you about
their disappearance, I must caution you, which
means you are under no obligation to tell us
anything. How do you know the Blavettes?
QP: I stayed with them here in France.
TD: As part of a cultural exchange program?
QP: Yes, I think . . . I can't remember everything
before my accident.

TD: When did you last see the Blavettes?

QP: I don't know. I can't remember.

TD: When were you last in their home?

QP: I don't know. I can remember being there, I think.

TD: Do you remember where you went on the night of July 27?

QP: No.

TD: This would be about ten days ago. Did you go somewhere with Noémie Blavette?

QP: I can't remember.

TD: Do you know the causes of the injuries sustained by Noémie Blavette?

QP: No.

TD: Did you have a good relationship with Noémie Blavette?

QP: I think so. I think we're friends.

TD: Then why did Noémie scream when she saw you in the caves at Les Yeux?

QP: I don't know. She was scared?

TD: In response to seeing you?

QP: No. Maybe. I don't know. Why would she be scared of me?

TD: Why did you decide to go to Les Yeux tonight?

QP: I just had . . . a feeling . . . if I went there, I could remember what happened to me there.

TD: And what did happen?

QP: I don't remember.

TD: The video recorded by Meredith Swift suggests that you did.

QP: Meredith Swift?

TD: You know her as Molly Perkins.

QP: My aunt . . . can I see my aunt?

TD: That's not your aunt. The name of that woman is Meredith Rose Swift, known as Molly. She's a journalist for an internet video channel.

QP: I don't believe you!

TD: She's not your friend, Quinn. Have you heard the term *trial by media?*

QP: Yes. I guess. Why . . . ? Where's Molly?

TD: Well, that's what is going on here. The media has not been your friend, especially Molly. She has, as you Americans say, hung you out to dry.

Quinn Perkins

JULY 23, 2015

Draft Blog Entry

Well, there were a lot of haters for the last post I put up. I get that that last thing I wrote about Raphael wanting to harm his family seemed extreme and freaked some people out, but he was mad. I'm sure it was only a figure of speech or whatever. Anyway, it doesn't make much difference. I don't have Wi-Fi, so I can't put this stuff online. Not sure I even want anyone to know what's going on. I'm not proud of myself tbh, the way things have gone. I'm only keeping up with this blog in Notes to stay sane. Then if anything happens to me, someone will know what it was. God, just saying that makes me think of those found-footage horror movies where you know the person's dead before they start speaking . . .

A lot has happened since I posted that last entry. For one thing, my brain is fried. Seems Raphael is thinking for both of us. He keeps telling me to stop worrying because he's made a plan so that we can be together and he keeps telling me what to do. I guess that's good? Everything feels miles from the real world. He says if we're going to make this work, we need to find another place to stay, one that feels safe.

I'm not sure why he thought that place would be the house of Stella Birch, the golden house on the cliff edge overlooking the sea. Maybe because we're already drunk as the bike rumbles along a dirt track, past the spooky trees that lead to Les Yeux, and stops at some secret parking place in the woods behind the fairy tale castle.

Stella answers the door in a tight black dress. She smiles and kisses us on both cheeks three times, the way they do here. Something's off, though.

"God, when I grow up I want to *be* you," I gush in an effort to be charming. "You look *amazing*."

Raphael rolls his eyes. "Americans, *hein* . . ."

"Amazing for my age," she says a little sharply. "Do come in." She ushers us through the white foyer with its sweep of stone staircase to the elegant living room.

I lean into Raphael, whispering, "Are you sure we're welcome here?"

He grabs me and pulls me out of Stella's sight behind the doorway, one hand clamped over my mouth, the other groping under my T-shirt, fumbling with the button of my jeans.

"I'll make it worthwhile for you," he says.

"Stop." I laugh, helpless from all the beer.

"Secretly you want me not to stop," he whispers.

"Don't," I say, feeling the moment go too far too fast, like everything we do now, going past the point of no return. "Seriously, she was weird at the door, don't you think?"

"She is always weird." He shrugs. His teeth graze my neck, sharp as a cat's.

"Stop. We're guests. It's rude."

"Who gives a fuck?" he whispers. "Prude."

"I do," I say weakly.

At that moment, Stella clears her throat and calls from the other room (in her best dowager duchess voice). "Everything all right, you two?"

I straighten my clothes and smooth my hair while Raphael flicks me a disdainful look.

"Chablis?" Stella doesn't wait for a reply. She hands us ice-cold crystal flutes. She's a little starchy compared to the last time I saw her, but I put it down to Émilie kicking me out.

"Thanks," I say, taking a glass.

"Not a problem, though I wasn't expecting company." There's something weird in her tone, her eyes. Something indefinably tart, and I can't tell if I'm drunk and paranoid or if she's . . . something . . . scared, maybe? No, that couldn't be.

Meanwhile, Raphael is prowling around the room, his eyes flicking over the delicate Tiffany boxes and small china ornaments scattered around the fireplace. If I didn't know better, I'd think he was casing the joint, but that's ridiculous. I guess Stella thinks so, too, though, 'cause she's following him around the room, eagle-eyed, watching his every move.

I need space, air. I walk outside, lured by the blue light of the infinity pool. I'm ragged, stumbling against the patio door, righting myself, carrying on along the paved path under the pergola. The air is thick with wisteria scent. I could strip off, go skinny-dipping. "Tragic Blonde Dead in Freak Pool Accident." I settle for rolling up my jeans and kicking my legs in the water instead, writing notes on my phone now that I have a chance. There's a bug drowning near my left foot. I fish it out and it drags its sodden wings along my toe. I name it Steve. Steve has big bug eyes and has seen better days. He reminds me of me.

A glass of wine is thrust into my hand, a lit joint eased between my lips. Raphael sits down next to me, kisses my neck, and plunges his fully clothed legs into the water. He smiles that wide, stoned, shit-eating grin of his. I don't smile back.

"That bad?" He tries to kiss me. "I made my shoes wet for you and not even a smile."

I shrug him off, pass him the joint. "I'm just crashing a bit. I guess we forgot to sleep the last couple days."

"And?" He takes a deep drag and coughs raucously.

"Well, it's been a pretty manic couple of days. I'm tired, y'know."

"Really?" he says, spluttering, eyes watering.

"Yeah, and I mean . . . maybe we should try and fix things with your mom. I don't like the feeling that your family is mad at you because of me and I seriously don't think we can stay here . . ." I take the joint back, suck on it.

"Don't worry," he says with a cynical laugh. "This is always coming around every once in a while. Like the cycles of the moon or something. When Noé and I were growing up we had star charts just so we wouldn't get caught out by one of Maman's hormones."

"You mean PMS or something?" I pass him back the joint.

He shrugs. "If PMS makes you a psycho."

I push him so hard he nearly falls into the pool.

Laughing, he grabs hold of me to save himself. "I hit a mark with PMS, *hein*? Lucky I borrowed the Midol out of Stella's medicine cabinet." He reaches into his jean pocket and pulls out a handful of round yellow pills, grinning wide.

"What the hell? Those aren't Midol. They're OxyContin. Have you stolen those? Have you taken anything else?"

"Maybe." He swallows two and chases them with Chablis. "Stop stressing. You're just on the downswing. Take these and you will feel better."

"Um, no. I'm on, like, about twenty different kinds of prescribed medicine, which you've watched me take. That could make me really sick, put me in a coma even. Also, stealing is wrong . . ."

He grabs me and kisses me long and deep. The little pill on his tongue melts in my mouth and swims down my throat and there's nothing I can do about it.

I find myself tumbling into the pool tangled together with him, not feeling the cold of the water, sinking under. We kiss hard. A smoke-trail of blood whispers up. I don't know which one of us is bleeding. I run out of breath and start to panic, clawing my way up. I break the water and gulp for air. He drags me under, kissing me again, tearing at my wet clothes.

The world is blood and blue and chlorine and it flickers. When he peels my shirt off I whisper, "She'll see us," but my words are so blurred even I can't translate them. Instead of answering me, Raphael ducks me under the water again, his hands holding my shoulders down. Silver bubbles speed up from my parted lips. The pool water stings my eyes and the cut on my lip. My lungs burn.

His hands slip away and I crash to the surface, coughing chlorine. "What the fuck? That's like what Freddie did to me when you—" *When you met me,* I think. *When you saved me. Weren't you nicer then?*

"Yes, me and Freddie like to play that game sometimes." He smiles, stroking my cheek. "Don't worry, it's only for fun. Don't you like fun?"

"Yeah, but—" My words blur and die in the night air.

The OxyContin hits too soon. Time speeds up and dilates and speeds again. In one of my moments of clarity, I find myself leaning over the side of the pool, my fingers pressing into the warm concrete.

Raphael is behind me. "I like playing with you, Quinn . . . very much," he whispers. "Don't you like playing with me?"

An electronic whine cuts through his words. I look up at the wall of the pool house. There, the small metal eye of the security camera follows our every move.

At first I don't know if what I'm seeing is real, or if I'm just tripping. But when I see colored lights flashing against the night and hear the buzz of a police radio, I start to think my most paranoid thoughts might be coming true.

Molly Swift

AUGUST 7, 2015

The car was silent except for the radio and the squeal of the wipers waltzing back and forth over the rain. The painkillers were starting to wear off and my whole body felt clenched, though not as clenched as Valentin looked. His face in profile was gray and tight, his hands white-knuckled on the steering wheel. Ever since the hospital, something felt off, and I couldn't help wondering exactly what "inquiries" Quinn was helping Valentin's colleagues with.

Valentin's overly tidy hotel room was no better. We drank whiskey and chain-smoked, watching the rain again, but this time the tremor in the air around us wasn't unspoken temptation. It was bad news that Valentin hadn't worked up the nerve to tell me. The longer he stayed silent, the surer I was of that.

I reached out the window and throttled my cigarette on a roof tile. Cold drops of rain lashed my skin, bracing me. I stood, brushing my hair out of my face and into a knot. My clothes were stiff with blood and dirt. I wanted nothing more than to take a long hot shower and sleep for a million years. I headed slowly towards the door, hoping he'd understand without me having to say anything.

He grabbed my wrist. His eyes were dark, his face fearful. "What?"

I spun around. "Look, I can't sit here waiting for the ax to fall. I know you know something you're not telling me. What I don't understand is why you're here babysitting me when you should be back with the others having some meeting or searching for the Blavettes or something."

"Please sit. We will talk. I just can't tell you all of it. I promised not to."

I sat down on the chair with a thump of my bruised butt. "Promised who?"

"My superior officer. I was forced to tell him of our . . . relationship. And so, for the moment, I am off the case. Before I spoke to him, there were things . . . coming to light about your niece that I—"

"What things?" I was surprised by the fear in my gut. Maybe I'd pretended to be her aunt so hard I'd begun to believe my own lies.

Valentin let his head fall in his hands. "Molly, I know how much you love her. Every time I see you together . . ." He looked up, his eyes shining. "It was lovely to see that. For me it has been like being in a family again. But family is complicated. And your niece, well, she will still seem like a little girl to you, I am sure. And perhaps you will hide things to protect her, but—"

"Hide what?" My heart drummed. "What are you talking about?"

"Things are coming to light in the information you handed to us, the blog and the things the Blavette girl has said. Someone anonymously has given a CCTV video to the media. It shows Quinn with an unidentified man in a swimming pool and it seems she is taking drugs perhaps, and, well . . ." He paused for a moment, seemingly embarrassed, before continuing in a hurried tone. "We have sent scrapings from underneath her fingernails to the laboratory . . . well, we will have to see, but it may be that Quinn has not told us the whole truth."

"Well, how could she?" I said indignantly. "She doesn't remember anything."

He looked away. "Believe me, Molly, I have done what I can. We are helping her to obtain some kind of representation."

"She needs a lawyer?"

He nodded. "I know we should have told you. I even told them that you should have been present inside the interview. But they replied that it might be dangerous if . . ."

"If?"

"If she had attacked you, too. The first responders reported that you were all victims of an attack. It was only after you had been examined that we began to piece together a picture."

"Yeah, well, Noémie attacked Quinn. I had to separate them."

He frowned. "It may be that before Noémie attacked Quinn, before we found her, that Quinn has caused some of her injuries. We are waiting for tests to return."

"And until they come back you won't really know for sure?"

"Indeed," he said, brightening. "And believe me, I wish her to be cleared. I have every faith. I have demanded that this not be released in the press, but the rescue of the girl will, and the rest I cannot control."

He pulled me to him and I let him sit me on his lap like a doll. I felt weak. The last few hours had caught up to me. "I hope you didn't lose your job because of me."

He kissed my neck. "Unlucky for them, they need me to work there."

I swallowed guiltily. "And Quinn . . . was it the iPhone that made her . . ."

"A suspect?"

The word jarred. I remembered her in that cave, her lost eyes staring, the terrified way she ran ahead of me.

"Not yet. I swear to you, I have done my best to protect both of you."

"I know." I let my forehead touch his. For all

his bluster and grumpiness, he had a big heart. When he carried me to the bed, murmuring sweet things in French, I let him do it, all of it, anything he wanted, because there was nothing else I could do.

Molly Swift

AUGUST 7, 2015

I watched Valentin sleep awhile, not because it's the sort of thing I ever do, but because it was oddly soothing, like CDs of white noise or whale song. As he fell asleep, he'd murmured that he loved me, which explained the weird vibe between us in part at least. I started to stutter something, but I wasn't sure what I felt, so in the end I said nothing. When the text noise went on his phone a little while later, I saw the message pop up and what it said: Quinn was being held under suspicion of murder.

When I read those words and mentally Google Translated them, it was like that horrible moment when you realize you have a stomach flu but you just haven't committed to vomiting yet. I couldn't help but wonder whether if I hadn't told all those lies and stirred shit up, Quinn would be in trouble.

I crept into my clothes, feeling as much like a dirty rat as I'd ever felt and trying not to let my attention wander to the glint of golden stubble on Valentin's face, the way his lips were full and curved as a girl's. It was surely the last time I'd see him that way.

Back in my room, I scrolled to the top of my speed dial. Mom was away from her phone, up to mischief, no doubt. Bill, as always, was in. The sound of Nina in the background busting his balls was curiously reassuring.

"You get the video?" I asked.

"Sure did." As soon as I heard his voice, I thought, *Bill sounds . . . different.*

"Watch it yet?"

"Uh-huh. And I'm not the only one." I realized what it was. He was pleased with himself.

"Okay. You sound chipper."

"Well, that was one hell of a video. I mean, it was long, but after a shrewd edit, it was good stuff."

"Thanks, I guess." Despite my general sense of disaster, I allowed myself a little smile. Praise from Bill used to be my whole goal in life.

"Seriously, though," he continued in his new, smug voice, "you went way above and beyond to get the truth and I think that's half of what people are responding to."

"Responding to?" My stomach dropped. "I sent that for your eyes only, Bill. Who else has seen it?"

"Try . . . the whole world." He sounded so full of glee I wished I could reach through the phone and throttle him.

"What?"

"I streamed it on the *American Confessional* channel."

"You streamed it? But who even edited it all together?"

"'Get with the times, Bill.' Isn't that what you're always telling me? And don't worry, I took out the bits with your boyfriend clucking over you."

"My what? You mean Valentin? Is that what this is about, Bill? You're jealous? You're taking revenge? You've fucked me, now. Everyone will know how I lied."

"Comes with the territory, Molly. Besides, you have the small recompense of journalistic celebrity."

"But I don't want—"

"To be famous? Every conversation we've ever had, that's just what you did want, more than anything. Now I've given you it."

"Yeah, I get it. Goodbye, Bill. Thanks for blowing my cover and everything . . ."

"So when's the next installment? The video's gone viral. The world's waiting."

I hung up the phone.

Quinn Perkins

JULY 24, 2015

Draft Blog Entry

I wasn't imagining things: it was the police coming to arrest us, question us, whatever. Stella called them when she found out that Raphael had taken the stuff from her medicine cabinet and a few little trinkets. It seems harsh for a family friend, "like a son to her" by his own account. There was no time to quibble with her, though, or even to get dressed. We had to slip out the back naked, through some secret gap in the fence Raphael knows about, which was pretty hard for me with OxyContin or Midol or whatever mixed with my meds and making my head weird. I remember shivering so badly I couldn't get my jeans fastened. Raphael said it didn't matter, to climb on the bike. Was it luck that made him park in those woods near the hole in Stella's fence?

He says we need to keep a low profile and that we need cash. Finding a place to stay will be even harder now, especially since, overnight, he's grown as paranoid as me. My mind's shut down for now. Today, I've just done everything as he's said, which isn't much except driving from one shitty apartment to the next, picking up twenty euros here, a promise note there, dodging into an alleyway every time we see blue and white stripes go by.

On this bumpy back road, the sea follows us, a blue dog speed-blurred. Every time a car passes, the bike tilts and I think we will fall. My thighs clutch hot metal. My knees press into the backs of Raphael's thighs. We get to St. Roch and carefully avoid the main drag. Not sure we should be here at all. When I catch a glimpse of the gendarmerie in one of the mirrors, I think my heart will burst. Flat, pale-faced shop buildings and soothing shutters over antiques and curios as the Sunday market winds down. The bike swerves, bumps over cobbles. Medieval buildings grow tall around us, leering down. Red awnings are cocked at irregular angles. Eccentric shopkeepers lean in doorways tutting at the bike. Or am I still being paranoid? *Slow down, Raphael,* I think. Our thoughts can't be that in tune 'cause he speeds up. We bump through a quaint square by the church, knocking over an empty café chair. Angry shouts swell and fade behind us.

In a dark side street, the bike stops. Raphael signals me to stay put. I do, afraid of following him through the flaking powder blue door. It looks shadier even than the others. Eyes glint from the darkness. Hungry. Suspicious. I hunch over the humming bike, shivering. In the shadowy street, it's suddenly cold. Raphael's gone a long time. I stare at the blue door and it stares back.

I already know what he's doing in there. Collecting money from some friend or other who owes him—what he's been doing all day, so we can "go somewhere nice, somewhere away from here." The trouble is, I'm not sure I want to go anymore.

The door creaks open and Raphael's back emerges, his head still talking in hushed tones to the person inside, who I now see is a young woman with dark hair, a bundle of cloth or rags tucked under one arm. She steps forward, leaning on the pale blue door, watches me with heavy lidded eyes. She smiles a knowing smile as if she knows something I don't know. Suddenly Raphael grabs the cloth bundle. Bolts from the door. The woman's mouth drops open, an agonized O of shock. She shouts something in French I don't catch.

"*Vite! Vite!* Come on!" Raphael elbows me back from the handles, jumps onto the bike.

The engine revs. The woman is screaming now. I want to get off, to run from this. But it's too late. The bike lurches forward, knocking me back. I cling on to Raphael to stop myself falling. The bike lurches over the cobbles. My head whips back in time to see the woman pull off one of her pink flip-flops. She screams in French, so loud I think her lungs might burst. Windows above fly open. Curious heads poke out. Her arm winds back and the flip-flop flies through the air. Falls pathetically to the ground. The bike speeds. I turn my head back, not wanting to see the woman or the street or the many pairs of eyes staring out in judgment.

We escape St. Roch. We are out on the road again, winding up where the fields give way to crops of rock and the road is steep. And then we are on a dirt track, juddering along so hard I think my teeth will smash. Maybe they should. That was way worse than what happened last night. Raphael wasn't just "borrowing" from an old family friend. He committed a crime. Or maybe that woman was mixed up in shady stuff herself and they're both thieves. Whichever way, I'm an accomplice to something much worse now.

The bike swerves to a halt, kicking up dust. It settles. I try to calm myself by looking around. It's hard when every tooth and bone in me is trembling. God, where are we now? In a nightmare. Or the set of a death metal video. Hard to know which. Rising all around us, ragged and blackened, staring down with gaping glassless windows of eyes, is an abandoned building.

"What the hell . . . ?" The words tumble out, then stop. I don't want to look at Raphael, speak to him. Not yet.

Out of the corner of my eye, I see him rub his hands over his face. Anxiety is eating away his charm and he does not smile. His curls are sweat slick. He shakes his head and a shower of salt beads spray me. I flinch back, eyes stinging where the salt hits.

"Don't you recognize it?" he says curtly. "It is the art block of the school, the part that was vandalized."

"What was that back there?" I say. I can't help it. I have to know what he's got me into.

"Nothing," he snaps. "Anyway, I must get something from here." In a few quick steps, he's climbed the broken steps where the Victorian children once lined up for their photograph. Then the door's toothless gape swallows him whole.

I hug my arms around myself. I unhug my arms. Should I run, call someone? I glance in dismay at the eight percent battery on my phone, the No Signal notification endemic to the St. Roch area. I straddle the bike and wonder if I could drive it out of here. To where? The police?

A car drives up, kicking up clouds of dust, actually not just a car, but a cherry red Chevy Impala. The low-slung door opens and a tall guy unfolds himself from behind the wheel. His policeman's uniform hangs loosely from his skinny frame. *Shit shit shit.* They're onto us, just as I feared. The police, come to arrest us, to question us.

"Good day to you," he says in heavily accented French.

It goes through my head that I should confess, come clean, turn Raphael in. Instead, I hear myself say, "Uh, my friend is in there, but he only went to get a photo or something. So he'll be out in a sec . . ." The words sound like the weak excuses they are. I stare at my dusty feet.

"Don't you know this is private property, that you are trespassing here?" He sounds mad, like he means business.

It's hard to keep my face calm, stop my hands shaking. And yet, there goes my mouth again, the easy explanations spilling out. "His family lives here, pretty much. Anyway, he'll be right out, and we'll be on our way, Officer." And then I smile. All that time I spend making up stories, rewriting my life to make it sound better, sure has made me good at this . . . at what? Covering my ass? Covering Raphael's?

The cop takes off his sunglasses slowly and I fully expect to get shouted at. His eyes are wide spaced and very blue. He looks me up and down coolly and then he breaks into a broad grin, showing crooked teeth.

"It's a joke! I am Raphael's friend. I meet him here."

An electric shock goes through me. Raphael

has a friend in the police. Is he part of this, some "well-disposed" cop keeping Raphael from getting arrested?

He grins wider, takes my hand, kisses it. "*Je m'appelle Léon*. And you, you are Quinn?"

"Um, yeah. He told you about me?"

"Yes, of course, the American girl. Ever since he left Paris, I hear of nothing else." When he leans down, his face is level with mine. He's not handsome like Raphael, but there is something nice about his smile that makes me feel a bit easier.

"Let's go," says Léon, starting towards the broken building.

I hang back a moment. This feels weird. Not just weird—bad. First the robbery, then some cop I don't know showing up at this rendezvous, a broken building. For what? To hang out? But I don't want to stay out here all by myself. So I follow him, picking my way through the rubble of the Old Schoolhouse, stepping over freaky curios: the mangled wire skeleton of a tailor's dummy, a shattered wooden desk, an old valise, a wooden crate with a dozen Kewpie dolls cheerily grinning through the frame of the burned-out past.

At the doorway to the school, my demon lover reappears, looking for a moment like an angry spirit, his skin pale, his beautiful lips down-turned. Do I know him at all?

Léon stops, hand cupped over his eyes as if he's straining to see this ghost-Raphael, the dead him like a prophetic vision. Raphael steps into the light and smiles charmingly, as if all of this is perfectly natural. He hugs Léon and does a complicated fist-bump thing. He pulls me close and I find it hard to resist, despite my misgivings. He stands with his arm draped over my neck, nuzzling me so that Léon fidgets with his watch. I wonder if he feels how tense I am, how much I don't want to be here.

"Come on, man," says Raphael, letting his arm drop away. "We better hurry."

"*Ouais, on y va.*" Léon nods.

I follow them into the darkness of the crumbling building. We weave our way through corridors with doors hanging off their hinges and the roofs caving in, until we get to a small room with no windows and no roof. Looks like maybe it was a dark-room once. There are vats of chemicals, developing trays, and camera lenses. In one corner is a pile of blankets covered with leaves and plaster. In another is a plastic tub full of half-dead electronic gear, a tripod, a broken clock radio. Raphael gestures to the blankets.

I hunch down, so pliant now I wonder if I'm getting Stockholm syndrome. He breaks out some beers, uncapping mine for me before passing it. Thirsty and headachy, I sip mine slowly while the other two sit on chairs talking in French. I hope this isn't going to be our hideout.

We sit for a long time. My head feels more and more vague, spinning, the room spinning, the sky above a twirling disk of blue. The sun starts burning my bare arms, chapping my lips. My blood pressure keeps on rising with the sense of anticipation, anxiety, unease—what are we doing here?

A lizard skitters over my foot and pauses to look at me, gold eye swiveling manically. My head pounds harder and harder and a metallic taste pools in my mouth. I don't understand why this one beer has made me so wasted. My eyes droop sleepily.

It's not long before I have cause to wake, sharply. Raphael and Léon are passing silver blister packs back and forth, sorting, counting. They have white boxes, like from a pharmacy, stacks and stacks of them. Dealing drugs. I want to be sick.

They stand and start fitting a video camera onto a tripod. All the while, they are smoking and laughing and speaking in French in low voices I can't quite hear. Neither of them looks at me. Then Raphael falls on the bed next to me, grinning his broad, easy pretty-boy grin. Léon gives us a sideways look and shucks his tab end into the dusty scrub grass growing through the broken floor. Raphael holds out his hand to Léon, beckoning with his fingers: *Gimme gimme*. Léon rolls his eyes and then, with a little sigh, reaches into the breast pocket of his immaculate shirt and pulls out a little Baggie. Raphael opens it, takes a little on his finger, and rubs it on his gums.

"*Danke schön, broheim*." He dabs his finger in more powder and offers me some.

"No," I say, turning my head away.

"She liked it last night," he says, winking at Léon, "and this morning. You were high as a kite, girl. Don't you remember?"

"Last night? But I—" I begin angrily. "I don't remember." Fuck. I really don't.

Léon shoots me an odd look, like I'm crazy or something. "*De rien*. Anyway, I go now." He hugs Raphael tight, clapping his back. "Be safe, man—" flinging his car keys on the bed "—take the keys for the Impala. I'll go home with your bike."

When Léon has gone, Raphael whispers in my ear, "Okay, baby?"

"Not really."

"What's up?"

"All of this." I gesture to the wreck of a room. "What happened earlier, the drugs. I didn't know you were mixed up in this kind of thing." My voice sounds high and tight and hysterical.

"Don't forget, you are, too." He winks at me,

his easy charm having returned. "Hey, it wasn't so bad today. Fun times, no? Exciting?" He turns back to rolling his joint.

I start shaking and can't stop. The worst thing is, he's not wrong. I could have run, told someone, called someone. But I didn't. I'm part of it now. When he passes me the joint, I don't say no. I want to take the edge off this, to not think. We stay till the stars come out, till we are so high we're almost up in them. Leaving this blog here in case stuff gets any worse. Glad the world can't see it, though. Glad . . . God . . . I'm in way over my head.

Molly Swift

AUGUST 8, 2015

It felt like I was coming down with swine flu or something. I was sweating. Everything hurt. I turned and turned in the starched sheets, the same thought circling through my head: *It's what I deserve, it's what I deserve.* Like an incubus coming to gloat over my stricken body, a message popped up on my phone. *Here's a link to the YouTube video. Bx*

I deleted it angrily and then set about deleting all my other texts from that backstabber Bill and even his contact details. God, how I'd despised the news coverage of that handheld footage of Quinn, the way the wolf pack took advantage of a terrified girl at her weakest moment. Now I'd done the same thing. By now, my video of the caves would be looping on the French news, the US news, every kind of news. Everyone would know how I'd lied. I ran to the bathroom, knelt over the bowl, and threw up.

Maybe it wouldn't be so bad, I reasoned. Maybe it would help with searching for the Blavettes somehow. Leaning my cheek on chilly porcelain, I tried to believe it. All the hot, prickly night as I lay awake sweating and hugging myself for comfort, I hoped for a knock on the door—Valentin checking on me one last time. A couple of hours ago, I'd crept away from him. Now that it was too late, I wished him back again.

In the morning, I woke to a different world, one where I was—in the words of Bill—an internet sensation. As soon as I dragged my exhausted body down to the hotel lobby, the journalists who'd been courting my attention a few days before turned their noses up in scorn. In the eyes of the world, I'd saved the day (or at least, a day). In the eyes of my fellow hacks, I was the lying scumbag who'd scooped them. As Bill always said, *Write what you like, but you never know how it's gonna play.*

Worst of all was the fact that Bill setting up a YouTube channel for *American Confessional* in the first place was my fault: I'd urged him to get with the times and now I'd created a monster. So I'd forced myself to watch it, every cringe-worthy moment. If you link through from the relevant episode of our #AmericanGirl serial, you come to the video's black title card of the same name, followed by portentous white-on-black text:

"In the middle of this riveting case, our investigations took a darker turn. Follow our roving reporter Molly Swift as she ventures into the notoriously dangerous caves known as Les Yeux to follow a lead in the Blavette disappearances. *WARNING: Some viewers may find the following footage disturbing.*"

Framed like some found-footage horror, the film cut in to my shaky GoPro-style camerawork, beginning at the entrance of Les Yeux and ending with the discovery of Noémie. It was hard to know which was worse, the obvious fear in my voice or the fact that Bill had used every word, uncut as far as I could tell. I only read five of the comments that spilled out underneath the clip. It was all I could stand. Vindictive comments about Quinn, her supposed guilt, the look on her face in the final frame—all misspelled in various lan-guages. I closed the YouTube app on my phone and deleted it with shaking hands.

It was naive to think I could escape it, though. The TV in the hotel bar replayed the same montage of clips over and over: me running into the big chamber to find the girls, followed by Noémie calling Quinn a murderer. This was being juxtaposed with a clip of Republic prosecutor Marcelline Masson reading out a statement about an American cultural exchange being questioned in relation to the disap-pearances. When I saw the way the two things had been spliced together, it was crystal clear where the guilt was being placed.

In the French papers, Quinn was being called

monstre and *démon*. A front-page feature in *Le Monde*—a publication that had previously celebrated the miracle of her waking from the coma—smoothly recast her as some kind of serial killer. To be fair, they had a decent circumstantial case against her. There was Noémie's reaction to seeing her in Les Yeux, the fact that she'd withheld her phone from the inquiry, and motive (discovered from her blog). Some bastard had followed the trail from Quinn's school records—reporting a term's absence coinciding with her mother's death—to three months spent in the secure psychiatric assessment unit at Boston Children's Hospital. Even the names of her medications had been published for all to see. She'd had no visitors at Sainte-Thérèse, which was taken as proof that she was a dangerous lone wolf, and there was that weird CCTV clip of her doing drugs and making out with some guy in a swimming pool, one that looked for all the world like the pool at Mas d'Or. On top of all this, a police interview had provoked her into a documented fit of rage.

A guest profiler whose qualifications were opaque to me had sketched her character, identifying her as a romantic obsessive suffering from borderline personality disorder. He went on to speculate that Quinn had fallen for Raphael Blavette so desperately that when Émilie got in the way, she killed the family and hid them some-where in the caves. Noémie barely escaped with her life and languished for a week without being discovered. No one seemed willing to mention that it was Quinn who had enabled Noémie's rescue.

It was all an obvious hatchet job, a classic trial by media. But thanks to me, there was an orgy of circumstantial evidence: stills of Quinn's disturbed-looking face from my video, and, I was horrified to see, the video I'd inadvertently taken of her meltdown in the hospital. It seemed that Bill had chosen his pitch long ago and been planning this for a while. A jokey Instagram picture of Quinn dressed as a vampire for Halloween was captioned *Bloodthirsty*. Under-neath it ran a quote from one of the horror stories on her blog. The news had already spread to the wider world: #AmericanMonster had been trending on Twitter for hours.

In the midst of my despairing iPhone news binge, a shadow fell across the table. I knew who it was even before I looked up. The expression on Valentin's face was somewhere north of anger. He cocked his head, his eyes flicking over me as if he was looking at an alien, trying to work out what made it tick and how he could kill it. I tried to hold his gaze, but couldn't. The way he was looking at me stung too much, as if I wasn't worthy of his anger. I stared down at he stubs of rouge-stained cigarettes in the overflowing ashtray. Between them were round molten scars of spent cherries fused with plastic.

"I'm sorry," I said.

He pulled out the chair opposite me with a squeal. I heard him take out a cigarette. "When are you flying back?"

"Dunno." I offered him my light.

He batted it away. "Well, maybe you should book a flight."

I lit my own cigarette, willing my fingers not to shake. "So I guess this is the sheriff with his six-shooter telling me I'm not welcome in this town."

He let out a cynical snort. "You Americans with your popular cultural references, always assuming we French know what you mean. Why is it so? Because our cafés sell your Coca-Cola, you imagine we are some small colony of yours, a holiday park where you come to stand bored in museums and learn a few words and fuck strangers and go home leaving a trail of broken bodies behind. Is this your notion of a holiday?"

"A holiday?" I stood up, turning over my chair. I could feel people's eyes on me, another scene hurtling out of control in this already overly dramatic town. "You call this a holiday? I wanted to help—"

"Always a mistake," he said, inhaling a lungful of smoke. "I suppose you mean you were helping that girl, the one who's in a prison cell. Oh yes, I see, when you pretended to be her aunt to get a news story, you were helping *her* and not yourself."

I could see how I looked to him, perhaps how I really was. What could I really say to justify my behavior? "I helped you," I muttered.

His blank mask dropped away. He looked angry. "*Quoi? Hein?*"

"And Noémie. She was trapped in there, dying. I—"

"Don't give yourself airs." He waved at the smoke hanging between us. "We all know what you were really doing in those caves. Your little art-house film."

I leaned over the table towards him, as angry as he was now. "I knew you were macho, but this is deluded. With every passing day you were losing that case. You need to get over yourself."

Valentin took a drag on his cigarette and exhaled slowly. Up until then, he had really succeeded in playing it cool. But he leaned forward then, pressing the knuckles of one hand into the table until they were white. "You bitch." He said it low so that our growing audience couldn't hear. "You hurt . . . people . . . without caring . . ." He stopped and looked away.

I reached out to touch his hand. "Whatever I did, I'm sorry." His skin was hot and tight. He didn't respond to my touch, but he didn't move away either. It gave me courage to finish. "Everything that happened with you was real. *Everything.*"

He frowned, his hand falling casually from under mine. "That's sad," he said, "because it was not so for me. I would have thought a woman of your experience would know pillow talk for what it was, but you American girls, you are all the same."

Quinn Perkins

JULY 26, 2015

Draft Blog Entry

So . . . if my American friends were here, they would stage an intervention or whatever. If Dad were here, I'd be headed back to the nuthouse. The theft from the woman, the drug dealing stuff . . . that was bad enough. Today was worse. Woke up in a strange bed in a strange, awful apartment. The windows were covered with newspaper, the floor littered with joint butts, and there was something weird covering the walls, every inch of them. Don't totally remember, though, 'cause my head was spinning around hard.

Ran to the bathroom to puke and the scabby toilet just made me feel sicker. The sink was filthy. I flung open the window, got vertigo. Must've been ten floors up. The worst thing: I didn't know how we even got there, or why we were sleeping on some stained mattress in a room with other people, or why the morning and afternoon had spun by without me noticing. Back in the bedroom, I tried asking Raphael, but he was in a nontalking mood, scowling down at his phone. All I could think was, *I'm in this now. We're in it together, God help me.*

Everything feels out of control. After the apartment, we ended up having an argument for most of the day—Raphael needed to borrow money and I didn't have enough. I drew out what there was, hoping Dad wouldn't notice. Raphael still gave me the silent treatment, though. A few times he left me on my own for a bit and I almost slipped away into the crowd of the street. But the thing is, I know the police are looking for us. It's why we've been keeping off the roads, blending in with the crowds. Maybe I'm better off sticking with him. He seems to know what he's doing.

We ended up at that shady club, La Gorda, again. I didn't know why we were there because Raphael still wouldn't talk to me. He just strolled in, nodding hello to this girl and that, while I trailed behind. Away from the outside world and the threat of arrest, he was up and charming again, introducing me to everyone: the unfriendly, hot, white-haired barmaid, Lolo; the bouncer, an old guy called Bruno with black Michael Bolton hair in a ponytail. Raphael ordered vodkas all around.

As Lolo poured, he said in my ear, "She is Latvian or something. She does not speak much French, but seriously she is the queen of La Gorda. Look at her go, man."

I don't know you, I wanted to say. It was true. I didn't know any of the new stuff I'd been finding out about Raphael—the drug dealing, the reckless driving, the mean streak when he didn't get his way. I didn't know what kind of boyfriend would keep feeding me pills that made me pass out and wake up in strange bedrooms. And I didn't know why I kept swallowing them, except that I was scared now. I felt stranded. Everything was happening too fast.

I sit at the bar of La Gorda, face drooping in my hands, drearily watching Lolo pour vodka shots, all skinny and commanding. After she pours out the drinks, she toasts Raphael with her Evian bottle and kisses him on both cheeks. It kind of bugs me that there's this weird vibe between them, but then there seems to be some weird vibe between Raphael and pretty much everyone. He's just one of those intense people who flirts with men, women . . . lampposts.

A large man comes up to us grinning broadly, an aging, jowly Gérard Depardieu type in jeans paired with a black suit coat and a wide white-collared shirt. He's a big man, not just in the sense of being fat or tall (though he's both), but in that he's impressive. For a moment he hovers behind Raphael, before clapping him on the back with great bonhomie.

"Raphael! Mon fils!"

For a moment—just a split second, really, so brief that I think I only notice it because I'm watching Raphael so closely—Raphael blanches. The expression on his face is even worse than that night at Stella's or yesterday after the robbery. Pure fear. Terror even. And then it's gone and he's grinning wide and kissing the older man, hugging him like a father.

We all hug and kiss and everyone is family and shots of flaming Sambuca follow vodka shots, sticky Sambuca with bitter coffee beans floating in it and the flame flickering blue in the darkness. Raphael and Séverin—the Depardieu guy—drink like Hemingway heroes, slamming palms down hard on the bar, downing each shot.

"Aha! *Fantastique!*" cries Séverin jovially after each one. Then he laughs until he's wheezing for breath, until you think he's about to die from a coronary.

It all seems like good fun, but that look of fear never quite fades from Raphael's face: he's pale, as if he has seen a ghost. His own ghost, maybe.

Perhaps because Raphael's so quiet, Séverin gets me talking—about where I'm from, what it's like at home. Really, though, he's more keen to talk about him than me. Soon he's in full flow, describing the farm he grew up on in Sicily and his French grandfather, who died a hero defying the Nazis during World War II. When he fleetingly inquires about my parents, I mention that my mom died. Suddenly we're best friends; Momma Séverin died last year and he dreams about her every night.

"The world lost its greatest gnocchi the day she died," he says, wiping away tears, "and its greatest meatballs."

Still, there are good things in life, stuff he loves: his stylish wife, Venetia ("that woman has given me everything worthwhile in life but, *mio Dio*, she thinks she's the boss"), his kids ("the girl is beautiful, but the boy is so lazy, a momma's boy"), his grandkids, and his brand-new kitchen cabinets. The longest time is spent talking about his Italian greyhound, Virgil, who was run over by a truck the same week his momma died.

"I loved that dog more than life. Since Momma and Virgil died, life has been hard. I work like a slave to keep this place going . . . and the other clubs, well . . ." He mops his brow.

Reading between the lines, though, I'd say he spends most of his time drinking Turkish coffee and keeping an eye on Lolo at the club, or at home, playing with his grandkids, being waited on hand and foot, cleaning a gun or two. Oh yes, he hunts wild boar. At least I think that's what he tells me. By this point, I'm wobbly from all the free drinks, the sticky sweetness of the Sambuca coating my mouth and skin. Suddenly

Raphael leans forward, lips at my cheek. I think he's going to kiss me.

Instead, he whispers in my ear, "He likes you. Keep him talking for me, will you?"

I nod hazily, not really getting it. As Séverin starts sharing his passion for breeding Italian greyhounds with me, Raphael weaves through the crowd towards the back of the club. I sit at the bar uneasy in the midst of all the Saturday night fun and high spirits. The punks in the club dance. Scowling Lolo keeps the drinks flowing. Bruno bustles behind the counter. He's always fixing things, Bruno, pulling the place together with another piece of gaffer tape. I kind of warm to him, watching his endless hopeless task, because looking around with newly cynical eyes, I notice that the place is practically held together by gaffer tape. Séverin talks and talks and I hardly listen. Raphael's not back. Could he be in the bathroom still?

Like a stone it hits me. He didn't go to the bathroom at all. *Keep him talking for me, will you,* he said. Meaning, *Keep him distracted. So I can . . . case the joint? Lift some cash?* Well, he's stolen something from everyone else. Why am I even surprised?

My stomach flips nonetheless. I feel sick, desperate to go, to not be in this. The other stuff was bad, but I was pretty much a bystander. This—whatever it is—is so much worse. I feel it. I'm no bystander either. I'm the decoy.

Not a very good one, as it turns out.

While I'm busy panicking, Séverin is telling me about his pet hates: bad wine, feminists, the clap, his cigar going out, his staff. "There's dissent in the ranks in these clubs. Isn't there always?" he growls. "And sometimes other people are just incompetent, don't you think?"

Yes? No? I have no clue what he's talking about and he sees that my mind has drifted away from his life story. With a grunt, he slips from the barstool, into the dancing crowd. If I was panicked before, now the feeling is ten times that bad. Feels like I'm having a heart attack. Fuck. What if he goes back there, finds Raphael?

A cough draws my attention. I look up to see Lolo craning her neck back and growling at someone in the gloom behind her. What she says seems to me to translate as "fat girl." Then, in English she asks me, "Who you say your name is?"

"Quinn," I say, trying not to sound too freaked.

She looks me up and down coolly. "Why you with Raphael?"

"I'm his girlfriend," I say wearily, palming sweat from my forehead.

Lolo cracks her face and at first I think she's having some kind of painful seizure. Then I realize she's laughing at me. Hard. The noise sounds unnatural coming out of her tiny throat, growly and a little bit unhealthy. She leans her head back into the darkness and coughs out a remark in French to the other barmaid. I translate their talk in my mind and wish I hadn't.

"This fat girl says she's Raffi's new girlfriend! Anyway, where's he run off to?"

"Fuck should I know," the other barmaid replies. "Run from her?" (pointing at me).

More raucous laughter. I gaze down at my hands, pale and splodgy, floating beneath the grimy cuffs of Raphael's hoodie. I wish I could just take off into the night, that I weren't trapped by Raphael being the one with the car, the one who knows how to cope with all this.

"Did Raphael tell you we used to be together?" Lolo folds her arms over her black T-shirt that says We Don't Give a Fuck and smirks.

I shrug and don't answer. Given the weird vibe between her and Raphael, I was already pretty sure they had recently been on a . . . friendly . . . basis. I knew that from their body language. But I buried it because . . . because what? I'm dumb? Or maybe because I seem to be willfully blind to everything about Raphael I don't want to see. None of it matters now, anyway. We'll get caught by Séverin and then either the cops will come (the real ones, not Léon), or some worse fate will befall us involving being fed to Italian grey-hounds or something.

Dark humor shimmers over Lolo's pretty, pale face. "Well, you are feeling stupid now, I think, because you can see I am better looking than you. Photos of me are much nicer than photos of you, too."

"Actually, I'm thinking I want to get the fuck out of this dump," I say, mad now as well as scared. "And I have no idea what you're trying to say about photos."

She guffaws like I just said the best thing ever. "*Putain*, you really do not know? You girls think you are educated, but you are always so slow."

She smiles and gestures broadly to what could be anything in the tense air between us. "It is a big piece of luck for you, though. You get to sleep with someone as nice as Raffi while it lasts, which is pretty good when you are . . ." She puffs her cheeks and spreads her arms on either side of her, growing exponentially, Kirby-style. "You get to be a porn star."

I look around and see Bruno lolling in the shadows, his hooded eyes flicking over my face, then away, to the girls at the bar, the door. Across the bar, Séverin flicks a look at me, then back to his ledger, his numbers, his Biro tapping at the paper. The end is chewed. Maybe all that drinking sobered me up, because the glamour has fallen from La Gorda. This place, the people in it, all at once look simply seedy.

I start to understand what's going on, a business run with little bags and boxes of drugs and Raphael's video camera . . . Film student, my ass! That night at Stella's, drugged up in the pool . . . that day in the caves . . . we weren't making love. We were making movies for my "boyfriend" to sell. I think of how many people could have streamed them by now, downloaded them from the internet. I don't know why I didn't notice it before, that day when the strange man came to the Blavettes' door with his grubby money. Maybe I just liked him too much and it blinded me to what I was really getting into, had already become part of even before he stole from that woman. My mind was caught like an old vinyl record, its needle jammed in a groove.

Now the needle's jumped.

Molly Swift

AUGUST 8, 2015

I knew times were tough when I went to La Grande Bouche and was disappointed not to find Marlene there. I slumped over my coffee, writing a bullet point list of everything I knew that might prove Quinn was innocent. It wasn't the greatest of lists. The main things that made Quinn seem sympathetic in her blog—her relationship with Raphael and Noémie, and Émilie's bad behavior to her—were the very things that were now being used as motive. Next there were the threatening Snapchats that may or may not have been from Freddie, but since these had vanished into the ether, I couldn't do much with them, or pin anything to Freddie apart from Quinn's words.

Third on the list was the Blavette family's own mediocre human rights record, namely the closing of the school and the death of Nicole Leclair. The jury seemed out on whether that was down to Marc or Émilie's poor decision-making, to take a tour of caves that made people go insane and now served as a haunt for local bad guys; but the caves themselves seemed key. Freddie had implied that not only Marc Blavette but Raphael was mixed up in something to do with bad people who used Les Yeux.

The question was, who were the bad people? I sat at one of the outdoor tables holding my phone all the way out, as far in the direction of the satellite as I could manage, attempting to catch a few rays of internet. Like magic, the Wi-Fi symbol rose to full and a message loaded in my in-box.

After a lot of digging around, I found an article in *Topix* dated 2013 about the disappearance of local businessman Marc Blavette, and put it through Google Translate.

There is fear in the small town of St. Roch after forty-one-year-old local businessman Marc Blavette has disappeared. His possible kidnapping is causing fear for his lot, and is being investigated by police. They do not yet want to label it a crime. It is entirely unclear where Blavette, owner of a chain of thriving local nightspots, is or why he disappeared. His family reported the missing person to police, who did a thorough investigation in the neighborhood, sent around a description. His regular haunts were searched, including his most well-known and popular club, La Gorda, situated in Place de la Préfecture.

It turned out that Marc Blavette was "a successful club owner, involved in the district association, and a tour guide at the local caves, popularly known as Les Yeux." Marlene Weiss, manager of La Grande Bouche, was even quoted as feeling uneasy in the wake of the disappearance. "St. Roch is like a small village. Everyone knows each other and everyone also knows

Marc. We are very shocked." Émilie Blavette, on the other hand, commented, "If I did know something, I wouldn't tell it to the papers."

After he vanished, police sealed La Gorda and an investigation began: *According to the head of the St. Roch police, Inspector Valentin, the police have also been to Blavette's other club, Inferno, to look at security footage.* It seemed that Blavette had been beaten by "unknown assailants" not long before he vanished. The owner of a shop near La Gorda reported that he had a dispute with these people, "but refused to be intimidated. They had a hold on him, though. I don't know if it was something to do with the club. I'm afraid this is more than just a missing-persons case."

La Gorda. That name stood out to me. I flicked through Quinn's Instagram again and sure enough: #clubbing, #lagorda, #thuglife, #crunk. Going through to the club's own feed, I found photos of a hip club and a map of its location.

I followed the map to the wrong side of the tracks in the land of the dirty bars. As I walked towards the door of the club, light gleamed from the sidewalk and I was struck by pavement blindness. I shoved my cheap shades onto my nose, scanning the white van parked outside, spray-painted on the side—Rise Up, Jonah in purple and Fatty's Junk below in yellow and bluish—plus other scrawls, other signatures, layered over and over and over, as if people felt compelled to keep contradicting each other on the side of that van.

Inside, the red outlines of Bud neons reflected in the glass, covering eerie art nudes that hung on the walls. The bar staff paced like caged animals, coiled around their own beauty and some savage tension of the place—as far as I could tell, a French heavy metal bar full of Japanese hipsters, cool Arabs in sock hats, and cigarette-thin Goth chicks with fierce eyebrows and long, black hair.

Leaning over the bar in my tight red dress, I was struck by what hard work it is being a young thing these days. Dirty work, too. The place stunk of sweat and stale smoke and warm beer, and I was pretty sure I saw a roach run over my shoe. I knocked back a double JD and chased it with a Red Bull and vodka before I worked up the nerve to draw the attention of the pretty bonehead chick with the spike earrings and breastbone tattoo, and say, "You know anyone called Blavette?"

Her forehead crumpled and she frowned. I couldn't tell if she didn't speak English or couldn't hear me, or both. I repeated the question in French.

The look remained, but with something extra added to it—a little touch of fear. She looked down at the glass she was polishing as if suddenly possessed by OCD. The punk guy next to her scowl-smiled and beckoned me closer. He lifted a pierced eyebrow and without speaking pointed towards the back of the room, though all I could see was a mosh pit full of headbangers enjoying the gig.

"You know about any people getting beaten up in this area?" I asked. "Turf warfare? Um, bad people?"

He shrugged. "Why don't you ask Séverin about it? He knows. Table at the back."

I headed for the mosh pit. The music throbbed. As soon as I got near the table the guy told me about, two heavies standing in front of it stepped closer together. I could see a guy I assumed was Séverin sitting behind them, hard to read behind his sunglasses. An expensive tailored suit was stretched over his vast frame, made blingier by the addition of a gold Rolex and matching cuff links. Suddenly he smiled and I realized that he reminded me of an older French version of Tony Soprano. He was probably good company, buying everyone lunch and dandling his grandkids until the moment he was cutting your thumbs off. I smiled back and waved. The lights changed, dyeing the man's face red when it lifted to watch me. They changed again, made his beckoning finger turn green. Maybe he recognized me from TV.

"Raoul. Pierre." Séverin snapped his fingers.

The bodyguards lumbered aside. I slid onto the cold leatherette next to him, glad for the shots I had downed at the bar that stopped my hands from shaking, that made it easy to smile.

He slipped his arm over the back of the couch. "And who might you be? I don't think we've been introduced, though it's hard to be sure."

"That's the trouble with wearing Ray-Bans in a nightclub. You can't see shit."

He cocked his head but didn't laugh. Jokes— they never translate.

"My name is Molly," I added.

"And to what do I owe this pleasure, Molly?"

"I'm trying to find someone called Blavette."

Séverin guffawed like I just said the best thing ever. "*Putain*, you are one of Raphael's little chicks? Aren't you a bit old for him?"

"No, I'm not one of his 'chicks.' I came here to find out what happened to Marc Blavette. Do you know?" It wasn't the smartest of interrogation techniques, but at least it cut to the chase.

So much so that the look on Séverin's face

shifted from one of benign contempt to barely repressed anger. "*Marc* Blavette? You come in asking for *Marc* Blavette?"

I seemed to have touched a nerve. "He used to own this club, didn't he?"

"Years ago," said Séverin slowly. "We were business partners actually. I bought La Gorda from Marc fair and square."

"Before he died, or after?"

Under the table, Séverin's hand grabbed my thigh, the nails digging in. "Who sent you? What do you know?" His fingers dug deeper, hurting me.

I flicked a look towards the dancing crowd, but could see nothing beyond the hulking bodies of the bodyguards. I was caught like a rat in a trap and now I understood the look on the bartender's face.

"You know," said Séverin, leaning close, "what happened to Marc can happen to anyone." His face was almost touching mine.

I pulled away, but he gripped my thigh tightly. There was a little knife in my purse, a sharp little folding blade my mom got me for my thirtieth birthday. It took serious subterfuge to get it through airport security. If only I could reach my bag, I thought. But it was down on the floor.

A man pushed in between the bodyguards. It was Valentin. He flashed his police badge. The bodyguards grudgingly moved aside. "Come on, slut," he bellowed. "I'm sorry, but this woman is a known prostitute and I have some questions to ask her."

"Questions? For her?" Séverin's hand slithered off of my knee.

"On your feet, whore," shouted Valentin.

As he led me away from the table, he continued to insult me, calling me a cheap tart, mutton dressed as lamb, and various other terms of endearment.

As soon as we were out of earshot and sight, I wriggled free of his grasp. "How dare you?"

"How dare I? I warned you once this morning. And here you are, talking to Séverin of all people—"

"I think he's got something to do with the Blavettes . . ." I began.

Valentin pulled me to him by the wrists. "Molly, why are you still putting your nose around, prying in my investigation? I have told you about this already."

"Told me?" I snapped. "*Threatened me* would be more accurate. I have a question. Why are you fucking up *my* investigation? Quinn is innocent and I'm trying to clear her name. I was just getting somewhere—"

"Molly." He touched my arm for a moment, before seeming to remember himself. "You were about to get hurt in some way. You are lucky that my snitch at the bar spotted you and called me in time. You do not know this man, Séverin."

"So he is a bad guy?"

"Yes, and he is serious in his business."

"I knew it," I said angrily. "So right here you have some bad guy who was Marc Blavette's business partner, who worked with Raphael, too. Yet instead of investigating him, you've arrested Quinn? You're just pinning this on her out of laziness or . . . I don't know . . . because she's an easy target."

"Listen, Molly. I have asked you once nicely to leave this place. I will ask you once more. The next time, you will be charged with putting your nose in places it does not belong." He turned on his heel and began to push between the dancers.

"I don't actually think that's a crime," I shouted after him, but he had already disappeared into the crowd.

Molly Swift

AUGUST 9, 2015

By way of an apology, Bill booked me a plane
ticket, using my ill-gotten gains. He forwarded
the e-ticket so that I could savor the prospect of
my cowardice. If I wanted his advice, he said, I
should catch the red-eye at six, read crappy
magazines, and eat peanuts and get so bored that
I would actually want to write up my notes. It
would be France detox, reminding me that this
whole St. Roch adventure had been nothing but
a wild journalistic bender. Bill and my beer
fridge and my sofa beckoned me home, and that
holy trinity would absolve all my sins.

It was tempting. The hacks that had followed
me when I was Quinn's aunt were following me
double now that I wasn't, hot-tailing up the main
drag, past the carrefour and the gas station,
scampering after me down cobblestoned
alleyways. They had big questions and I didn't
even have small answers.

Seeking sanctuary, I ducked into the maritime
church in the middle of St. Roch, solemn with
stained glass and boat-shaped votives, hung
from the nave to thank God for showing mercy

during shipwrecks. Up front, an unseen organist played melancholy chords. Beside him, behind the altar, sat a pietà carved out of marble, a sad, beautiful statue of the body of Jesus on the lap of His mother, Mary, after the Crucifixion, after they'd both given up hope. Valentin had told me his ancestors dragged the stone for it from the mountain quarries, hacking one great, unbroken piece from the high cliffs over the beach for the artist to carve. Light, tinted blue and green, fell slowly over the stone, as if life itself had distilled over centuries and become nothing more than still air.

A hand settled on my shoulder. For a moment I held my breath, feeling sure that it was either some divine intervention or the long arm of the law again seeking retribution. I was about to tell Valentin to get lost when a husky voice murmured in my ear. I turned to see Marlene's carmine lips split in a conspiratorial smile.

"The woman of the moment," she whispered, though her indoor voice was so loud it made the organist stop midarpeggio.

"Just kick me when I'm down, Marlene."

"Oh, Molly, Molly." She squeezed into the pew beside me. "Everywhere I go, they are asking me what you are like, squeezing me for the juicy details."

"I hope you gave them the full P. T. Barnum experience."

"No, no." She laughed. "I just told them all about the *real you*."

"And what's the real me like?"

"Look in *Grazia* if you want to know," she said, "or *Paris Match*. You are a celebrity, Molly. What are you going to do with all this fame?" Her blue eyes glittered like pebbles in a stream.

"I just want to climb on the plane, take some pill or other, and wake up in the States," I said truthfully.

Marlene pouted. "*Ach, nein! Wirklich*? That is very party pooper of you. And anyway, what about poor Quinn? Is she to languish in prison when you go?" She sure knew how to twist the knife.

"I don't know how to help her," I said pathetically. "Her dad's suddenly decided to hire this top-notch lawyer. I suppose he cares now that it's his family's reputation at stake and not just his kid's welfare. No one will let me talk to her, of course, even though I *actually* care."

She stroked my arm. "It's okay, *chérie*. Marlene understands. Of course you don't want to see her. That girl could have killed you in Les Yeux, after all."

"No. Of course she wouldn't have," I protested. "I never thought . . ."

She tutted knowingly. "I told everyone that is what you would say, because you are a true saint. But we all know she won't stop asking for

348

you from that jail cell of hers. It's obvious she just wants you close enough." Marlene mimed a stab to my guts and laughed her gravelly laugh.

"What?" I couldn't tell if she was joking or not.

"*Vraiment.* She has been asking for you. What a joke, considering you put her there. Maybe she really is insane, as they say." She twisted her finger next to her temple. "So far gone she still believes you're her aunt."

I was now haunted by a horrible image: Quinn languishing in a jail cell, as feverish and confused as the first time she woke, not knowing what was real and what was her mind playing tricks on her. "Where did you hear this, Marlene?"

"From your lover, of course, where else?" She clapped me on the back. "*Scheiße*, you really stepped on his heart, poor Valentin. He looks like a train has run him down."

"Thanks, Marlene," I said, rising from the pew to a new flurry of *Phantom of the Opera* chords. "I feel a whole lot better now."

Quinn Perkins

JULY 26, 2015

Draft Blog Entry

"You fucked me up," shouts Raphael. "It was one simple thing. Keep him busy. That was all which I asked." He slams his fist on the hood of his car, one eye still on the flow of new punters into the club, paranoid.

The scene regulars swarm in there, craving it the way addicts do. Shaking now I'm out, I bend double on the street and puke my guts out. There's not much to puke. I haven't eaten for days. Raphael turns from me, disgusted.

"You didn't tell me what you were doing," I croak. "Anyway, whatever it was is totally wrong." I puke again, like it was punctuation.

"Are you done? We need to go." He pulls open the door, the anger coming off him in waves.

"It's not as if he caught you," I say in my own defense, thinking of the way we slipped out under Séverin's nose, the thick stack of bills stuffed in my bag on top of pills and powders that—it turned out—had been in there all night, anyway. "You got away with it." I spit the last words.

"*We* got away with it," he says. "Though that doesn't mean they won't come for us."

In the car, on the road, Raphael twists a dial. A radio buzzes on, some tinny French channel crackling to life. He gives me a pill he says is for nausea and flat Coke to knock it back, lights two cigarettes, hands me one. My head lolls back on the leatherette seat and my eyes vaguely see the dusty road lit by headlights and the moon domineering over the sea. My ears half hear the crickets striking up their freaking constant song. Everything in this paradise depresses me now. *We got away with it. In it together.* Like Bonnie and goddamn Clyde. We're on the back roads again and Raphael's eyes are on the rearview mirror twice as often as the road.

I know I should run, but it's as if I've become Raphael's prisoner, trapped by my complicity in his life of crime. The new Quinn keeps drugs in her bag and acts as her boyfriend's decoy. The new Quinn has made a porno or two and eats pills like they were candy.

Raphael turns to me, scowling, says, "What was really so hard about talking to Séverin, keeping him busy for a few moments? You need . . . what is it you say?—" he taps the top of his head angrily "—a doctor to look inside the brain."

"I don't need . . . what you were doing. You still

haven't told me," I snap. It's hard to remember now what we were like before this.

"Why do you think I drive around like this all the time?" He taps his head again, as if the gesture will make me understand and regret my own stupidity. "Séverin is my boss. I work for him. Ever since Papa . . . my mother, she has sucked up every penny of what was left. That place is where my money comes from."

Blood hurtles to a stop on the highway of my heart, remembering the money he made me draw out, realizing what he truly wanted me for all along. Cash. He'll probably want more of that, of everything. More films, more help stealing from other criminals, until I'm in so deep there's no way I can ever go back.

"Stop the car," I say suddenly.

"*Quoi?*"

"You heard me. Fucking stop. Right now."

He does. I open the door and climb out in the dark and try not to freak when he gets out and follows me down the gutter that runs the length of the dusty road.

"Quinn. Quinn. Hey! Talk to me." His voice sounds needy now, appeasing.

I turn around, pulling the crumpled photo out of my pocket and letting it fall in the dust. "I just want to go home."

"Home where?"

"To the States. Where d'you think?"

Raphael's eyes widen. "You don't want to be with me? Baby, why?"

"Because you're not . . . you're not who I thought you were. I mean, the drugs are bad enough. But you made films of us, of me, to sell." Tears prick my eyes.

"No, baby, believe me, I would never do that to you. I love you so much I could never hurt you." Slowly, calmly, he edges closer, like a Samaritan inching towards a jumper on a ledge or a mon-goose creeping up on a snake.

"But Lolo said—"

"Lolo is just jealous," he says with a shrug. "Why would you believe her over me?"

Because every word out of your mouth is a lie.

But now we are face-to-face, I remember why I liked him in the first place, that childlike openness to him—not just his face, his eyes, but radiating from him somehow. Calmness that makes you calm just to be near it.

"Why don't you trust me, my love?" He touches my cheek.

I push his hand away. "What do you do for Séverin? Do you hurt people?"

He wipes his nose, avoiding my eyes. "I just . . . deliver packages . . . That's it. And sometimes I look after people, stop them from being beaten. After Papa left us, we had nothing. And now Maman has lost her job. Oh, Quinn, I'm so ashamed of myself." His eyes flood with tears.

"Don't lie. You're a drug dealer. I know you are."

"No! Stop listening to Lolo. She's a bitch. Don't let her drive us apart." He cries pitifully, wiping his face on his sleeve.

"Whatever. I still want to go home," I say, looking away.

He falls on his knees in the road. "Listen, baby, I can see you're homesick. Tomorrow, I'll help you book a ticket home. I will get some money together and pay you back as soon as I can. I'd do anything for you, believe me. You'll be safe, I promise."

Raphael is singing along to French hip-hop under his breath. I squeeze my eyes shut for a moment, not able to make sense of the things he said, the things I think might be true. I want to believe him because I don't know who else to trust.

In the alley behind the seedy apartment I woke up in, he pulls out a pack of American Spirit, asks me if I want one. "You know, there's so much I want to show you here, that will help you understand me." He says the words quietly, tentatively even. "Don't you want to know who I really am?"

I take a cigarette with a shaking hand and smoke it, the hit making me heady. I shrug.

The silence spools out between us, unknowable as any moment when we face up to our aloneness in the universe. Raphael says nothing more. Tin cans and assorted trash crumple under the vintage chassis. Shrill street talk and hip-hop are as one. The engine stills.

Raphael's hand brushes my knee, just enough to make me look around at him. "Remember," he says. "I love you." He smiles his charming smile.

Lies, I think.

"Don't you love me?" He looks sad.

My hand moves to the door handle. Grinning to hide my fear, I say, " 'Course I do." The lies falling from my lips once more.

"Don't be frightened," he says. "If they come for us now, because you didn't distract him enough, or even if the police found out, I wouldn't speak of you. Would you tell anyone about me?" His eyes flick anxiously upwards in the direction of the scummy apartment where we will sleep among other lowlifes too stoned to care what we've done.

"Your secret's safe," I say slowly, hating myself more with every word.

Molly Swift

AUGUST 9, 2015

When I first came in, Quinn didn't see me. She was sitting on a narrow metal bunk in a small cubicle that held nothing else but a metal john with no lid and a crappy folding chair. The Plexiglas screen dividing us blocked sound from the cell, but I could tell she was muttering low and crazy as a drunk at a bus station. I stared for a moment, thrown by this picture of her. What if she'd really cracked? Then I went to the side of the glass and pushed the intercom button. I tried to think of something light and cheering to say, but all I could think of was *How's the food?*

Better to say nothing at all. She turned to face me, her eyes looking stung. Even through the heavy-duty glass, I could feel the awkward vibe between us. Well, awkward didn't cover it. She got up and started to pace the cell.

When she finally spoke, the words were darts, sharp and carefully aimed at my head. "They told me you got close to me to use me."

The darts hit their mark and burned there. "It wasn't as clear-cut as that . . ." I said, lost for a way of explaining it better. However I really felt, though, there was no denying the truth of what she said. "They told me everything you said was a lie, too, so maybe we're even."

"Well, they're wrong," Quinn shot back, kicking the bunk.

A long silence rolled out between us, gray and uncertain as the coast road that wrapped around this town like a noose. I felt sick and hurt and from the looks I stole at her I was pretty sure she did, too. After a while, I looked at my watch. Four P.M. My flight left in two hours and this visit was a waste of time and emotion. I should be in a taxi by now, headed to my terminal, putting my ticket and passport in a place I'd be able to find them later. I should be waving goodbye.

As if she'd read my mind, Quinn came closer, her palms pressing on the thick glass. "I know this is weird, but I liked . . . having family . . . I mean, I know it was fake, but . . ."

"Yeah," I said, "me, too." And I meant it. "I wish there was something I could do, but it's—"

"Yeah, yeah, out of your hands." Her hands dropped from the glass. "My dad said he was coming, but in the end he just sent a lawyer instead." She rolled her eyes. "Like, thanks for your support, Dad, I guess."

"Well, maybe even if he can't help you himself—" I fidgeted with the half-empty cigarette packet in my pocket "—it's good that he knows how to help you." I gave her a lame smile that tried and failed to be reassuring.

"Whatever that means." She kicked the metal chair. It flew into the cement wall with a crash, knocking a chunk loose. The thought flashed through my head that she could be the person they said she was. I'd met killers before, seen them flit between sentimentality and rage. "Fuck it! Fuck you all. Fuck you all!" she screamed.

The guard materialized behind me and I realized he must have been hovering just out of sight the whole time, maybe listening, too.

"I guess I better go," I said, turning to him.

"Wait." The voice she spoke in was Quinn again, soft and intent through the intercom's crackle. "Please . . . come here. Just for a minute."

I did as she said, a ticklish feeling in my bones, as if I was crossing some unseen line and those four short steps foreshadowed more than I could know.

She waited until I was a hairbreadth from the cell to speak again. "I didn't do it." Her eyes held mine.

The glass between us seemed to drop away. "I believe you," I said.

Quinn smiled wryly. "You don't really. And if you do, you're the only one." She bit her cracked bottom lip.

"They will believe you. It takes time to build a case—" I began.

"Don't leave me." She pressed her hand to the glass, the pads of her fingers flattening into pale circles.

"Quinn—" I laid my hand over hers.

The door behind me swung open. In reflection, I saw two gendarmes flanking a guy in a suit and sunglasses.

"*Pardon, madame.* I think your interview is over?" It was the younger of the gendarmes who said it. Didier. Palely mirrored between Quinn and me in the layers of glass, he looked almost apologetic.

Quinn held my gaze, refusing to look beyond me to whatever was hurtling towards her next.

I turned to the gendarmes. "Would you mind if I stayed?" I addressed my words to Didier, sensing a sympathetic audience.

He shrugged and looked at the guy in the suit.

"I'd like a moment with my client." Brisk. American. This was the lawyer her dad sent.

"Quinn, this is the best . . ." I couldn't finish my treacherous sentence. I ran outside.

The flint of my pink Bic lighter had seen better days. Minutes of strumming the wheel and not even sparks would come out. I tossed it at the bin, trying for a rim shot, but the lighter just bounced off the metal lip, landing inches away, a visual representation of the current state of my karma. I leaned back on the wall of the gendarmerie with a disgusted sigh, the sun in my eyes, an unlit Gauloise hanging from my bottom lip. Italian leather squeaked a few feet away from me, footsteps bearing down from the parking lot. *Oh, great,* I thought, *the guilt-trip police.*

"Recording the next episode?" Valentin's voice dripped contempt. "Or just taking photos for Facebook?"

"It's a free country, bud." My cigarette hung limply. My soul hung limply. I didn't even want to look at him.

"What does that mean actually?" he said coolly. "A world in which you sell tickets to other people's misery, like some giant freak show?"

"It means . . ." I threw the cigarette at the bin and it didn't even bounce off the rim this time. "If I want to stay here and help Quinn, then I will."

Valentin took off his shades and looked into my eyes for a moment. He frowned a little, as if he was trying to decide whether or not to arrest me. "Okay," he began in a gentler tone, "but . . ." He stopped himself midsentence and pointed to the sad, fallen cigarette and lighter. "Just stop littering while you are here."

Molly Swift

AUGUST 9, 2015

I wasn't drinking to get drunk. It was a valid coping mechanism. Besides, where could I go except the bar? I didn't know what to do, where to look next. All I knew was, I couldn't leave Quinn, not after she said I was the only one who believed in her.

Ever since whiskey number four, the barman had been giving me that look, like, *Will I have to call someone to get rid of her?* As long as he kept topping up my drink, I didn't care. I took small sips, trying to pace myself. Against my better judgment, my eyes kept flicking back to the wall-mounted TV, a flickering magic lantern show of familiar clips and punchy sound bites about the American girl. I didn't need the sound on. Quinn's predicament was televisual wallpaper, constant and irritating and there to stay.

My whiskey glass was empty. I looked up for the barman, struggling to contort my numb lips into a charming smile. I was sloppy drunk and he shouldn't serve me. He should just get someone to roll me home . . . or somewhere. I looked up and down the bar for him and finally saw him sitting at one of the tables, eyes fixed on the TV. I waved and grinned at him, but he didn't see me. Whatever was on was clearly pretty fascinating.

When I squinted up at the TV, all I saw was the same old #AmericanGirl news story, punctuated with clips of me yelling because I had my ass stuck in a cave tunnel and a smiling family photo of Noémie, Émilie, and Raphael, captioned *Time is running out for the Blavettes*. Then the picture changed to something I hadn't seen before, new footage of microphones and flashing camera lights, a man in a suit holding his hand up to the camera. Behind his head hung the worn sign of the gendarmerie. From beneath it emerged Quinn, blinking in the false dawn of photographers' flashes.

My vision finally cleared enough to see the caption running across the bottom of the screen. *Suspect in Blavette case released from questioning, ordered not to leave country.* I let out a breath I hadn't realized I was holding. I wondered what had happened. Maybe the lawyer had found a loophole, or maybe the physical evidence had come back inconclusive. Watching the faces of the crowd as she passed by, her hand shielding her face, I suspected her troubles were just beginning, though. She may have been free for the moment, but in the eyes of the world she was still a criminal.

The clip ended with a limo driving up and the

smooth lawyer folding Quinn into a leather seat behind dark glass.

Then the item ended and the barman approached with a sigh. "*Encore?*"

I shook my head. "I need to make a phone call."

I was chain-smoking in the lobby when the elegant limo pulled up—for me this time. The driver's door opened and a man in a crisp chauffeur's uniform got out.

"Mademoiselle Swift?" He bowed very slightly in my direction.

"Guess that's still me." I grabbed the handle of my bag and started towards him.

"*Excusez-moi?*" He took off his shades. He was tanned and young and looked untouched by life's vicissitudes.

"Quinn did send you, didn't she?" I asked, momentarily paranoid.

"*Oui.*" He nodded, flashing a row of bright white teeth. He began hauling my bag into the factory-fresh well of the trunk.

About ten minutes later, the limo idled outside Mas d'Or. Between baroque twists of wrought iron, I saw the tastefully floodlit palace in its regal glory. It looked even classier at night. As the gates inched open, the dark glass obscuring the front of the limo lightened and a voice rang from a speaker hidden near my seat.

"*Nous sommes arrivés.*"

The limo swung into the driveway and my fetching chauffeur slipped out and carried my case inside. In the purple evening, soft with bats and moonlight and lovesick moths, the whole scene seemed like a fairy tale. The butler ushered me through the gleaming foyer, into the refined sitting room where Stella and Quinn sat sipping Shirley Temples. Stella rose to greet me rather more stiffly than the last time.

"Miss Perkins that was," she said crisply. "Or should I say Miss Swift?"

I smiled awkwardly, craning around to the foyer to catch sight of my bag disappearing upstairs. "You sure it's okay for me to stay here?"

"Of course," Quinn said, smiling and getting up. "Thank you for coming." She gave me a hug.

The way Stella averted her eyes you would have thought we were in the throes of a satanic orgy. She stood, coolly smoothing her linen dress. "I've a dinner to attend. Any objections if I leave you two to it?"

Quinn shook her head.

In the doorway, Stella turned her sleek head and looked austerely at us. I watched the butler fold her into her pashmina. She looked as expensively elegant as a crystal wine stem. As soon as the front door closed behind her, Quinn collapsed back into the overstuffed chair, her legs folding under her. I followed suit.

"I don't think Stella likes me," I said wryly.

"No," Quinn replied in a quiet voice. "It's not that. She just didn't really want me to bring you here. And she can be quite . . ."

"The bitch?"

"Determined," Quinn said, even laughed. "I had to talk her around a bit."

"So how'd you end up here after . . . ?" I didn't want to say *the hoosegow*.

"Well . . ." Quinn unfolded and refolded her legs beneath herself. She looked ganglier than I remembered, as if someone had stretched her out cartoon-style and pinged her back in a rubbery heap. "Dad's lawyer fixed it up for me. Stella rents out a lot of properties here, so he contacted her to see if she knew any place I could hide out while I have to . . . you know . . . stay put. He was keen for me to be somewhere with gates and cameras, somewhere the press wouldn't find me. Stella said I could stay here, which was nice considering I don't actually remember her."

"No?" I looked around the obnoxiously tasteful living room, a shiver going down my spine— the same vibe I got from the place before. "So you went to all this trouble to hide from the press and then you invited me over?"

"I thought you invited yourself," Quinn said.

"Yes, you're right. I guess I just wanted to say sorry, offer help if I could. You must blame me

365

for all this, a little bit at least?" I couldn't meet her eyes, so I stared awkwardly at the log fire crackling away in its vainglorious marble hearth.

She said nothing. Her eyes followed mine to the fire, the golden flames glittering. Eventually she said, "I remembered some things . . . while I was locked up."

She had my attention. I turned to her. "What sort of things?"

"I think I was mixed up in some pretty bad stuff." She twisted a length of hair around her finger and stuck it in her mouth. "It's kind of hazy . . . the details. I remember a dark place. Pain." She chewed hard on her hair.

"Jesus, Quinn. Are you sure that's, like . . . a real memory?"

"What, as opposed to a fake recovered one?" Her eyes flashed angrily.

"Have you told the police . . . your lawyer?"

She took another length of hair, wound it meticulously around her finger and began chewing that. "I need to know what really happened first." She dropped the hair and hugged her arms around her knees. "I'm not psychic. I mean, I'm still a suspect, I know. I have half a memory, if that. I just have . . . this feeling." She turned to me, fixing me with those green eyes, full of fire and mystery. "When you came to see me, things started coming back, as if being with you . . . I think you're the one who can help me remember the truth."

I thought about my encounter with Séverin, the warning Valentin had given me at the club. "That could be really fucking dangerous, Quinn."

"I know," she said, looking back at the fire again. "But being locked up is worse."

Quinn Perkins

AUGUST 9, 2015

Video Diary: Session 7

[Quinn sits in a white wicker chair in a taste-fully expensive white room. She looks fragile, hunched, and drums her fingers nervously as she speaks]

No chance of me sleeping, that's for sure. Not after the police and the prison and Noémie screaming and everything that's gone on. The stuff I've remembered . . . it's bad, but kind of vague. I've given Molly a password I found on my phone in Hush-Hush Calculator.

[She flicks through her phone]

This app, see? Looks like an innocent little calculator where—the app store tells me—you keep all the secret notes and pics you don't want folks to find. It was filed under "blog" because it opens up the drafts of my blog I kept private. Maybe that will help her. I refuse to look at it myself.

[Quinn puts the phone down on a side table]

Well, I, um, gave up trying to sleep a while ago and got up. It's hot, you know, but I feel cold. I walked to the window, undid the shutter, and opened it. Hey, I'll show you Stella's garden.

[She walks to the window and pans the phone around the garden]

Stella's not short of cash. Can you tell?

[Pause]

So many shadows down there, though you can just make out the white of the roses, the bench. No one there. Not that I can see, anyway. Still, I have this feeling someone is watching me. Time to close the shutters.

[Quinn fastens the latch and goes over to the bed, where she sits down]

Thought I saw something there. Out of the corner of my eye. Think it might've been a stink bug stuck on the mesh. Caught like me.

No chance of sleep. Not now.

[Quinn starts pacing, lights a cigarette]

I know this is wrong, right? But it eases the tension.

Um, there's another password I've remembered and it's for this phone. It unlocks a folder of videos, and ever since I remembered it, I've been watching them.

[Quinn picks up her phone again]

Eighteen percent, says the little battery. I can maybe watch this three or four times more before the phone dies.

[She flicks to videos]

Turning the sound low . . .

[Pressing Play, Quinn shows us a video clip, images flickering in golds and blues]

All these beach colors. California colors. Toned guys in Speedos and skinny girls in bikinis, like some dumb *Spring Break Vines* compilation. It's weird, um, watching the old me as if I were a stranger. I was so . . . loud . . . a total tomboy, straddling that guy's shoulders in the pool, playing volleyball, swearing in French, screaming as I fall in the water.

[Quinn searches for a different clip]

On to the next. So, uh, this one shows me and Raphael huddling under a beach towel, shivering. We must be cold from going in the sea, 'cause we're wet, too. Sunny day. Must've been Freddie filming, maybe? See, there's Noémie behind us. Reading her book, plugged into her iPod. She looks kinda sad. Émilie buttering a baguette, making sandwiches for us.

It's weird . . . the police kept asking if I liked them, got on with them. I mean, um, I was like, "How would I know? Did they like me?" Seems like the police think I've been a bad girl.

[Quinn stops the video]

I hate them both, those two—Raphael and the old, oblivious me. I don't even know why I'm watching these videos. I mean, what am I even looking for? A sign? A clue?

[Quinn flicks through to another clip. When she sees it, she looks shocked. She shows us the

370

phone. There is darkness and flashes of flesh and red and frightened eyes, someone sobbing and gasping for air. Quinn's hands shake as she tries to turn the clip off. When it does not, she crawls under the bed until she is hidden from view. Finally, the video ends and the sound of crying stops]

Molly Swift

AUGUST 9, 2015

Among the fragments Quinn recovered from her iPhone was a password, which she gave to me. Like the key to the forbidden room in Bluebeard's mansion, it opened up a dark space, in this case a virtual one—drafts of blog entries I hadn't seen before because she never put them online, the last few entries journaling her holiday in France, before it all went so wrong. After Quinn crawled up to bed, I sat by the dying fire and began to read about what happened after Émilie Blavette kicked her out. I had just looked at the first entry when my phone buzzed in my pocket, the sudden noise shocking me in the silent house. I fished it out.

"Bill?"

"When should I expect you, Molly?"

"I decided to stay a little longer."

He sighed. "Oh, Molly, why are you like this?"

"Like what?"

"Not happy unless you're where the drama is."

"Hmm, I can't think. Maybe because you're my substitute father figure and that's how you taught me to be."

"Oy, always with the Freud."

"We all have our foibles. Anyway, the Queen Bitch has given me a place to stay."

"The Queen Bitch?" said a voice from the doorway.

I jumped like a child caught midmischief and dropped my phone. "Evening," I said brightly. From down the side of the chair, I could hear Bill's muffled voice, "Molly, you're worrying me." My thumb groped down and dropped the call. Bill wouldn't mind. Stella walked towards me, slipping off her shoes and earrings as she went.

"Nice night?" I asked, a nervous laugh dying in my throat.

She crouched low by the fire, the slit in her linen dress opening to show a flash of expensively tanned thigh. Picking up a poker, she stoked the embers, before dropping it with a clang and curling herself into a chair. Her dark blue eyes considered me as if I were a pesky stain someone had left on one of her spotless chairs. She reached over to the polished table beside her and poured two glasses of something amber from a decanter, handing me one with such authority I didn't dare refuse.

"I didn't approve of Quinn asking you here, you know." She held her glass up. "Cheers."

"Um, cheers." I took a sip. "Fuck. This is some badass Japanese single malt."

"Good nose," she said, doing that admiring frown thing. "You were rotten to that girl, tricking her when she was at her most vulnerable. You hurt her."

I squirmed uncomfortably. I'd rather she'd hit me with the poker than another guilt trip. "Quinn knows what I did, but she still asked me here. What's your excuse?"

"I shouldn't imagine I need an excuse for being a kind host." She sipped slowly, relishing her drink.

"What did the TV stations pay for that CCTV clip of Quinn in the pool, out of interest?" It was just a hunch I was going on.

Stella's poker face was perfect. She never even flinched. "I don't believe in discussing my finances, Miss Swift. I've done some questionable things, most with good reason. It doesn't mean I'm the villain of the piece."

"Didn't say you were." I was dying for a smoke but didn't dare. It was like being in Catholic school again, with the nuns.

"But you've heard things . . . on the trusty St. Roch grapevine. Marlene perhaps?"

I sipped my whiskey to hide my knowing smile. "Whatever I heard, I heard in a professional capacity. I don't judge."

"You heard that I was having an affair with Marc Blavette under the nose of my best friend, Émilie. You heard that I broke up their marriage, destroyed their family, that when Marc disappeared everyone blamed me. You see, he was planning to leave them for me. He was gathering funds. And Marc, well, he was all charm, but he was weak and he had fallen into some very bad habits, befriended the wrong people. And when he started pressing people for money he was owed . . ." She trailed off, staring at the red shapes between clumps of burned log.

"He got deeper into trouble?"

She frowned a little, her pinched features contorting in what would have looked like sadness on another person. "I never found out the truth. I pulled myself together." She let out a bitter little laugh. "People said I was heartless, especially since Émilie was trailing her misery around St. Roch." She looked at me significantly.

"You think *she* did something to Marc?"

Stella looked at me as if I was being very stupid. "Molly, that's a tad literal, if you don't mind my saying so. This isn't murder mystery television. It's life. Might I finish?"

"Sorry. Please go on."

"What nobody saw behind her show of grief was the way she treated the children. No one except me perhaps. As a child, Noémie was always daddy's little angel, but after he left, she was too much of a reminder of Marc. She grieved for him. Émilie couldn't stand it. She made her daughter's life a misery, while Raphael could do no wrong. One child was golden, the other the scapegoat . . . and Raffi was always a charmer. Why, even as a young boy, he could . . ." She let out a girlish giggle.

"He could what?"

She rolled her eyes. "Oh, well, never mind. We had a connection. I taught him English, helped him get into the Sorbonne. I was the first to know he had a place and the first to know he'd dropped out."

"Dropped out? No one said . . ."

She shrugged. "He was the golden boy here. He wasn't about to come back and tell people to stop worshipping him. No one noticed him going the way of his father."

"Was he involved with the same people?"

She shrugged. "I don't know the details. In the end, I was the last person he would have confided in. You see, he was trying to blackmail me for rather a substantial sum of money. That is the reason I recorded the footage in the pool. I thought if he knew I had something on him, he might release me from what had become a heavy financial commitment. In the end, his scheme left me one choice: lose this house or sell my little film to the highest bidder."

I almost spat my whiskey out. "What in God's name was he blackmailing you for?"

She laughed, an eerie, high little laugh, like some forties melodrama queen going insane. "If that was the sort of thing I was willing to divulge to a journalist, do you really think the blackmail would have worked?"

Molly Swift

AUGUST 10, 2015

Stella lent us a black Buick Electra 225, the same make of car Jayne Mansfield was decapitated in. I tried not to take it as a hint. The car had been customized to reflect the needs of the times: a built-in navigation system with soothing voices that told you when you were about to fuck stuff up, and—I was pretty sure—bulletproof glass on the windows. We were headed into a different part of town, following Quinn's instinct that the things she remembered had happened there *somewhere*. So far it seemed to me that a cop car was likely to follow us at a not-so-discreet distance wherever we went.

I kept one hand on the wheel, one on the dial of the radio until I found a channel apparently devoted to the early work of Dolly Parton. Quinn was lolling in her jean shorts and Black Sabbath T-shirt, looking more like the teenager she was than I'd yet seen, one bare foot stuck out the window, the other crossed in her lap, the better to paint her nails with creamy matte polish called Siren in Scarlet.

"I don't know how you can paint them on a road like this," I said.

She did a snort-laugh. "Practice."

"Since when have you practiced painting your toenails in a Buick Electra on a French country road?"

"I have amnesia," she said, her tongue probing the corner of her mouth as she licked red over her big toenail. "How would I know?"

"Good point." A bubble of anxiety writhed up from my stomach. I hadn't yet found the nerve to relay Stella's confession from the previous night. In the short space of the morning, I'd seen Quinn pitch between depression and manic glee at small things like finding the nail polish. Her mood seemed unstable. I felt responsible for keeping her calm while we took this road trip to the dark corners of her mind.

In a falsely cheery voice, I said, "Fuck me, it's a beautiful day. The sun is shining. We have a fast car, cigarettes, and Dolly. I don't know about you, but I feel like something out of *Thelma & Louise.*"

"What's *Thelma & Louise*?" she said, nonplussed.

Still on my psycho pep squad high, I said, "An amazing film as well as a classic piece of nineties feminism. More my generation than yours, I'll admit."

She yawned and dropped a finished foot, toes spread simian-style. She picked up the other with her hands, crossed it over her leg. "What happens in it?"

"These friends go on the road to escape their shitty lives, husbands, kids, whatever. And then the younger one—Thelma—keeps getting them in all kinds of trouble."

Painting the big toe first. "What kind of trouble?"

"Well, first her husband is hitting her. Then she meets a guy in a bar and he nearly rapes her and Louise has to shoot him. Then they rob a bank and Thelma, well, she . . . romances a guy in a hotel room . . ."

"Romances? You mean fucks." She blobbed scarlet onto her middle toe.

I looked over at her, suppressing a laugh. "What, were you raised by sailors?"

Her foot dropped with a soft thud. "Stop the car."

A bubble of panic rose and popped. "What did I say?"

"Stop the car. Stop the car. Stop the car." Her hands flailed, flicking spots of scarlet on the dashboard. The nail polish rolled to the floor, glugging its blood-colored contents into a gleaming puddle.

I pulled hard into a dusty turnout. A truck sped by on my left, blaring its horn. The police cruiser slowed, then went around us somewhat reluctantly. I waved to the gendarmes as they went by, sure they would circle around and find us again.

"What is it?" Tentatively, I touched her arm.

Her skin was raised in a sharp braille of goose pimples. Shaking, she fell forward, her head between her knees. Her pale fingers clawed at her hair, raising beads of blood.

"Sweetie, stop!" I pulled her hand away from her hair and lifted her up, propping her against the seat. It surprised me how light she was, as if her bones had gradually hollowed over the last few days. Her head lolled. I smelled piss. Looking down, I saw the dark stain spreading in her shorts.

"That place. That . . . I was there. I was there!" She screamed the last word, her spine jolting her straight.

"Shhh, shhh," I said, stroking her hair. "It's okay. You're safe."

Her face turned slowly towards me, a blue vein popping on her forehead as if someone else inside were trying to break through. "No, I'm not."

Quinn Perkins

Draft Blog Entry

Raphael kept one of his promises to me at least. He took me to the Blavette house so I could pick up my stuff. He texted Noé first to make sure Émilie was out and we drove along the back roads, our eyes so busy checking in the rearview for the police or Séverin's men we never once looked at each other. *We're fugitives now,* I thought, and almost laughed. It sounded so dumb. At his mom's, he lounged out front and I borrowed his keys, the better to creep inside with. I felt like Goldilocks. Or the big bad wolf. I don't know what I'm gonna do with my stuff when I get it. Don't know if I should believe Raphael about my plane ticket. Can't help but think it would be good to get far away from here, though, if I can.

I've just packed up my room when I hear a little noise from down the hall. I freeze, listening. The sound comes again. A cough or a sob, then a steadier noise like someone crying. My heart sinks. I know at once it's Noémie and I suddenly think about the whole thing from her point of view. It was bad enough when we were all here, but now she's alone with Maman.

In her pale pink bedroom with its airbrushed ballerinas and china unicorns and Channing Tatum pinup pages torn out of teen magazines, Noémie sits on her floral bedspread. Her ballerina books are arranged in neat pastel rows on the pine shelf, the dusty classics stowed underneath: *Madame Bovary*, *Thérèse Desqueyrous*, *Dr. Jekyll et Mr. Hyde*. After my road adventures, her room seems childlike.

On top of the bookshelf, flanked by rainbow Beanie Babies and an old-school My Little Pony collectible, is a faded photo in a seashell frame. The picture inside shows a beaming, plump little girl, her shiny dark hair falling down either side of her face in long braids. Cheek to cheek with her is a man who looks an awful lot like Raphael, except stubblier, craggier, with streaks of silver in his brown hair.

I walk over to the photo. "You and your dad?"

"*Ouais*," she says, blowing her nose inside the neck of her T-shirt.

I sit down on the bed next to her. "You miss him?"

"Not really." She shrugs her skinny shoulders. "I mean, it's pretty hard to remember him. It's been a while since I've seen him."

"That's so awful. I can't imagine not knowing what happened to him. I mean, at least when my mom died, I knew the score." Awkwardly, I pat her hand.

She smiles sadly and I realize I've lost the script of life and stuff somewhere in the last few days. Reaching into my pocket, I pull out a crumpled pack of American Spirit and offer her one. She takes it, gesturing to the window. We poke our heads out. The rain has stopped and the air smells clean. There are bats flying, or maybe owls. As we smoke, we watch their progress across the mauve sky.

"I think I do know what happened to my father." Her voice has a hard edge when she says this.

"How come?"

She shakes her head, exhales. "It wasn't just like happy families and then one day, poof! Papa is gone. Things were bad for a long time before that. He had an affair and Maman thought it ended, but . . ."

I feel a chill, thinking of Raphael's bitterness about his family, this place. Thinking of my own teen years, crouching behind doors to over-hear snippets of rows, my dad's rumbling drunk logic interspersed with my mom's shrill accusations—*Tell me where you've been! How could you . . . with her? I hate you!*

"Your mom and dad were fighting?"

She nods, looks away, inhales smoke. "And now she fights all the time with me, about not eating enough or not telling her things. Sometimes it is only because I remind her of him, I think. Maman can be . . . You have noticed maybe she will go on the attack if she thinks people are leaving her."

Abandonment issues, huh? Yes, I had noticed Émilie shouting at Noé constantly and now I know why. The cogs of my mind grind. "You think she might have done something to your dad?" Is that it? Is the whole family rotten somehow?

"Sometimes. The last time I saw him was before he went to the caves and . . ." Noémie lets out a little sob, then stifles it, looks at me wide-eyed. She takes a last shaky drag, crushes out the cherry, and drops the butt. "There are other times I imagine him happy somewhere in the world with whoever she is. I dream that's how he is living now. I just wish that I knew."

I offer her another smoke. She takes it, smiles ruefully. "Quinn, listen to me. I am sorry for what I did . . ."

I rub my hand over my face. "It's okay," I say, "your mom can be kind of . . ."

"Scary." She takes a deep drag. "Raphael probably takes after her in that way."

I smoke hard, trying not to give away my own feelings on the subject. "Really, you think so?" I say guilelessly. "I'm sure he doesn't mean to be . . . scary."

She shrugs, runs a hand through greasy hair. "I

know you like him, Quinn, but you do not know him very well."

I look at her from the corner of my eyes, trying to stop my panic from surfacing. I don't know whether I should own up to what the last few days have been like, or whether she'll just go and tell him. "I know you two have your issues," I say, deflecting it back on to her.

"He has said that?" Noé sounds stung.

I try to soften my words. "Not exactly."

She crumples up like a used cigarette packet falling to the sidewalk. "I am so worried," she mumbles. "I just sometimes . . . I think my family is very broken. That everything will end . . ."

"End . . . ?"

"Badly, you know. Something terrible will happen, like it did to Papa."

I put my arm around her shoulders and give her a little squeeze. "You know, I thought that a lot . . . after my mom . . . that I would just stop existing. Or my dad would. I dunno . . . I think it's just how you feel after a train hits your life. It'll be okay."

She looks up at me with big, brown, wistful eyes. "I do like you, Quinn. A lot. If things had been somehow different I think we would be good friends."

"That was my fault probably," I say, reflecting on how my crush on Raphael clouded my judgment of everything here.

She smiles a big, toothy smile and I see something that I've never really noticed in her before—the kid sister, just wanting approval. "Let me show you something."

On her bedroom wall is a big picture frame with lots of photos of kids our age. They are ranged around a map and their faces are labeled with their names and cute little bios and arrows pointing to where on a map of the world they came from.

"These are all the other ones that came. There were exchanges from all over the world: Russia, China, Ireland, Pakistan, Belgium, Ukraine. There's Dushka and Ruth and Sita and Gemma. Gemma was so nice," she says, stroking the face of a pretty red-haired girl.

"The other ones? Exchanges?"

"Yeah, they always came from so far away and I would be friends with them for a while, go to the pool and be happy, enjoy the sun. And then the same thing would always happen. They would like Raphael and Maman would get really mad. And then they always go away from me. This happens every time. By the time you came, I didn't even really want to make friends because I knew I would lose you in the end. Oh, Quinn, I'm so lonely. And so afraid. I just want it to stop."

A tingle of *the fear* again. "What happened to them?"

She doesn't answer. Her eyes are wide, focused on a point behind my head.

I spin around, expecting to see Émilie, but it is Raphael who stands there, his dark eyes unreadable. He stands in the doorway for . . . I don't know . . . ten seconds. Thirty. Ninety. His face goes dark. His whole expression changes and he looks as demonic as something out of the legends of Les Yeux. Just for a second or two. And then his lips split into that Colgate grin, the one it's impossible to resist.

"Having fun, *mes filles*?"

I smile a little nervously. "Just saying goodbye," I say.

He grabs me by the waist, leans me low and kisses me, like we're the doomed leads of a film noir. When he's finished kissing me, he looks at Noémie and she looks at him and I look away, because there's some weird vibe between them.

"Everything is ready," says Raphael.

"Ready?" I say.

"Your bag is in the car."

I smile nervously and I don't know why. I don't know why I am so scared.

"Well, kiss Noé goodbye," he says.

I turn to her and pull her close, noticing as I kiss her cheek that she is trembling. We hold each other close for a moment. Then she kisses my other cheek and the first one again, southern French–style, and whispers in my ear, a warning for me only.

"Take care."

Molly Swift

AUGUST 10, 2015

We stood in the street, looking up at a bland apartment building. This was the place Quinn had directed us to, seeming to feel her way by some magnetic force rather than exactly remembering it. The closer we came, the more rigidly she sat, hands nervously scratching her thighs until it was hard to believe that an hour before she'd been painting her nails and cracking jokes at my expense. Just before we got here, I'd channeled my inner Steve McQueen and managed to slip the police detail, but now I wondered if that was so smart, after all.

"You sure this is the place?" I asked, casting a nervous glance at the quiet street stretching on either side.

Quinn nodded mutely and reached for my hand. We rode the lift up to the tenth floor. The fluorescent tube light flickered on and off, pulsing between darkness and a vision of our ghost selves back to front in the smeared mirror. Apart from the sound of the pulleys hoisting us skywards, the building was eerily silent—no radios blaring or children laughing or even the sounds of people arguing. As I thought about it, there hadn't been many people outside either. In the mirror, I saw the hollows of Quinn's eyes, but not the expression in them. Behind her head, vivid fronts of graffiti unfurled like horns. In the momentary darkness, I saw her again, running through the caves, a whisper in the darkness ahead.

I touched her hand. "Who took you here, Quinn?"

She looked at me strangely. "Raphael."

All down the corridor with its peeling paint, Quinn walked like a small, broken robot, eyes straight ahead, feet moving just a little slow. Disconnected from the world until she found door number twelve. Then she stopped. The door was open a crack.

"This one?" I asked, as if anywhere else in the building showed signs of life.

She nodded. "Why don't you film it?"

I shrugged. "Okay." Who was I to argue after all that I'd already filmed? I went to Video on my phone and pressed Record, pushing the door open with the toe of my boot. We tiptoed in, past the grotty kitchen, the lino blackened with mold and half ripped from the floor, the stove scattered with cigarette butts. The place had been abandoned for a while by the look of things.

I turned to Quinn. "You okay, kiddo?"

She didn't answer. I touched her arm.

She jumped as if I'd burned her and turned from me. "In here," she said hoarsely.

I followed after her through the doorway. Pressed close in the half dark, I could hear the raspy catch in her throat. We came into a small, dark room with a single bed. Sheets of torn paper lay on the floor around it, along with pages torn from porn magazines. Quinn crossed the room and perched on the edge of the bed. She stroked the mattress as tenderly as she might touch a lover. "He brought me here." She looked up at me, her eyes wide.

"Why?" I said, even though I could guess.

"He stayed here sometimes," she said listlessly, as if the words didn't mean much of anything, "after his college kicked him out." She flicked a nervous glance up at me. "We smoked a bit." She gulped. "I think there were other people, too, and we drank, took pills, danced. I can remember it seemed like fun for a while."

She stared at the window, where one clean square of sky hung like a topaz amid the grime of old newspaper pasted to the glass. That bright square shone down on the sad scene and made it all somehow bleaker.

I looked for an equally clear spot on the boards in front of her, knelt down, and looked up at her. "What happened next?"

She frowned, her eyes flicking to the right, straining to remember.

"He said we should play a game. He really liked games." She broke off, rubbing her face so hard I thought she would scratch it again. I pulled her hand away. She stared at me, suddenly intent. "It was kind of like strip poker . . ." Her eyes blurred. She looked up at the topaz square. "And we were just messing around, snapping pictures of each other . . . and that was when I noticed it."

"What?"

"The wall." She pointed behind my head.

I turned around and it was hard to believe I hadn't noticed it before. Taped all over it like wallpaper were photos of girls, some blurred close-ups, smiling or blowing kisses, others more intimate, topless or nude, posing as if they were auditioning for a men's magazine. On some of the photos were words written in Sharpie pen. Taking a step closer, I saw that each photo had a caption: *The Russian Girl, The British Girl, The Italian Girl.* I let my eyes scan over the wall, looking for another photo I thought might be there. It didn't take me long to find it. Quinn stared at the camera, smiling vaguely, her eyes heavy-lidded, half aware. In another she sat cross-legged on the floor. This one was captioned in Sharpie like the rest: *The American Girl.*

"It's like he was collecting them," I said, half to myself.

"He said I was special, that he loved me," said Quinn, staring at the photos. "But it was just what he said to all of them . . ."

"Some of them look . . . kind of familiar," I said, peering at the wall.

"Some of the others were exchanges, too." She walked up to the wall and touched a photo of a girl with red hair. "Gemma . . ." She went to another. "Ruth."

I remembered where I'd seen them before: a bunch of photos in Noémie's room at the Blavette house, a cheerful map of cultural exchanges, little bios glued underneath.

"The weird thing is that we all must have come in this room at some time or other, but we were all too out of it to notice each other."

"Too stoned on pills," I said, thinking back to her blog.

"Too in love," she added bitterly, kicking the papers around our feet.

One landed on my shoe. I bent down and picked it up. It showed a crude drawing of a dinosaur shaded in Biro, the way you might do a doodle in the middle of a boring class. Looking closer I saw a list scrawled in blocky writing. My French was just good enough to guess at it.

- Play the game
- Take the photos
- Collect the money

The last item grabbed my attention. *Collect the money.* Stella Birch had told me Raphael was blackmailing her, though she wouldn't say why. I translated the scribbled title: *Things that will un-fuck the situation.* This was Raphael's planning document.

I made a pile of everything on the floor and stuffed it into my bag. There might be something in here that would lead us further along the trail. One page gave me pause: a photo was stapled to it. Well, two halves of a photo, torn in the middle. It was old and crumpled, but I'd seen it before at the Blavette house—the Blavette family before Marc left. It was easy to recognize them, even though Émilie and Noémie had their eyes scribbled out until they looked black and Marc had big fat tears drawn onto his face. Across the bottom of the photos, *assholes* was written in big block letters.

"This is disturbing," I said, pointing at the photo.

She took it from me. "Yeah, he really hated his family," she said. "He blamed them for everything that was bad in his life."

Molly Swift

AUGUST 10, 2015

Everyone loves a carnival, though the masquerade drowning the streets of St. Roch in glitter wasn't a true Mardi Gras affair after a grueling Lenten fast. It was just thrown to keep the tourists happy and the costume salesmen in work.

Still, it was pretty. There was carnival royalty in gold masks and peacock feather cloaks, mermaids on floats, bare midriffs gleaming from iridescent plastic fish scales, and fifty-foot clowns farting fire. Only we weren't in the mood. The masked, grinning world danced past us as we slouched over a sidewalk café table nursing cherry sodas like it was our last meal on this earth.

It felt as if we were a 78 record playing at 45. Everyone else was fast, hard, hilarious, laughing at us from behind rented masks. Leather-clad boys with the faces of devils whirled streamers in our faces. Stilt-clad street jugglers bent low to mock us. Buskers playing Beatles hits on their acoustic guitars were simply oblivious to the gallery of conquests we had seen in the empty apartment and what those photos meant. Neither Quinn nor I knew where those girls were now.

I couldn't guess what Quinn was thinking. She stared at the revelers as if they were extras in some confusing foreign film, as if human beings suddenly made no sense at all. Maybe they didn't.

She slipped to the bathroom often, and judging from her red eyes when she returned, she was going there to cry. Each time she disappeared, I fished furtively in my bag and pulled out another of the papers. So far, I'd managed to work out that Raphael had been living in that place ever since he was kicked out of the Sorbonne a year before. He clearly dealt drugs from there for Séverin, too. Séverin's name was mentioned in the notes along with people called Bruno and Léon. His scribbled lists and doodles—organized like a hypermanic double-entry bookkeeping system—showed his incomings and outgoings in a sort of code that I'd sort of deciphered. There were symbols standing in for types of drugs, accounts settled, and people in debt. On other pages were lists of names, including some of the girls on the wall.

The list gave me the overwhelming urge to go home and wash my hands about a hundred times and never go out into the world again. But I knew this nauseous feeling was the feeling of having found something that might help Quinn, maybe other people, too. A sigh at my elbow made me look up. I didn't know how long Quinn had been sitting there, reading over my shoulder.

Her face looked ten years older than it had that morning. I folded the papers and stuffed them in my bag.

"No, don't," she said. "I need to know. Can I?" She took the papers, holding them tentatively. "Is this . . . ?"

I nodded my head. "It's stuff from Raphael's business."

"What . . ." Her voice was tight. "What was he doing in there?"

"I think that was a place he went to sell drugs and stuff."

"And these?" She ran her finger over the lines of writing as if she might find Raphael there.

"I think it's something to do with those—"

"Wait." She held up her hand, her face trembling feverishly. "I know this one." Her finger jabbed at a line of writing so hard I thought it would tear through the paper.

"Sixty-six rue de Rivoli?"

She nodded. "I think we should go there."

"Okay, but not tonight. It's late and we need some sleep."

"Sleep?" She laughed bitterly and grabbed up her cherry soda as if it was liquid peace of mind and tipped it back. A single drop rolled onto her outstretched tongue.

"I'll getcha another one." I winked at the waiter who was buzzing about in his black apron. "*Garçon*?"

A man at the table in front of us twisted around. He had on a red mask with a long, phallic nose and high cheekbones. "Fairly certain the waiters here don't appreciate that." He grinned. His accent was crisp and English. His eyes flicked to take Quinn in. Even though they were partly hidden by his mask, the look of prurient interest that suddenly filled them was unmistakable. "Why, I'll be damned. It's the . . ."

"Come on," I said, grabbing Quinn's wrist. "We'd better go."

The dick-nosed man had alerted his companion, a fellow in a gold cat mask with long, jeweled fangs. "It is! It's that American bitch."

More people turned around. Of course they all spoke English in this carnival town, this holiday mecca. Of course they'd all seen us on TV. Everyone in the world had. We worked our way between the tables, turning our hips sideways to squeeze past chairs, knocking over empty glasses and toppling cutlery. People turned to complain. Some had their phones out and were pointing them at us. The waiter, all ears now, rushed over with the check in his hand.

"I've done it!" I cried, pointing at the table with its scatter of coins. "I've paid."

Someone tugged at my shirt. I spun around to see an old guy, a benign, smiling granddad type. "Say cheese, honey!" He grinned, snapping a photo.

Quinn fell against me. I half carried her into the street, but as soon as we got there, a flash went off in our faces.

"How do you feel about the result of the bail hearing, Quinn?" A woman shoved a mike in our faces.

"Fuck off," I snarled, whisking her away from them and running towards the river of masked faces.

In the manic crowd, I thought we were free of them, but every time I glanced around, all I saw were cameras pointed at us. Finally, we slipped down a cobbled alleyway where the walls were barely shoulder-width apart. Music trickled from an open door. I saw darkness inside.

"Good enough for me."

When we were safely inside and Quinn asked for something stronger than cherry soda, I didn't say no. We drank our Cherry Bs and bourbon in the noisy dark of the roughest dive in town. Grubby guys propped up the bar and from time to time they tried to talk to us. I leered back. We'd already made all the wrong choices, Quinn and I. There were no worse ones left to make.

Molly Swift

AUGUST 11, 2015

Like most people my age, I've been a teenager. In those heady times, I learned many things: to drive a car, to smoke a range of substances, and to dress like my friends and do whatever they told me. When I was done with band camp and its sequel, delinquency, I learned the most important lesson of all: how not to be an asshole. Quinn has yet to study this most vital element in the curriculum of life. Though in the current circumstances, I couldn't really fault her for rolling out of bed in our rented fleapit room and telling me to fuck off, or stealing my cigarettes and locking herself in the bathroom for eternity.

"But I need to pee," I pleaded.

"Go away," she said calmly.

I figured she'd be in there awhile, enough time for me to buy cigarettes, anyhow. Working at speed, I pulled on my jeans and sneakers. I ran down to the street, where I spotted a café just opening, and dodged a large lamb kebab that a vendor was chasing down the middle of the road to get to it. A weary man let me in the door with minimal protest and seemed not to care when I bolted to the bathroom. Squatting over the porcelain before my bladder burst, I realized how very few fucks I gave about stuff that would have alarmed me a week before. Maybe that youthful wilderness training did me some good, after all.

I walked back into the café and leaned over the bar to order a double espresso and a packet of Gauloises Blondes. The barman looked me up and down with a curious leer and I discovered I was wearing a white strappy tank top with no bra and that my nipples were plainly visible. I couldn't help but laugh.

"Yeah, I wore this to my prom," I said.

"Well, I wish I had been there that night." The voice behind me sent lightning bolts to my brain. I spun around. "Valentin?"

"It is nice to see you, Molly Swift."

"Really. That's not what you said last time," I said, starting to walk away.

"Maybe I was a little mad."

I sighed. He'd been pretty mean the last few times I'd seen him, but I guess I'd kind of deserved it. Also, I needed him on my side right about then.

We sat at an outdoor table and I kept one eye on the door of the fleapit hotel in case Quinn tried to make a run for it.

"Stalk much?" I asked, smiling at him.

He chuckled. "It is very simple actually to track

your phone. You should beware when using Google Maps, for example."

"Um, okay," I said, feeling a bit freaked out.

"Hey, I'm just saying. You're playing detective, poking around. Be careful. Don't be a sitting duck."

I bristled. "Is that what you came here to tell me? *Watch out, little girl . . .*"

He sighed. "You think I am being like a dad."

I looked him up and down—his khaki pants with the crease at the front, his button down oxford and panama hat. "Don't you?"

"Perhaps I just wanted to see you," he said softly.

"Maybe you should call next time."

"Sure. I will." He sipped his coffee for a moment. "Fancy a quickie? Then at least my trip wouldn't be wasted."

I snorted a laugh. "Actually, there is something." Scrabbling in my pocket, I found the crumpled sheet of paper with the addresses written on it. "We found this in an abandoned apartment near here. It's some list of Raphael Blavette's. That one there." I pointed to the one that Quinn nearly put her finger through. "I wondered if you could check it out for me? She wants to go there, but I don't want to just walk in if it's—"

"Dangerous?" He raised an eyebrow. "Do you know what you're doing, Molly?"

"Helping a friend," I said firmly.

He stared at the paper dubiously. "And if this address is important to the investigation, to finding the Blavettes?"

"Then I know you'll hand it on to the right people."

"I'll do what I can." He folded the paper and tucked it into his breast pocket, then lit a cigarette.

"How are things going with the investigation now?"

"Same, I guess." He exhaled, his eyes avoiding mine. "They looked in the caves again. Found nothing again. That's pretty much all I hear."

"Is Quinn still . . ."

"A suspect?" He frowned. "They do not have anything solid but they have quite a few circumstantial things. I cannot tell you more than that."

I nodded, trying to take in what he was saying without getting too freaked out. I decided to change tack a little. "Is it weird to be so far away from it when you were so close to it?"

He shrugged. "The minute they found out I was seeing you, I was off the case for sure. And when they found out you'd pulled the wool over my eyes, that went double."

Batting my eyelashes, I said, "Aren't you mad at me, for messing up your job?"

He laughed. "I was, but finally I realize I got

the better deal . . . no work and the hottest lay."
He leaned over and kissed my cheek.

"Ever the charmer."

He pulled me close for a moment. When we drew apart, his eyes were sad. He stroked my cheek with his thumb. "I said a lot of bad things to you that I did not mean, but I said one thing to you when we were in the hotel that I did."

I was embarrassed to feel tears sting my eyes. "Me, too."

"But you never said anything." He took my hand and kissed it. "Am I just your holiday romance?"

"You pass the time."

He cleared his throat. "About this paper, this address. I'm going to check it out, see what is what. Then I will call you and tell you it is nothing to worry about, just a normal house. Then you can stop feeling stressful, okay?" He leaned forward, twisting a lock of my unkempt hair around his finger. "You really are sure about helping Quinn Perkins? I know they've not arrested her, but she's still—"

I stopped his lips with my finger. "She's just a kid."

He kissed me once more and then he was gone, his panama hat dissolving into the sunlit hustle of the street.

Molly Swift

AUGUST 11, 2015

It took a quart of coffee to jolt Quinn from her slump. I felt for her, enough that I knew the last thing she wanted was embarrassing grown-up empathy. We grabbed croissants from a *boulangerie* and it felt like a huge victory when she took a few grudging bites of one. It was such a relief to find Stella's car in one piece and graffiti-free that I sent up a little prayer of gratitude, hurling the keys into the well, hearing the smooth voice of the navigator guiding me forward.

And this time we really needed it. Quinn didn't seem to recognize the streets or houses as we wound our way around the suburbs to the wrong side of the tracks. Driving through an industrial estate, flanked by juddering trucks and anonymous white vans, I wondered if the address even meant anything at all, especially when we pulled up in front of a row of blank-eyed storage units, their metal shutters pulled down, their prefab concrete frames squat and identical.

"You think this is it?" I asked, flicking my gaze between Quinn and the navigation, dinging its praise that I'd managed to reach the checkered flag.

Quinn looked a little bit frightened. "I don't know."

"You recognize anything . . . on the way, or here?"

She shook her head. She looked miserable now and I couldn't help but feel sorry for her. I could tell she wanted this to be the end of it all, the key to the mystery that would simultaneously solve the missing-persons case, unlock her lost memories, and clear her name. I wanted that, too, and I felt the tug of disappointment in my gut, the sense that our quest had hit a cul-de-sac.

"Well, only one way to find out." The car lighter popped out with a beep to punctuate my thoughts. I lit up a Gauloise and opened the door.

I'd just locked the car when my phone buzzed in my pocket. Valentin.

"Hey. You find anything?" I asked hopefully.

"Yep. Anything and also nothing."

"How d'you mean?"

"I checked it on the computer and I drove by and took a look, too. It's literally nothing, an empty lot." I could hear the sound of him inhaling cigarette smoke, exhaling coolly. He sounded sure he had his facts straight. "Yeah, babe. Nothing to worry about."

I said nothing, leaning against the side of the

car, its warmth ticking out of it, just looking at the place, wondering if he'd even checked it out for me. It might not be the right place, but it was sure as hell not an empty lot.

"So anyway, I thought I'd call, save you a trip. Maybe Quinn thought she remembered something and . . . you know . . . the mind is a tricky place."

"Yeah, I know," I said, glancing at Quinn. Perhaps she was wrong, after all.

"Bye, *chérie*, love you." His voice sounded far away.

If there's one thing a survivalist childhood teaches you, it's how to pick locks. As a kid, I did nothing more useful with this skill than break into the padlocked sheds and outbuildings of the farmers who encroached on my dad's Emersonian independence. Once in, I'd consider how best to sate my desire for petty delinquency, my options ranging from stealing fertilizer with which to mix my own backyard explosives to "rescuing" any neglected-looking livestock I found. Perhaps breaking into places in order to solve crimes was my weird way of making amends.

Inside, the place was bigger than I'd imagined, a long room with dull cement walls and a concrete floor that tapered into darkness beyond the light falling under the shutter.

"Smells weird . . ." said Quinn, shivering.

"Yeah," I said, breathing through my mouth. "Remember this place?"

Quinn shook her head and folded her arms across her chest protectively. "Maybe you should film it again? In case we find something . . ."

I frowned. She seemed big with the video thing these days. I pressed the Record button, anyway, to humor her if nothing else. "Want to wait in the car while I look around?"

She shook her head. "It's so dark. You think there's a light?"

I groped along the edge of the wall. Somewhere out of sight was the drip-drip of a leaky tap, slow and sad. A grimy switch hung from frayed wires. I pressed the buttons. Fluorescent lights flickered on with a metallic plink, lighting the room about halfway. I tried another switch, but the end of the room remained dark. There wasn't much to see, anyway. I panned the phone's camera across a few piles of boxes stacked against the walls. From one I pulled a cheap china cup with a sketch of the castle and *Visit St. Roch* written on it. I checked another box. The same.

"Tourist tat," I said. "This place just looks industrial, don't you think?"

Quinn took my hand. "I think we should look down there." She pointed into the dark half of the room.

"Sure," I said, trying to sound casual. "There won't be anything there, though. I mean, it just looks ordinary, doesn't it? Unless that stuff is crack cleverly disguised as cups."

Quinn didn't answer. The further we walked, the more out of it she looked.

"Quinn?"

"Noémie. She came here, too," she said with that blank, wide-eyed stare that told me she was remembering something.

Slowly my eyes adjusted to see what lay beyond the light, though at first I saw it in fragments. Beside me, I felt Quinn quivering, her flesh shaking so hard it barely looked solid or anything more than a moth's wing fluttering in the gloom. Slowly the outlines of small objects came clear: the spiky feet of a tripod, the gleam of a camera's glass eye. That's when I knew what the place was for.

"Quinn, I think you should . . ."

She was already running towards the shutters. I heard the sound of her retching on the sidewalk.

Quinn Perkins

JULY 27, 2015

Draft Blog Entry

U left passport, says the text from Noémie that wakes me. *Come 2day.*

Weird, I think . . . I cast my mind back to the house, my room, clean and neat and swept of all my stuff. *Weird,* I think again, sneaking out of bed to rummage in my suitcase in the gloom of the scabby bedsit that's become our temporary home.

I scrabble around, frantic, trying to be quiet. I check under the mattress, in Raphael's jean pocket in case he took it. It's gross here. There are pictures of girls on the walls. Naked ones. It stinks of weed and urine. Feels like the cops might raid it at any moment. Shit! The passport is nowhere.

I have a paranoid thought. Could Noémie have stolen it so that I wouldn't pack it, so that I'd have to come back? But why?

I talk Raphael into dropping me there to pick it up. It's not that hard. He has stuff to do and doesn't seem to want me with him, anyway. He drops me a few minutes down the road and tells me he'll come get me in an hour or so.

When I reach the Blavette house, I knock, but there's no answer, so I try the front door handle. The door swings open easily. I creep through the house, up the stairs.

Noémie's in her pink princess bedroom, sitting on the edge of her neatly made bed. She's dressed in black, skinny jeans and black sneakers, a black Metallica T-shirt that must have been Raphael's or her dad's. I have the ridiculous thought that she's dressed like a ninja.

As I come closer and the sun moves out of my eyes, I see that she has a black eye to match her outfit.

I sit on the bed next to her, my hand on hers. "Who did this to you?"

She presses her finger to her lips, reaches into her back pocket, and pulls out my passport, handing it to me. Then she says, "There is something I need to show you."

On soft feet, we cross the hallway. Downstairs, Émilie's shoe leather squeaks as she moves around. We pause, listen to the rush of water pouring from the faucet, the clink of cups. Noémie flinches at each noise. I can almost feel the knobs of her spine drawing tight. We come to it, then, the forbidden door, the one Émilie said I am never to open.

Noémie pulls out an old key, dark with age. She slips it in the lock, which clicks open too loud. She cocks her head, listening, then her hand grasps the handle, slipping around because of the sweat on it. It doesn't turn. She jiggles it. The metal squeaks, stiff from underuse. My heart beats faster, louder, more insistently than a biblical plague of cicadas. It's all I can hear in the silence of the house.

I hear a noise coming from the floor below, like the sound of shoe leather squeaking, moving from the kitchen to the stairs. My calm New Quinn self takes over. The one that steals and lies. I move Noémie aside and turn the handle all the way to the right. The door gives way onto thick darkness. The stairs creak below us, the noise moving closer. We slip through the door and I close it behind me, wondering how long it will take Émilie to work out which door we went through. Despite the gloom of the Blavette house, it takes a moment for my eyes to adjust to the deeper darkness of the Old Schoolhouse.

"Keep moving," says Noémie, pulling on my sleeve.

We stumble on along the corridor, where the shutters are closed against the summer light. I listen for the door opening behind me, but hear nothing. My phone buzzes in my pocket and I duck into a classroom to silence it.

Raphael: *Done here. Where are u?*

One sec, I text, and stuff the phone back in my pocket, knocking my hip on a desk as I head out of the classroom.

From the dark gape of an open door at the far end of the corridor, Noé's eyes meet mine.

"*Vite*," she whispers.

I sprint to her, hitting a race stride—"using the fear," as Coach used to say. When I reach her I take her hand and squeeze it. Let Émilie come after us. We will run.

So we go, through the beige doors with their graph paper glass that whip up a dust cloud in our wake. In the dark stairwell, I grip onto the banister, feeling my way down. We are on the ground floor now, pushing forward on autopilot. From where we stand, I see big double doors where the daylight streams in, where the graph paper glass slices squares of sun onto the dusty floor.

It's padlocked. No way out.

A clock ticks on the wall above us, marking down the minutes. I look at Noémie. She looks back at me and I see how swollen and red her eye is, how broken she looks. She takes my hand and guides me towards a half-open door. She smoothly unfastens it and shimmies through the door. I follow. Inside is a computer room, a bank of dusty PCs that must have been abandoned when the school was closed.

"What's this?" I say, panicked. "There's no way out."

She puts her finger to her lips again. "Shhh, come sit." She pulls out one of the wheeled office chairs and sits down.

My ears strain towards the door, ready to hear footsteps in the corridor outside. She pulls me down onto the chair next to her and switches on the Jurassic era PC. It boots up noisily, all flashing lights and humming hard drive.

"Noémie, we don't have time for this."

She says nothing. The PC blinks and judders to life. Noémie takes out her phone, scrolling through the apps until she gets to photos. She hands the phone to me. It shows a screen-grab of a Snapchat conversation. Well, not quite a conversation—just two Snapchats to me, a video, and a text.

I take the phone from her, hands shaking. "How . . . how did you get this?" But I already know the answer.

"I sent those texts to you and the video," she says distractedly, her hand on the mouse, rolling the cursor across the screen to a folder sitting on the desktop. *Mes filles*, it says. She double-clicks on it, her eyes turning to me, one bruised closed, the other wide open. "I was so afraid of getting in trouble if anybody found out what I know, what my family has done. I could not just tell you face-to-face . . . but I had to warn you."

Before the first file opens, I know what I'm going to see next. I wish I could close my eyes.

Molly Swift

AUGUST 11, 2015

If I'd expected the police to be grateful somehow, to pat me on the head for my excellent
detective work, I would have been wrong. As it
happened, I'd phoned them on autopilot while
Quinn crouched on the pavement beside me, her
arms wrapped around her knees. A couple of
officers came and poked around the place and
took statements. I pointed out the camera and
the mattress, told them the hunch that had
brought us there, and showed them the pages of
Raphael's journal.

They looked at my clutch of grubby notes as if
I were a child handing them a crayon drawing
and listened to my story in the same spirit.
Throughout, I could sense their hostility, seeing
Quinn there. I tried to keep her out of it, which
wasn't hard because she refused to say any
more, even to repeat what she'd said about
Noémie being there.

It was frustrating. When I'd seen the video
camera—so obviously rigged up for making films
of his hapless girlfriends—and Quinn's reaction,
I'd been sure this was the detail that would
break the case. Looking around with the

gendarmes, I could see I was wrong. Whoever had been using the place had been very careful to leave no evidence of their identity behind.

"Will you at least check out who rented the place?" I asked.

The gendarme taking notes frowned at me. "I thought you said this was your unit, that you were reporting a break-in?"

"No," I said. "I mean, I know my French is bad, but I thought I made it pretty clear I was handing over important evidence in the Blavette case."

"So it was you two that broke in?" he asked incredulously.

The police commissariat on rue Gargoulleau was an old stucco building, foursquare and wicked to the eyes of thieves like us. We sat in a small room with flaking red paint on the walls. We'd be very lucky, the policewoman who took my revised statement said, if whoever owned the place didn't press charges. Sitting at a plastic table, waiting for Valentin to come and talk us out of the trouble I'd gotten us in, I felt eight years old again: the time Tommy Lutz and I scrawled all the bad words we knew on the sidewalk in chalk, and I spent the rest of the week convinced Tommy would narc on me and I'd go down for it and be thrown in Sing Sing for life.

On the plus side, I had time to dwell on why the lockup seemed significant. As the police kept pointing out, it was just a lockup with a mattress in it. Maybe someone had been sleeping in it—so what? It was all so frustrating. We'd finally found something that might help with the Blavette case. Quinn had remembered nearly enough to go on, and nobody believed us. If only they'd seen the way Quinn reacted to that room, they'd believe there was a connection.

That last thought gave me an idea. If my videos had hurt Quinn before, maybe they could help her now. Keeping my phone under the table in case one of the angry policemen came in again, I put the two videos in an email to Bill. Luckily, I'd photographed Raphael's notes before I handed them over, so I sent those, too, along with my thoughts on what had been happening. Right before I pressed Send, I remembered the card that Aurelia Perla had given me. Her email address was on there. I copied her in for good measure. Bill might not be able to get anything together in time, but that woman looked like a trash-news pro.

Through all this, Quinn sat, catatonic, her head turned towards the half-open window of the stuffy room. Outside in the street, there was reggae music playing: the masquerade swinging into its second day. It sounded so festive, so happy, the voices of people just enjoying their lives.

Molly Swift

AUGUST 11, 2015

Valentin drove us to Stella's house without speaking. The radio was on, the top ten, then the news headlines, a local interest item about mountain hamsters as far as I could tell from the chirpy DJ joking and kidding around with the day's guests. He wouldn't even turn to look at me, though sometimes I caught a glimpse of his eyes reflected in the rearview mirror, watching me. I got the feeling it had cost him a lot to get us out of there.

We turned into the drive of Mas d'Or. The mansion rose up like a pale face, its eyes half shuttered. As soon as the car stopped, I tugged at the door handle and got out. Like some kind of movie montage, I saw the sunshine and the sea stretching out all around, the roses twining the pergola. It seemed surreal after all that had happened. Quinn, her eyes blank, her lips still sealed, got out and walked inside the house. I was about to follow her when Valentin caught hold of my arm.

"I don't think you should be doing this, Molly. If you poke a stick in a nest of the hornets like this, the bees they will sting you. It always happens."

I tried not to laugh at the weirdness of his metaphor, especially after all I'd put him through that afternoon. "The bees, from the hornet's nest? You were the one who said there was nothing at that lockup. I found things, important things. No one believes me, so who else is supposed to poke the stick or whatever?"

"*I* believe you," he said, his jaw tightening. "I just worry about what you are getting involved with."

"Like what?" I asked defiantly.

He shook his head. "Staying here will not do you good. I mean, take a look at you. You seem to have some sentimental feeling for Quinn, but she is okay. She is free. And remember, she is not your niece, after all."

"Valentin, I'm a journalist. And this here—" I pointed vaguely in Quinn's direction "—is a story. So as far as you're concerned I'm just like any other hack in this town, following leads, writing words, grubbing for a paycheck. Okay?"

He rubbed his fingers over the bridge of his nose in that familiar gesture. "So you are not going to stop this goose chase?"

"No."

"Then what is the next place on your list?"

"The hospital," I said, "to see Noémie."

He bit his lip, rubbed his nose again. When he finally spoke, his voice was hoarse with emotion. "There will be a big search in the caves tomorrow, early. The locals are helping this time and we hope . . . They want me to be there, but I can meet you at the hospital afterwards, perhaps two o'clock?"

"Okay," I said, "as long as you don't interfere."

"Interfere? You are infuriating, truly." He pulled me close and kissed me. I felt his hands on my back.

Out of the corner of my eye, I thought I saw a flicker, as if someone pale and silent was watching us from the darkness of the doorway, but when I looked, there was no one. I pulled away. "Look, I'll see you tomorrow at two."

Valentin straightened his panama hat and drove off without another word.

Stella looked stricken when I told her the Jayne Mansfield Buick was parked down a side street in the seedy part of St. Roch. She dispatched her chauffeur and butler to retrieve it and I escaped upstairs to take a bath and avoid further recriminations. I'd just filled the tub to the brim and scattered in some of Stella's hundred-dollar organic bath salts when Bill called.

"Wow," was all he would say for the first five minutes.

"I know," I said, climbing into the tub, my thighs turning instantly pink.

"I mean, that's . . . Jesus, I didn't see the story going that way."

"I know." I sank down into the neck-deep bubbles.

"We can't use it all." I could hear him nervously scratching his comb-over. "I mean, we can use some of it . . ."

"You didn't hesitate to use the first video. This one will be just as good and maybe it will persuade people that Quinn is innocent."

"It's kind of scrappy, Molly . . ." I heard him take off his glasses and polish them.

"Bill, listen. I'll have more by tomorrow."

"Molly." Bill's voice was stern. "What are you going to do? I mean, shouldn't you leave it to the police now? This Séverin person you mentioned in your email sounds dangerous."

"I'm not going to do anything stupid. I just . . . if Quinn wants to stop this now, I'll stop. But if she wants to keep on . . . I mean, this guy she was involved with was sick. I can't see her put in prison when there was clearly more to it."

Molly Swift

AUGUST 12, 2015

I woke up bleary in my room at Stella's to find that Quinn's bedroom was empty. For a second, I panicked, until I returned to my room and found her curled up under my bed sucking her thumb. I let her sleep, drove down to the *tabac* to get cigarettes. And there my short-lived calm abruptly ended. Covering the news rack like some weirdly patterned wallpaper was the same smiling photograph. It was one I'd seen before—Quinn and Raphael at Les Yeux, him smiling his assured smile, her scrunching her nose up in a playful snarl, both with red-eye from the camera flash. On her blog, she'd joked that the red-eye made them look like devils from the caves. I grabbed a paper off the rack.

"Police Hunt for Victims of Demon Lovers." *Quinn et Raffi: Folie à deux*? read the caption under the photograph, leading to a think-piece on page six by the "leading profiler" from before, this time claiming that from his analysis of Quinn's blog and Raphael's journal pages, the combination of their personalities must have created a "perfect storm of psychosis," a recipe for murder. I recognized the photo of the hack who had written the piece: Aurelia Perla. She'd used the stuff I sent, clearly. She'd just completely ignored everything I'd written to explain it. I shoved the tabloid back in the rack in disgust. It tore a little as I walked away with my cigarettes, the tobacconist hurling abuse at me for my vandalism.

On the drive to the Hôpital Sainte-Thérèse, Quinn was silent, no cracks about my music taste, no red nail polish. Her hair was tied back tight, her face scrubbed clean as a penitent's, or a convict headed for the gallows. I didn't know if she'd seen the papers or not. I hurried her past the *tabacs* and cafés, buckling her into her seat like a child and dumping a bag of pastries in her lap. When we drove over a bump in the road, they fell to the floor in a flurry of buttery crumbs and she didn't move to pick them up. She just stared out the window, biting her nails. I could hear the click-click of teeth piercing nail through the smoke of Patsy Cline singing "Crazy" on the radio.

When we pulled into the parking lot of the hospital, she sat up and cupped her face to the window.

"Look familiar?"

"Why are we here?" She looked flustered, as if she thought I'd taken her back here to be locked up again.

I slung the car crookedly between the dotted lines of a space, leaving the engine running. "I just need to slip in and ask a few questions. Why don't you stay here, eat a croissant, unless you need to pee or something?"

She nodded vacantly. "You won't be long?"

"I'll be back in two shakes of a lamb's tail."

In the long, green-painted room where the nuns' sneakers squeaked on the polished floor, the skinny girl in the bed could have been mistaken for Quinn. Her bony knees barely tented the covers. Noémie wore a floppy sun hat over the cuts and bruises on her cropped head and it hid her pale face, the sunken shadows of her eyes. When I sat down in the plastic bucket seat beside her, she looked up uncertainly.

"Who are you?" she asked in French.

I hesitated, no longer as slick and certain as I once was. The truth was I didn't know what to tell her. A lie . . . The truth? That I'd been to a weird porn lockup the day before and Quinn might have had a memory of Noémie being there? It seemed like a pretty thin pretext, even to me. In the end, she saved me the trouble.

In tentative English, she said, "You found me in the cave. You saved me."

I half nodded. "*Saved* might be too strong a word."

The nuance was lost in translation. Her pale

423

twig-arm reached out and her delicate fingers settled on my wrist. "Thank you."

"You're welcome," I said. I wished I really had saved her. But looking at her, tiny and emaciated in her hospital bed, I wondered if anyone could.

We exchanged pleasantries for a while, in broken English and worse French. I discovered a sweet girl who sometimes struggled to meet my eye, quite a different creature from the sulky beauty of Quinn's blog, aloof and cruel by turns. This Noémie spoke to me haltingly, asking me, at long last, if there was any news about her family.

"No. I'm sorry, Noémie."

She frowned, but it was an odd little frown. Behind it was an emotion other than sadness. Relief. "You know, a journalist came yesterday to talk," she said, "until the nuns got mad and dragged her away!" She let out an odd little laugh.

"Oh?" I said, a picture of Aurelia forming unpleasantly in my mind. "I'm surprised they let a hack like her in."

Noémie gave me an odd look, as if she knew more about me than I imagined, saw through me somehow. "She said the police found a locker place where Raphael took girls to. She asked if I remembered it."

"And did you?" I asked, holding my breath for the answer.

"I told her I did not." She stared at her bony hands. "But that was a lie."

"You do remember?"

"I wish I didn't. I wish I was forgetful . . ." She met my eye and I saw something underlying her shy look. A question. Or a challenge. "Am I on these films?"

"What films?"

"You haven't seen?" She put her hands over her face, peering at me from between her fingers. "After our father left, my brother missed him, like I did. And after a while, he followed him into the family business, working at the club. It was easy for him to sell the films to them, to threaten . . . to get money from girls this way. Then when they went home to their own countries, he would blackmail them to keep his secret."

"You mentioned the club? Did you mean La Gorda?"

She nodded. "It was a bad thing he did to these girls." Noémie started to cry. Her heavy head fell into her hands and she sobbed brokenly. Her cries rose and became wails until the other patients started stirring, looking around at the source of the disturbance.

Quinn Perkins

Draft Blog Entry

He found me on the road. Don't know why I didn't go through the woods, seeing what I saw, knowing what I knew . . .

After Noémie's confession, I'd walked out of the Old Schoolhouse in a red haze. Couldn't think. I ran through the woods, my mind telling me the steps I needed to take: getting my clothes, my ticket, catching a bus to the airport. As soon as that picture had formed, my thoughts would double back to that dusty computer room—how could I leave Noémie there?

She was so scared that if anyone knew how long she'd been in on it all—the videos of girls, the pay site, the blackmail—she'd go to prison. Her brother certainly would. Either way, her life would be ruined. But as she put it, "Now I am not sure I would mind that very much."

I had to help her somehow—like she'd tried to help me with the Snapchats. I was up to my neck in all this. We both were.

Raphael leaned out the low-slung window, yelling like an angry cabdriver. "I waited outside. Maman went crazy at me. Where were you?"

"Didn't see you," I said lamely, eyeing the distance to the tree line, trying to picture the town I couldn't quite make out on the horizon.

"Fuck, Quinn." He slammed his hands down on the steering wheel.

I kept walking, my feet moving as fast as they could without actually running.

He followed me at a crawl, the wheels crunching the road, right on my heels. The next time he spoke his voice was different, even and inviting, that voice that only a couple of weeks ago I thought was the only one he ever spoke in. "C'mon, babe, get into the car. We'll go to the woods, have some beer, a little party, then tomorrow you fly. God, I'm gonna miss you soooooo much. Gonna miss your eyes . . ."

And still I kept walking, steady, eyes on the road in front of me, closing my ears to everything he said.

I heard the engine rev, felt the air rush as the car swerved around. Relief came, tsunami-style. Maybe he was going to leave me alone. Then he stopped, just a little way ahead of me, and I saw the light glint off a piece of white paper.

"My e-ticket."

"I printed it out for you." Raphael smiled. "See, I can be a nice and helpful boyfriend sometimes."

"Thanks," I said, grabbing for it, falling forward as the car inched out of my reach.

"Not so hurrying, Quinn. You'll get it when you get in." The e-ticket vanished inside.

"I don't need it, anyway. I can just ask for another at check-in," I said, brushing the road off my jeans.

The car stopped. "Come on, babe. What do I have to do to prove that I love you? Don't be so hard on me . . . I'm trying."

Don't judge me, even if I seem like one of those girls who goes back to him over and over again. I was so tired, so confused, after days of pills and crazy and not sleeping. It was hard to think of what to say when Raphael looked at me that way. I thought we'd be in the car five minutes, then Stella's, then the airport, like some montage at the end of a Disney film. I didn't know we'd still be creeping around on a full tank of gas hours later trying to lose some car on our tail. Raphael says it's an undercover cop car. He knows from the dark glass. Other times he says it's Séverin. He's smoked more in the past hour than most people do their whole lives.

Night is falling, but when I look in the wing mirror, I still see the car with the dark glass a few meters behind. I've started to think Raphael's right. We are being followed, but the way it's happening fills me with dread. Surely if it were the police, they'd have stopped us by now? And if not the police . . . ? The road sprawls like hair, cut loose and held high by the witch. We drive into a fire-engine sunset that will take your days-long hangover and raise you a brain aneurysm, take your pounding head and run it through a wood-chipper *Fargo*-style. The radio plays the French charts. Three months into my stay, I knew every verse of French rap, every bridge to a Johnny Hallyday song.

Raphael smokes furiously and flings Gitanes at me without sparing me a look. He drives with one hand on the wheel, the other fidgeting with something under his coat. Something tells me that it's a gun and I wonder which would be worse, to be stopped by whoever's in the car, or to keep on with him in this frame of mind.

I know now that he is broken beyond repair. I didn't see it at first, or for a long time, but now I see nothing else. Something is wrong with every part of him, or rather with the way the parts don't fit together: the sweet smile, the cute broken English, the way he acts easygoing but is actually pulled tighter than a garrote wire. Something happened to him when his dad disappeared, to his whole family, and they cannot come back from it. I thought I was broken after my mom died, but the Blavettes could run circles around me in the dysfunction department. They have me beat.

I could ask why he's keeping me with him, but I don't want to hear him speak the words in my head: that somehow he knows what I know and he doesn't want me to tell.

Molly Swift

AUGUST 12, 2015

I moved near to Noémie on the bed, trying to calm her, but she was beyond me, somewhere else entirely. On the edge of my vision, I saw the gray forms of habits approaching along the ward. In a moment, I would look up and see the angry face of Sister Eglantine, who would be incredu-lous to see me here in her hospital again, causing more trouble.

"Noémie," I whispered, "Quinn's here. She remembers things. She told me—"

Noémie stopped wailing and looked up through a haze of tears. "Quinn is here?"

I expected her to really freak out then, like she had in the caves, but her response surprised me far more. "Can I see?" she asked in a child-like voice.

"We need you to go now," said a voice from the foot of the bed. "You're upsetting her." It wasn't Sister Eglantine. It was one of her jackbooted lackeys. I remembered this one throwing me out on my ear once before.

"Of course, Sister," I said, flashing her a big, fake smile, but before I got up from the bed, I whispered in Noémie's ear. "She's in the parking

430

lot in a black Buick. I'll wait until you come out." I walked away, looking over my shoulder at the tiny shape in the bed, the one slowly shrinking from view.

In reception, I stopped, my attention caught by a strange scene. All the patients waiting to be treated were crowded around the television in the corner. The nurses and doctors, too. Even the receptionist had left her post to go investigate. The crowd was so dense I couldn't see or hear the TV at the center of it. Whatever was on must have been compelling stuff. *Well, good,* I thought. This way Noémie could sneak out and go talk to Quinn. I was curious to see what effect bringing the two of them together might produce.

I was about to walk out to the parking lot when I saw the silhouette of a panama hat in the light flooding in from the entrance. Valentin walked towards me, a grim expression weighing down his cherubic face. When he saw me, he took off his hat and ran a hand through his blond curls. He came to rest about a foot away from me, his eyes downcast, his lips twitching. I remembered then how he had spent the morning—part of one last futile search party through Les Yeux. I imagined their flashlights glowing, their voices echoing through the maze of tunnels. It must be a bleak feeling to have to give up on people like that, to leave them lost somewhere.

"So you have seen Noémie?" he said distractedly. He sounded out of breath.

"I did. We talked until the nuns booted me out."

"And—" he flicked a look around the waiting room, his eyes resting briefly on the crowd around the television "—did she seem okay?" His forehead shone with sweat.

I laid my hand across it. "You're feverish," I said. "What's wrong?"

He swallowed hard. "We found the Blavettes," he said, seeming amazed at his own words. His eyes pricked with tears and he wiped them away.

I was too shocked to feel anything. "That's amazing," I said, my brain not really processing the words. "Will they be okay?"

He shook his head. "No, Molly . . . you don't understand. We found two bodies in the caves this morning and we have not identified them yet . . . but we think it may be Émilie and Raphael. I just went in the ambulance to the hospital morgue and then I came here, as we agreed." He looked around again distractedly. "Where's Quinn?"

"Out in the car," I said. "She didn't feel like—"

His eyes bugged. "We must go get her in this very moment."

"And tell her, I know. But wait—"

"No." He grabbed me by both arms, shaking

me. "I don't want her to find out by the radio or something. I have to be with her when—"

"When what?" His panic was spreading through me, shocking me out of my numbness.

"They are planning to arrest her again, Molly, for the murder of the Blavettes."

We ran outside, but it was too late. The Buick was gone. Quinn must have heard it on the radio, just as Valentin had feared.

There was worse to come. When we checked the ward, we found Noémie was gone, too. Ever the bad influence, I'd encouraged her to sneak out and she had. She'd even managed to creep past Valentin and me, too caught up in each other to see her.

There was only one conclusion to make: that Quinn had driven off with her. I called and called, but Quinn wouldn't pick up her phone. I could only imagine how scared she must be, her worst fears having come true.

Molly Swift

AUGUST 12, 2015

In a white-tiled room in the belly of the hospital lay the intertwined bodies the police believed were Émilie and Raphael Blavette. The search team had been on the point of giving up when they made a wrong turn, turned down a tunnel, and found the wooden door that hid them from view. Behind it, in a dark chamber formed in the rock millions of years ago, the two bodies were huddled.

Hushed as medieval pilgrims traveling to a shrine, Valentin and I were paying the remains a visit. A subdued mood wrapped around us like smoke as we followed the pathologist through a plastic-chaired waiting room, where a clock ticked too loudly and people sat waiting for bad news.

"When we found them, the male was lying on the female's lap," said Valentin. "She was bent over him just like a mother bends over her child. The first thing I thought of was the pietà in the church."

In my mind's eye, I saw the statue he was talking about, the one that dominated the apse of the St. Roch church: Mary in her veil, leaning over the prone body of the dying Christ, His head bound in thorns.

"How long have these people been dead?"

The pathologist, who must have been listening to us talk, turned around. "More or less two weeks, so it fits the time frame. They are so decomposed they must be recognized from their teeth, though, and some of the skin it has fused together. They will be hard to separate." His hands moved to the swinging doors of the morgue.

Time slowed. The hospital bustling around us felt somehow comic and awful and wholly inadequate all at once. Inside, it was too bright.

"We think they died from inhaling poison gas," said the pathologist as he pushed the doors open. "It is produced naturally by the rocks there and with the door shut and bolted anyone trapped inside would die within hours."

A cold, chemical smell hit my face. "But who would have shut it?"

Both men looked at me silently, then at each other, clearly struck by some unspoken thought. I blinked against the sudden blurriness in my eyes, hearing the subtle flick of the sheet in the pathologist's hands. There was no way to avoid seeing what the sheet revealed. Lit so brightly, the two bodies looked less like a pietà and more like some bloated, leathery sculpture. The eyes bulged. The teeth were bared. I looked down at the tiled floor, hearing the pathologist's words as if underwater.

"The male was naked when he died, though the female was clothed. We don't know why. There was a picnic blanket, wine, dried grapes, a radio."

"As if they were having a party in there," said Valentin darkly.

"Strange as it sounds," said the pathologist with a chuckle.

I turned around and walked through the swinging doors. They'd seen this before, who knew how many times. They could do the coffin humor thing. I couldn't. My head spun with fragments of ideas and memories. The caves. Noémie. Quinn. The section from her blog when Raphael told her the history of Les Yeux in the seventeenth century: when a Blavette who was Witchfinder General decided to kill his family by shutting them inside that terrible chamber, adding a door to make sure they could not escape. Whoever these people were, they had died the same way.

The morgue door shushed closed behind me. On the way to reception I dialed Quinn's number. It went to voice mail. I hung up and tried again. Eventually I left her a message, begging her to call me back. In reception, the TV had lost its crowd of moths. I could see the image flickering on it now: a photo of Quinn and

Noémie. Running under the photo was a request that anyone who saw them call the police. Not only was Quinn wanted for murder, but everyone thought she had kidnapped Noémie.

Everyone except for me.

Molly Swift

AUGUST 12, 2015

Evening fell and La Gorda drew the bon vivants close. In their black leathers and drainpipe jeans, they swarmed the closed doors, reminding me of those hot summer days when the queen ant flies and the melting world suddenly crawls with winged insects, biting, mating, hunting a crack in the sidewalk to hide in.

Police had been sent to the woods, Mas d'Or, and the Blavette house to search for the girls. I'd told Valentin what Noémie had told me about her father and Raphael's involvement in La Gorda, and though we had different views about recent developments, we'd gone to the club on a hunch—my hunch—that we might find some clue to their whereabouts inside.

We sat in the car, waiting for the crowd to thin. Valentin smoked. I tapped the dashboard, hoping to glimpse a flail of blond hair, a frightened face, to see Quinn and Noémie together and safe. Valentin pointed a pack of American Spirit at me. He looked weary, older.

"Light?" he asked.

"Sure."

He flicked on the little yellow tongue of flame and I breathed the fire deeply.

"Did Noémie tell you what her father and brother did here?" he asked.

"Worked, I guess, though judging from Raphael's journal and all the other evidence, I would have said their occupation was drugs and girls."

"I would not have called that evidence," he said.

"It's more than you've got on Quinn."

"There will be solid evidence soon, I think," he said, staring out at the stream of club-going ants. "Then it will be official." The way he said it made it all too clear: he thinks she did it.

I took a deep drag of American Spirit and swallowed back my anger. "Don't imagine I didn't notice the police following us around even before you found the bodies, and you had your eye on her before that. If you want to know what I think, you decided it was her right from the start and you've never even considered—"

"That is unfair, Molly," he snapped. "If you wish to know what I feel, it is that you are believing Quinn instead of me, choosing her over me."

"If I am, it's because you say dumb things like that." I jettisoned my cigarette and closed the window.

"I am just worried about the trouble you seem

to be getting yourself into. I only want to protect you, Molly."

I turned to face him. "By lying to me. Is that how you protected me?"

He looked confused. "What do you mean?"

"About the address, the lockup? Why did you tell me there was nothing there . . . when . . . when there was everything there?" I spat out the words, feeling sick.

He wiped the sweat off his forehead. "Jesus. I did not even check it. I did not think you actually had anything."

"What, because I'm not a cop? Because I'm a woman?"

"Don't be absurd." He rolled down the window, angry now, lit another cigarette, and smoked hard. "She's not who you think she is. But I guess you'll only work that out when it's too late."

We sat in angry silence, until, like some surreal music video, I saw a whip of blond hair in the crowd, a tight red dress I thought I recognized. Like Persephone sneaking back into hell, the blond girl pushed through the black-clad crowd and into the gaping maw of La Gorda. In the time it took Valentin to exhale again, I was out of the car and at the door, squeezing between punks and into the dark.

Molly Swift

AUGUST 12, 2015

Inside, white lights pulsed on red walls. Punk rock crackled from the back of the room. The club hyperventilated, its denizens parting and merging in front of me, swallowing the last glimpse of the girl in the red dress. I looked around to see Valentin trailing behind me. I could hear him—just—like some French spoken word track weaving into the music, telling me to slow down, to stop.

But I couldn't. She was just ahead of me, always just out of reach, Eurydice to my Orpheus as we sank into the depths of the club, drawn to the growl of the band, the black cage mesh layered over boudoir red on the back walls, the photos of long dead stars staring down in nonchalant judgment like gods.

We were at the back of the club. The singer's raw growl shook the ground from under me. Dancers thrashed their long dreadlocked hair, showed pale bellies, metal-spiked, wild arms like mascaraed lashes. I saw them in strobe, saw her, the red of her dress iridescent under the black lights.

"Quinn!" I called to her. The music drowned

my voice. I felt Valentin's hand on my arm, whirling me around to face him.

His face was angry, anxious. "Molly, stop," he mouthed. "Open your eyes."

"What do you mean?"

He spun me back around. "Look."

A door opened in the trompe-l'oeil wall in front of the blond girl, a hidden one I hadn't even seen. A man poked his head around: Bruno, the stern-faced bouncer. The girl turned then; her lips moved in profile. It wasn't Quinn, after all. Bruno beckoned her in, the red door closing over her red dress like a hungry mouth. I turned to talk to Valentin, but he was moving towards the stage, the hidden door. He looked back a couple of times, his face jowly with consternation, signaling me to stay.

As soon as he was out of sight, I pressed towards the back of the club and the door I wasn't sure I should open. When I got there, I tried the handle. It opened onto a narrow corridor. I looked one way and the other, checking for Bruno, then closed the door carefully behind me and crept down to one end, where I tried the first promising-looking door. It was locked. I stopped for a moment. It was then that I heard voices coming from the opposite end of the corridor. Raised voices, arguing.

Walking as quietly as possible, I headed down

to it, finding a door marked Cagibi. Through the crack in the hinge, I glimpsed Valentin and Séverin. They were having what sounded like a stressful conversation in French. It was too rapid for me to translate. My fingers grappled for my phone, slid to my little translator app. I flicked on the video recorder, too, and pointed the phone at the door.

"You have found them, then?" Séverin said.

"You have known where they were all this time, Séverin," Valentin spat. "You must have. You have been using that place to get rid of people for years."

Séverin shrugged. "And you police, you have been turning a blind eye to it for years. Why are you surprised about it this time?"

"Because these were not your rivals or your clients . . . this was a normal family." Valentin banged a fist on the table Séverin sat behind.

Séverin laughed. "There was *nothing* normal about that family, believe me."

"They still did not deserve to die."

"Listen," said Séverin. "If you wish to protect bad people like that, simply offer them the same kind of arrangement you make for me. Though if I were you, I would not bother. Whatever has happened to them, I wasn't personally involved. In fact, you have been far more involved, stealing papers from this annoying journalist, following her, removing evidence from the house of the Blavettes. It seems you are in up to your neck."

"If you say so," said Valentin, "but these are only small things. *You* are the one who knew they were in that chamber."

"Perhaps," Séverin said amiably. "Who can say? For a long time now, I have tried to pry my money out of Raphael Blavette's greedy hands."

A hand closed over my mouth. I smelled cigarettes and meat and beer. I bit at the fingers but they just squeezed harder, yanking me against a barrel chest. My neck screamed pain. I saw spots of color. The man forced my arm around my back, pushing me into the storage room.

"This woman!" Séverin exclaimed. "She seems to follow on our heels like some small dog."

"Let her go," Valentin spat. "She has nothing to do with this."

Séverin turned to him angrily. "If that is true, you should not have brought her in here. But I do not think you are telling the truth, or she would not be here."

"Let her go," Valentin shouted, banging the desk again. "Or you'll find the custom of silence around here will end very quickly."

"Very well," snapped Séverin. "Bruno, let the new Madame Valentin go."

Molly Swift

AUGUST 12, 2015

In the middle of the writhing crowd, I stood stunned, feeling everything I thought I knew fall away. Valentin had hold of my arm and was maneuvering me through the crowd. Valentin had been involved in this the whole time. No wonder he couldn't solve the case. Not couldn't. Wouldn't.

A dancer slammed into me. With all my strength, I flung Valentin towards her. She spun around and punched him, flooring him. He lay like a grounded fish, panting hard breaths while the DM-booted, spike-toed feet of headbangers jumped around him. Nobody offered to help him up, including me. I just let the world reel angrily around us until the song stopped and the feet fell silent.

"Molly . . ." he said, struggling to get up.

"I heard everything, Valentin," I said, my foot poised to kick him in the balls if he dared to make a move. "I understood everything."

"*Dieu* . . ." He turned his head away. His hand moved to his stomach and he groaned, breathing hard.

"You hurt? Because you deserve it," I said.

"I can't believe I let myself like you . . . love you even. It makes me feel sick."

His eyes turned to me. "Be careful, Molly. You are in danger," he said.

I let out a bitter laugh. "Do you really think there's anything you'll say that I'll believe?" I said. "All that time you were pretending to investigate, to actually find the Blavettes, and you knew all along. You knew and you were covering up for Séverin. Did you know about the girls, too?"

He shook his head. "No. Of course not . . ."

"I don't believe you." I took him by the lapel and shook him. "Why d'you do it. Why'd you lie?"

"Tradition." He half smiled. "Or perhaps habit. Same as you perhaps."

"No," I said, "I may be a jerk sometimes but there's a difference. I would never lie like that."

I left him lying there and pushed my way through the crowd, shaking so hard I could barely walk straight. When I got outside, I sent the video and translation to Bill with a new subject line: *Police corruption in St. Roch area leads to Blavette murders*. I didn't know if that was the whole truth, but it would get his attention.

The moment the pinwheel stopped turning and the message was sent, a text popped into my phone. I didn't recognize the number, but one of the words in it jumped out at me straight-away. Quinn.

Take out one thousand euros in notes and come to the Old Schoolhouse if you don't want Quinn to get hurt.

Quinn Perkins

JULY 27, 2015

Draft Blog Entry

If you're reading this, it's because something happened to me and you've found my phone. Maybe it's the last part of me that will remain, unless I manage to turn things around. I'm in the caves, waiting for Raphael and Noé . . . typing these last words and not knowing who they are for or what will happen after now. The last few hours have been the edgiest of my life. I itch to escape, but not yet.

In the car, I kept checking that the lock on the door of Raphael's car was up. I needed to know I was still free to go. He was strumming the wheel of his Bic, offering me a light.

"Do you," he began, "have everything packed for tomorrow?"

Third time he'd asked me that.

I took a deep drag, stared out the window. Because he *knew*. He'd been looking at my phone, had cracked my password somehow. He'd already read this blog, seen that I'd been spilling his secrets here and now he wanted to stop me showing anyone else. *All the more reason to keep on with it,* I thought, *in case I don't make it, so at least people know what really happened.* Now I know that his charm's just part of a game we're playing to pass the time. In less than an hour, there'll be a party in these caves, the last taste of France, *farewell to Quinn.*

"Noémie will be there," he told me, "some others, too. There'll be dancing, a few drinks, and a bonfire. Sounds good, doesn't it? How your first trip far from home is supposed to be."

When the party's over, I can take that ticket from him and use it to get home. *Home.* I close my eyes . . . try to imagine it. All I can see is a black video screen whirling.

Dushka and Ruth, Sita and Gemma . . . and Quinn. The girls come and they go away quietly every time. But where? Noémie doesn't know. She's just afraid the same thing will happen to me, that she'll lose me like all the others. She's afraid of being left alone again, with nothing but Maman and Raffi and her nightmares.

After two hours of driving through ditches and rural back roads, we lost our tail. So we thought at least. The road by the sea was empty except for us. On Raphael's side, wheat fields reeled past in a golden blur. On mine, the sea was a strip of blue. With each turn of the tires, my guts curled tighter around ground glass at the thought of tonight. Woods sprang up from the yellow dirt at the rim of a cornfield, sudden and sparse, not the acne-scarred plane trees that crowd the village roads but sad black beech trees waving their skinny arms. Like a legion of emos at a Jimmy Eat World concert—a scene from my old life.

The road twisted around hidden little beaches full of washed-up trash, dark cave pockets hacked into the coastline. I watched Raphael's face watching the road, the features unreadable. I wanted to know what he knew, what he had planned, but I didn't want to open another box I couldn't close. I stared out the window, wishing I still had my cigarette, the sun tattooing disco lights into my eyes. That's when I saw the turn into the woods, the dirt track leading up to the caves, and I would soon find out what he wanted with me. He'd find a few things out, too.

In the darkness of this cave, with its constant drip of water, I squeeze my eyes shut, see an image of us standing in the ashes of burned wood and cigarette cartons, sucking beer from a keg, the beat from the sound system pounding the ground, moving us despite ourselves. White pills, blue pills. Me dancing in the white dress I put on this morning because it made me feel less . . . sullied, my sandals shucked off, my feet bare, almost a child again. At the center of the gathering: Raphael Pan-like, demonic, doomed. Or that's how I imagine my last night in this place could be. I don't want to dream up the alternative versions . . .

We parked between ancient trees and walked under their witch fingers. I felt a last twitch of uncertainty. It might have been better to do something, anything than come here, after all. Raphael turned to me, unsmiling. Without his sunglasses, his eyes looked cold.

"Where's Noémie?" I asked, trying to sound casual.

He pressed his finger to his lips, *Shhh*.

Then he was on the phone, snapping questions or instructions. Nodding. Frowning. He hung up, pulled a cigarette out of the pack, and tapped it, front-loading the nicotine hit.

"Time to play one last game, Quinn: hide and go seek."

My hands were shaking. I shoved them into my pockets. "I guess it is." *Two can play at that game,* I thought, eyeing the caves up ahead.

"Let's go a little further up, then." He smiled that half smile I used to find cute, gesturing me forward as if I were a sheep.

We moved deeper into the woods, into darkness.

Les Yeux, we meet again. The eyes of the caves watch us as if they remember.

When we got close, we stood still for a moment, on the edge of something. Raphael drew deep on his cigarette, dropped it, ground it out with his heel. I had the weird feeling of looking at his expensive shoes, his black shirt. Looking at everything about him closer than before. I was struck by how beautiful his skin was, the most flawless skin I'd ever seen, I thought. And his hands were beautiful, too. Delicately veined. An artist's hands.

Now I can feel the caves' weird hatefulness. I remember that terrible crimes happened in| here. Do they lurk somewhere, those nightmares? Have they soaked inside the rock and loam like ghosts? Are they trapped there, howling their pain forever?

It's dark. After a long silence, Raphael flicks on his phone, shines its dim flashlight into the darkness. "We've waited ages. Don't think Noé is coming . . ." he says. He sounds nervous all of a sudden.

"She said she'd show and she will." The grit in my voice surprises me.

"Well, I guess this is my new hideout . . . those guys in the car will never find us here."

"No, never," I say, steeling myself for what will come next. The word is lost in the darkness, the endless cool, sardonic laugh of the caves. They swallow my thoughts in a mocking echo. *So so so so . . . so what?* they seem to say.

We go deeper, edging through one more narrow hole that leads into one of the bigger chambers. The light of his flashlight flicks and gleams off corners of rock, casting huge shadows into the next chamber like monsters with mouths full of teeth. On the threshold of the room, my body tenses. This was the chamber he took me to, where we lay naked together, trusted each other, but that was a long time ago.

Molly Swift

AUGUST 12, 2015

I climbed in through the same window as before
and ran down the corridor, past the coldly
gleaming trophy cabinet and the staged school
photographs. When I came to the double doors
at the end of the corridor, a flashing light caught
my attention. It filtered through the squared glass
window in a closed door, carved into fragments
of shifting colored light on the floor in front of
me. I walked to the door and peered in. Inside
were banks of dusty PCs. Behind them, blurred
pink shapes squirmed and swam, writ large on
the white wall. I pushed the door open.

A projector hummed, beaming flickering images
through its single eye. The film it flung onto the
wall played soundlessly. It was a film of a girl's
face with plastic film pulled tight over her nose
and lips. The room around her was dark and it
was hard to see the details of her pale face, but I
recognized her, anyway. Nicole Leclair's mouth
sucked the plastic wrap in and out, her breath
making a vapor. Her eyes were wild, afraid. The
covering tightened over her face, until, after a
few choppy frames, she fell still. It was the clip

Quinn had been sent via Snapchat back when all of this began.

I followed the projector lead to one of the prehistoric-looking PCs. It was switched on. The same film played there. I clicked the little *x* in the corner, closing it, and saw that the desktop was covered with .mov files. Video clips. Littered with them, in no particular order, jumbled on top of each other, some of them piles deep. Snowdrifts of video. As soon as I'd closed the first, another opened automatically. New grainy footage was beamed onto the wall: a girl lying prone on a bed, smiling happily, another girl chatting away, naked to the waist. I closed them and there came another and another, spewing out of the computer like vomit. In every one there was a girl, some faces familiar from Raphael's wall of trophies in the La Rochelle squat.

As I looked at these girls, it seemed that they'd trusted the cameraman. Perhaps, like Quinn, they'd let themselves be filmed willingly, believing Raphael loved them, not knowing what he wanted the films for. The unpleasant words *revenge porn* came into my head. Another video opened up: a woman dancing naked, her back to the camera. She turned to face the lens and I recognized Stella Birch. As soon as I closed that, something different spun open, an Excel document logging more code names of girls, alongside email addresses. It was an organized operation—seducing girls, filming them, black-mailing them to pay up and stay quiet.

I clicked the spreadsheet shut, my sweaty hands slipping on the keys. Another film opened. In this, the room was different again. It was light, pretty, familiar somehow. A skinny girl lay on her side, her dark hair falling in front of her face. Behind her, just visible on the bookshelf, was a family photo, a mom and dad smiling at the beach with their tanned kids. Then she turned her sad eyes to the camera: Noémie Blavette.

Bile rose in my throat. I smashed my hand on the keyboard, desperate to block the images out. But all that happened was more videos opened, many of them at once, smiling, laughing, innocent of the humiliation to come. I covered my ears, seeing, in among them, a darker film, even grainer than the rest. I recognized Quinn, her soft lips pressed against another girl's. Noémie. Inside the chamber of a cave, they kissed and touched, sighed and gasped. The camera moved around them, panning in and out, egging on their performance.

Another video opened up beside it, filmed in the same dark chamber. This one showed Raphael, lit by a single spotlight. He stood on a picnic blanket, a bottle of wine and some stained glasses tumbled beside him, the same things with which he'd been found. Raphael's face was contorted in an angry frown. He began to undress, beginning with his shirt, then his shoes. The striptease looked forced, unwilling. As he stripped, the other videos playing on the screen slowly ended and closed on their own.

In the spotlight, Raphael turned his face first to one person, then another, hidden behind the camera, protesting alternately in English, in French. When he was completely naked, he stood with his hand over his privates, looking every bit as vulnerable as the girls in the videos he'd made. Another figure entered the frame. It was Émilie Blavette, her face red and furious. First she ran to her son, hugging him protectively, then she lunged at the camera, her hand hitting the lens. The file closed and the screen of the PC fragmented, its colors shivering. Then it turned blue.

There was a cough behind me. I turned around to see Quinn, her face dyed blue by the final projector image. Beside her stood Noémie and their hands were joined, Noémie's delicate fingers squeezing Quinn's strong, tanned hand.

"Oh my God, are you guys okay?" I asked, taking a step towards them until something in the way Quinn looked at me made me stop. Something in the way they were both looking at me, as it happened.

Quinn Perkins

JULY 27, 2015

Draft Blog Entry

After we watched the videos in the school computer room, Noé and I sat in the woods while the sky grew dark. She didn't want to go back to the house again and I didn't want to leave her alone. Not that I had anywhere to go myself.

Sitting with our backs pressed against the white bark of a tree, our bodies vanished into the night and our voices became all of us. When I asked her the question *How did things get this way?* it seemed to me that the door that had been closed over the story of her life for so long had been opened. The secrets tumbling forth were unstoppable. I smoked and listened as she told me the story of what happened that day two years ago when her father supervised a school trip to the caves.

Nicole was Noémie's best friend in the school, but neither of them was popular. The cool kids like Freddie, Sophie, and Raphael pushed them around probably the average amount that uncool nerd kids get pushed around. A little while before the trip to the caves, though,

Raphael and Freddie kicked the bullying up a notch. What had been ordinary geek-oppression like getting splashed in the face during swimming lessons became the dunking game. And then there were the running games of truth or dare that everyone felt pressured to be part of. It was just that the dares kept getting worse and, for her part, Émilie turned a blind eye to it. She thought her son could do no wrong. The other teachers were too poorly paid to care.

During one game, the dare was holding a square of plastic wrap from one of Raphael's sandwiches over your mouth until he said you could stop. Most of the kids got off with a few seconds. When it came to Nicole's turn, Raphael kept timing her until she passed out and made a film of her humiliation. Hence the video Noé first sent me. When they were alone together, she pleaded with her brother to stop, but he just made fun of her. He seemed to take pleasure in what he was doing, and after her protest, the things he did to Nicole just got worse. Sometimes Noé wondered if it was the vicious fights her parents had that had made her brother turn cruel. She told her father what was going on and he promised he'd have a talk with Émilie, but of course that just turned into a fight, too.

The day of the school trip, Émilie had a migraine, so Marc took the kids to Les Yeux alone. Raphael was in his element. He'd been to the caves so many times with his father that his knowledge of their tunnels and chambers was second only to Marc's. At some point—Noé wasn't quite sure how—she and Nicole ended up with Freddie and Raphael, separated from the rest of the party. Raphael wanted to play a game. He knew about the hidden chamber from his father. It was a family legend, a special secret, and he knew just how to use it. He led the girls into it and told them its gruesome history—the reason it was created, the gas in the rock, the people who had died in there centuries before. Noémie had heard it before, but Nicole started to freak out. She didn't like it. She had to get out. That was when Raphael shut the two of them inside.

Noé remembers banging on the door, begging her brother to open it, remembers Nicole crumpling in a heap against her, so terrified all she could do was cry. Afraid of the rocks around her, she started gasping for air, having some sort of panic attack. It was Freddie who weakened and undid the bolt in the end. By then, Nicole was unconscious. Even when Marc carried her out into the sun-shine, she never woke up. The doctors said later that she had a heart defect, that it ran in her family. No one could have known that the fear she felt inside that chamber would kill her.

It didn't stop the board of governors from shutting the school, though. Émilie, who had thrown every atom of her energy into her head-mistress role, was furious. But she didn't take her anger out on Raphael. She'd painstakingly protected him through the initial inquiry and afterwards it was Marc who took the brunt of her wrath. He was the grown-up in charge. He was also weak, a disappointment, and she knew he was having an affair. Marc had already been struggling. His nightclub business was failing. He'd used up what money was left to bribe contacts in the local police force to drop their investigation into Nicole's death and the Blavettes could no longer afford Mas d'Or. Émilie's wrath seemed to push him beyond the breaking point. One day after they'd closed the school and closed the caves and St. Roch was trying to salvage its tarnished image for the tourists, Marc walked out and never came back.

Noé cries when she tells me about the black hole that opened up after her father disappeared, how she didn't know if he had got lost in the caves or just run away. Sometimes she didn't care and sometimes she thought about little else. Life moved on in St. Roch. Nicole's parents left. A new school opened up and the students took lessons from their new teachers there. Since the incident had been kept quiet, tourists still came to the town and Émilie was able to sign Noémie up to exchange programs, hosting students in return for a pittance, but it was never enough.

Émilie was out of control. She would swing

between manic weeks when she would shop and socialize as if nothing had happened and weeks of sitting in an armchair all day, not moving, stricken with guilt that Nicole died on her watch. She ran up debts that Stella had to help her with. She went out partying and came home late or not at all. Worst of all, she seemed to blame Noémie for everything now that Marc wasn't there anymore to shout at.

Yes, that was the hardest part, to hear how her mother hated her, the main reason being that she was too like her father: her looks, her mannerisms, her weakness. Everything about Noé reminded her mother of that bastard. She would see that look in her mother's eyes after she'd been drinking, as if she was thinking of revenging herself, as if she had confused the two of them. That look terrified her. That was why Noé started starving and cutting herself. If she vanished, her mother wouldn't have to look at her anymore.

All the while, Raphael shone ever more golden, the town hero. He won sports medals, scored straight A's, a scholarship to the Sorbonne. Noé never noticed him suffer a day of guilt for what he had done to Nicole. In fact, it seemed to inspire him to play more cruel games, as if they had become some kind of addiction. When he came home from Paris with a video camera, Maman was so pleased. Her son was going to be a famous film director, a star! One day Noémie looked at what was on the camera and found out the kind of films he'd been making and in a video of one of their exchanges the girl looked scared. She took it and showed it to Maman.

That night, Émilie locked Noémie in her room and didn't let her out for three days. She said it was for "her own good." After that, Noé sometimes heard her mother wheedling with Raphael to stay away from the girls, to "be a nice boy." Maybe one reason she'd been so hard on Noé . . . she feared she'd be next. But Maman was trapped: Raphael had been giving her money he made from blackmailing girls and his new job working for Séverin and she depended on the income he provided. More than that, the money made her his accomplice.

After a long time, Noémie's words stop. She falls so quiet, it's eerie, hearing the bats and the owls call, the crickets' endless chanting. I reach out for her, to reassure myself that she's still with me, that she hasn't vanished as she said she wanted to.

"I'm so sorry all of this happened to you," I say.

"Tomorrow," she says darkly, "Raphael will say he wants to play one last game with you. Don't go with him, please."

My hand finds her cheek. A tear runs over my fingers, its salt stinging some hangnail or paper cut I hadn't even noticed. "No," I hear myself saying. "I am going. We both are. We'll all play his little game together."

Molly Swift

AUGUST 12, 2015

The girls and I stood facing each other across that blue-lit room, not moving, not speaking. I felt numb. When I'd visited Noémie in the hospital, she'd seemed so vulnerable. I couldn't get my head around the way she blocked the door now, her eyes not moving from mine.

In the last few days, I'd grown to know Quinn (at least I thought I had), her tremulous swing between light moods and dark ones, her shy sweetness. I'd only really seen the pair of them together once before, when the jagged energy of their meeting ricocheted around the walls of Les Yeux. Now that I saw them holding hands in the doorway, I thought I understood why Noémie had screamed that day when the friend who must have abandoned her there came back for her after a week. Now I could see why their strange meeting had held the world's attention. There was some-thing electric about the two of them together, something that terrified me.

Long minutes dragged by before Quinn ended the staring contest. She flicked a glance past me at the blue screen of death on the PC monitor, her face oddly void of emotion, as if she was trying to be hard. "We put a program on there," she said, "so it would play the videos one after the other and wipe the hard drive after the last one."

"Why?" I asked softly, though deep down, I'd begun to guess.

"Why play them or why erase them?"

"Why any of it, Quinn?"

"We played them for you so you could see what happened to us," said Noémie. Her dark eyes glistened with unshed tears.

"And we erased them because we know how you are with videos," Quinn said in her new fake-tough voice, "and we didn't want you to be tempted. Did you bring the money?"

"Yes," I said. I'd been wondering how long it would take her to ask me for it. "But this isn't the way. It isn't even enough to get you—"

"You don't need to worry about that," she said sharply, then in a softer voice, she added, "I'm sorry, but we needed enough to get away from here." She turned to Noémie and I caught a hint of anxiety behind her bravado.

"You have to believe, we only wanted to scare Raphael," Noémie said suddenly, "to make him see the bad of what he was doing and stop it. We never meant to harm him. But then Maman had followed me there and things went—"

"He wanted us to play a game with him and we

did play his game, but not the way he wanted us to," said Quinn.

"It was an accident," said Noé, rubbing her hand across her eyes, "but we knew no one would believe us."

"Fuck," I said, putting my trembling hands to my face, "what are you going to do now?"

Noémie's lips trembled. "We need to get away from here, I think—"

"Yeah." I took out the money and looked at it in my hands, thinking it would never be enough for them, that I should stop them from making things worse for themselves. "I don't know, shouldn't you . . . ?" But in the end, I didn't know what the right thing to tell them was, so I crossed the room and handed the money to Quinn. "You should turn yourself in," I said. "They'll be easier on you."

But they were already half in the hallway, ebbing from the blue light into the dark.

Quinn Perkins

AUGUST 17, 2015

Video Diary: Session 8

[Quinn sits by a window, smoking. The wall behind her head flakes blue paint; the furniture is bright and cheap, a hotel room, maybe, in a hot country. Outside the window, car horns blare and the sun is blinding]

Well . . . we never meant to hurt anyone. Maybe you don't believe me, but it's true.

[She stubs out the first cigarette and lights another]

So, um, by the time Raphael told Noémie to meet us at Les Yeux, we'd come up with kind of a plan: we would make a video of him, get him back for all those videos he made, all those poor girls he blackmailed. You know, like, play him at his own game, right? Make him feel scared like he made Nicole feel . . . like he made us feel, I guess.

[Quinn smokes]

It wasn't hard to get him there. All I had to do was make him think he was in charge. Easy enough—he got off on that. He had his own plans for the night, anyway. We met Noé, went inside the caves. He started handing out the pills and alcohol. It was dark, so, easy enough to pretend to swallow them, stay sober while he got more and more out of it. Soon there was like this three-person party going on in that big bit of the cave like a cathedral vault. Creepy place, that, where his ancestors were put to death all that time ago . . .

[Quinn stares at the chaotic life outside the window]

He asked us to start kissing while he filmed us, so we did as he said. After a bit, I said, "Let's go look in that little chamber through the bolted door, the one you told me about."

He jumped at that, 'cause in there, well, um, he could play the game he'd wanted to play with us all along. It was Noé who brought a knife, just to scare him a bit, so he'd do what we said. It was so much easier than I thought to make him strip, make fun of him in front of the camera, like he did to us. So, anyway, uh, Noé bolted the door . . . behind him and Émilie. We panicked then. I guess we weren't really in control anymore.

[Pause]

Yeah, I lost track of her in those caves, when she fell, sprained her ankle. I ran out in the woods, feeling God . . . so bad . . . like, I should go back and find them, open the door. But what stopped me? Well, I remember feeling so scared of what they would do to me if I went back, and at the same time, I thought, what would happen if I let them die?

[Quinn lights another cigarette and smokes furiously]

I remember running towards that guy in the car, thinking maybe he would help me fix it somehow.

[Pause]

So, not all of the videos were lies. At first, I really couldn't remember much. Honest to God. But then, slowly, I started to. But by then I didn't know who to trust. Anyway, we all told a few lies, didn't we? Émilie and Raphael and Noémie, the inspector, and Molly, too.

Wasn't expecting Molly's last lie to get us off the hook, though. That last clip she took in the club, her recording of Valentin and Séverin? It's front-page news now: *Police corruption in Charente-Maritime. Local mob questioned over role in Blavette slaying.* Since they couldn't find any real, um, physical evidence. That film we made of Raphael in the caves uploaded to the site before we could stop it, but deleted itself after Molly watched it. Only she knows what we've done. Her film from the club distracted the media away from us, gave us time to get away.

[Quinn takes a deep drag on her cigarette]

Last I heard, they're not even interested in us now. This woman Marcelline Masson, the Republic prosecutor, she's reinvestigating every-thing—the Blavette case, corruption in the local police force, everything . . . Seems like the powers that be were turning a blind eye to Séverin's business ventures since long before Valentin took charge. In actual fact, it was so well known that he dumped bodies in the caves, the police didn't even look in them properly to start with. They thought Séverin was their man, the guy behind the family's disappearance—they just couldn't say that. As soon as they started this new investigation, the prosecutor's team found other remains—the body of Marc Blavette. He'd been in those caves since he vanished two years before. No way of knowing, I guess, if Séverin killed him over money, or if Émilie did it . . . or if he just had enough of everything and wandered off one day.

[Long pause as Quinn stares out of the window]

One mystery is left, I guess. See, I keep hassling Noémie, trying to get her to tell me the truth, um, about how Émilie found us in the caves that day, right? Noé, she says her mom just followed us there to that chamber on a maternal hunch of some kind. But whatever. I mean, I don't see how that could be, 'cause it was deep in the caves, that room, where only the Blavette family could find it . . . so the legend said. So how could it be true that Émilie just randomly wandered in there . . . unless Noé told her?

[Quinn stubs out her cigarette and flicks the butt out of the window]

Still, we're far away now, starting a new life.

Think I'm gonna have to stop asking her about it. Only bugs her when I do. She says we have to trust each other now.

It's true. We're all we have.

[She taps her pack of Lucky Strikes, but there are none left]

Damn. Hey, you ever have one of those Magic 8 Balls as a kid? Yeah, they're cheesy but I like 'em. Can't see one in a junk shop these days without remembering my little pink bed with the daisy-pattern comforter on it. And that makes me think of my mom. She picked out that bedspread with me at Sears when I was eleven . . . Now I think that there never really was anything for me to stick around for at home after she died, not my dad, anyway. Not my friends either—I mean, none of them even sent a card, though they all had time for Fox News interviews.

I have this theory . . . our lives are all a bit like those Magic 8 Balls. You can shake 'em around, hoping for the right answer, the one that will make you happy, but you never really know which of those sharp little pieces is going to bubble to the surface.

[Pause]

If you find you can't live with the message on that cheap plastic triangle, though, I have some advice for you: *ask again later*. You never know what's waiting inside those mysterious globes of plastic . . . hidden away in the dark.

Molly Swift

AUGUST 18, 2015

My flight was leaving for Logan International in a couple of hours, and this time I really didn't want to miss it. Things back home were taking off. Our latest episode of *American Confessional* brought in our best viewing figures yet and, despite my beef with Bill, I had to admit it was perfect the way he edited together my clip from the club with a bunch of the earlier footage of Quinn's quest for the truth. Our focus on the police cover-up and the way the murders were wrongly pinned on Quinn had done double duty: we redeemed her in the public eye at the same time that we condemned Séverin and his co-conspirators.

That final show exonerating Quinn proved beyond doubt that the local mob had been in cahoots with the police the whole time, covering up their murders as well as their drug dealing . . . well, you can imagine. It was like Watergate all over again for Bill. He says if it had just been a story about small-town corruption in France, it wouldn't have played too well: it was the #AmericanGirl aspect that brought in viewers, who now had a chance to rant about the injustice of the whole #AmericanMonster vilification. No one needed to know the real role she and Noé had played, not when what they'd done was justice, of a kind. I made sure we gave them a bit of cover by insisting Bill add one last line to the narrative of the last episode: "Quinn is now living under witness protection for her own safety." By the time the furor dies down and people realize she's really gone . . . well, I hope she and Noé have had time to vanish for good. It's what they wanted.

In place of a farewell drink, Marlene and I were holding one final meeting of the St. Roch coffee klatch, at where else but La Grande Bouche?

It was oddly comforting to watch her on the go, refilling our coffees and dumping a pound of stollen loaf on the table in front of me. I didn't need to test my theory that it had the consistency of cement peppered with lead shot by tasting it; sometimes you just know these things. She sat down across from me, a satisfied smile on her face. I'd already thrown her some tidbits about Stella's affair with Raphael and the way she leaked that video to the press. I was in her good books for now.

"You are flavor of the month here, Molly, and not only with your listeners. Marcelline Masson has sung some of your praises, I hear."

"Yeah, well, it's not all it's cracked up to be," I said modestly. "After a life spent as a nonentity, celebrity's too crazy for me. I've been screening my boss's calls and everyone else's. I haven't even seen that last episode." It was true. I had to do what I did, shape the story the best way I could to keep Quinn and Noé out of the spotlight. And if the whole thing ended Valentin's career, he deserved it, didn't he, the way he'd lied? That was what I kept telling myself.

"Perhaps you are not so popular with the local police force, though." Marlene flicked a glance around the café, pretty empty now that her cop regulars were either in jail or avoiding her.

"I feel bad about that," I say, sipping black coffee and avoiding eye contact with the stollen. "They were bad to the bone, but they still bought your coffee. And I'm worried, you know, when I leave, that there might still be some of Séverin's people out there who might want to hurt you. You were pretty involved in it all."

She snorted a cynical laugh. "You think Marlene will be lost without Molly the Pit Bull to defend her. Bah! Most of them are gone down, anyhow. Is that how you say it? In the clink. As for the rest, I will make short work with them. I was tough girl long before you, Molly Swift."

"I know, but I mean . . . Séverin will have connections on the outside still, family. Don't be a hero, Marlene."

She threw her head back in a raucous laugh. "I am of course a hero, always, as you tried to be, too, I think. I have seen your film, busting into the club, punching your boyfriend on the ground. Being so macho. I was like proud momma when I saw it."

I tried to laugh along, but the sight of Valentin lying prone on the floor lodged in my head and I stopped, rubbing my eyes wearily. "I guess it had to happen. I mean, they were up to their necks in it. I still don't understand how Séverin even knew all that stuff, about Valentin following me, stealing my papers . . ."

"I think it is obvious," said Marlene. "They were plotting together all the time; the police, they were taking some bribes to turn a blind eye to Séverin's drugs and murders so they could skim the top off the proceeds."

"Okay, but why did they want me followed in the first place?"

Marlene rolled her eyes. "Séverin knew Quinn. When Raphael disappeared with his money, he had men looking inside the hospital, and his dogsbody Valentin following the 'aunt,' you, to see what she might know. It is all on the internet, Molly. Really, you Americans can be such ignoramuses."

"So he did trust me . . ." I said, more to myself than to her. It's been bothering me—not knowing whether Valentin ever really believed I was

Quinn's aunt, whether anything between us was real. He seemed so hurt when he found out I'd lied. "But anyway, he told way worse lies and I believed them all," I said, trying to sound cynical rather than hurt.

Marlene didn't miss a trick, though. She gripped my hand in a slightly terrifying show of solidarity. "That dummkopf deserved to be kicked, Molly. He deserves prison, too, coming in here, drinking my coffee and eating my stollen, pretending to be nice. If he were here I would take this knife and with it cut off his . . ."

"No cutting off things after I'm gone," I said, trying and failing to disarm her. "Anyway, you wouldn't get very far with this table knife."

"Why not? I have the muscles of a woman who makes her own bratwurst. I would make quick work of these dirty cops, who didn't even investigate the crimes of our town because they were taking with both hands from the till." The stollen took the worst of her wrath with the knife, an image that will haunt my dreams.

When I stood, Marlene heaved herself out of the booth and enveloped me in possibly the most perfumed and definitely the most bosomy hug I'd ever had.

"I will miss you, Molly Swift," she said.

I don't do sentiment, not really, but it was one of those moments.

"I'll miss you, too, Marlene Weiss." It was true.

She was the only one who'd been honest with me, after all. As for Valentin—in the end, our relationship was based on lies on both sides, and in that sense, at least, we were a good match.

Marlene deftly undercut our *Casablanca* moment by stuffing a Tupperware tub of what I felt fairly certain was sauerkraut into my handbag. "For your trip."

"This win any awards at the festival?"

Marlene looked affronted. "Do you truly need to ask?"

I waved goodbye before we could get onto the thorny subject of German versus French recipes for pickled cabbage, and headed to the taxi stand. Climbing into the back with a murmured request, I leaned back and let St. Roch flow by me in all its dust and sunlight and beauty and ridiculousness, bidding goodbye to the gas station and the medieval church and the gendarmerie. There were exciting times ahead, according to Bill. We would go places, he said, be people. I should be excited to get back to it. Still, I found myself leaning my head against the window, my eye caught on a blue streak of sea panting alongside the car. At that bend in the woods, the one where they found her, I couldn't help checking to see if there was a young girl wandering the road in her white dress, somehow lost. I told myself there were two of them now and they were holding hands, their eyes fixed on the road ahead.

Acknowledgments

I'd like to thank Oliver Munson, Lee Horsley, and Kevin Wignall for liking the idea for this book and sticking with it from its first moments until the bitter end; and Duane Swierczynski, whose LitReactor masterclass was invaluable in helping me develop the novel at an early stage. Thanks to Trish Daly and Marguerite Weisman at William Morrow for their excellent editorial skills. Thanks to the family I stayed with as an exchange student in the South of France during my mis-spent youth for doing their best to teach me a little bit of French. Finally, thanks to my own family for being so lovably weird.

Center Point Large Print
600 Brooks Road / PO Box 1
Thorndike, ME 04986-0001 USA

(207) 568-3717

US & Canada:
1 800 929-9108
www.centerpointlargeprint.com